Conservatism, Consumer Choice, and the Food and Drug Administration during the Reagan Era

Conservatism, Consumer Choice, and the Food and Drug Administration during the Reagan Era

A Prescription for Scandal

Lucas Richert

LEXINGTON BOOKS
Lanham • Boulder • New York • Toronto • Plymouth, UK

Published by Lexington Books
A wholly owned subsidiary of Rowman & Littlefield
4501 Forbes Boulevard, Suite 200, Lanham, Maryland 20706
www.rowman.com

10 Thornbury Road, Plymouth PL6 7PP, United Kingdom

Copyright © 2014 by Lexington Books

British Library Cataloguing in Publication Information Available

Library of Congress Cataloging-in-Publication Data

Richert, Lucas, 1979-
Conservatism, consumer choice, and the Food and Drug Administration during the Reagan era : a prescription for scandal / Lucas Richert.
pages cm
Includes bibliographical references.
ISBN 978-0-7391-8258-1 (cloth : alk. paper) -- ISBN 978-0-7391-8259-8 (electronic)
1. United States. Food and Drug Administration. 2. Pharmaceutical policy--United States--History--20th century. 3. Drug development--United States--History--20th century. 4. Drugs--Law and legislation--United States--History--20th century. 5. Pharmaceutical industry--Government policy--United States--History--20th century. 6. Consumer protection--Political aspects--United States--History--20th century. I. Title.
RA401.A3R53 2014
338.4'76151--dc23
2014008754

Printed in the United States of America

Contents

Acknowledgments

This project would not have been possible without the generous support of institutions and archives in Canada, the United States, and Great Britain. I received much needed funding from the American Politics Group, British Royal Historical Society, European Association for American Studies, Institute for the Study of the Americas, University of London, and Wellcome Trust Foundation. In addition, I must thank the Social Science and Humanities Research Council of Canada and the UK Overseas Student Research Awards Scheme.

I would like to convey my sincerest gratitude to the helpful staff, archivists, and librarians at the National Library of Medicine on the National Institutes of Health Campus, the FDA Biomedical Sciences Library in the FDA, Library of Congress in Washington, D.C., University of Pennsylvania Rare Book and Manuscript Library, and the Chemical Heritage Foundation's Oral History Collection. Thanks also to the Business History Conference, Centre for Addiction and Mental Health, Mater Dei Institute at the University of Dublin, University of Heidelberg, University of Saskatchewan, Robert J. Dole Library, Reagan Presidential Library, Carter Presidential Library, and Society for the Social History of Medicine for funding my travel to communicate parts of my research to a broader audience.

Many senior scholars have been generous with their time and support. Erika Dyck has been an inspiration as both a historian and person. Iwan Morgan offered his continual encouragement for this project and his importance to my work is immeasurable. Robert Mason was kind enough to suffer through my early writing and has extended himself on my behalf for years, whereas Jeffrey Weinberg, during his time in London, shared his expertise and proved an exceptional critic.

I must also thank James Dunkerley, Maxine Molyneux, Kevin Middlebrook, Timothy Lynch, Diego Sanchez Ancochea, Rachel Seider, and Natasha Warikoo for their many fine suggestions and sage criticisms. Others who deserve thanks include Taylor Bassingthwaite, Lesley Biggs, Nicolas Bouchet, Ryan Buhay, Theresa Callan, Robert Clark, Shereen Colvin, Mark Cooke, Alexander and Catherine Davies, Linda Dietz, Christopher Dummitt, Jim Handy, Ian Hart, Michael J. Heale, David Herzberg, Greg Higby, Geoffrey Hudson, Kalinda Hughes, Simonne Horwitz, Kathleen Kendall, Maurice Jr. LaBelle, Man-Kam Leung, Dan Mallek, Stephen Mawdsley, Mark Meyers, Jonathan Metzl, Jim Miller, Adam Montgomery, Tom Packer, Nadine Penner, Karen Perkins, Marc Polachic, John Porter, Gary Teare, Dominique Tobbell, Lisa Smith, Larry Stewart, Alex Waddan, and Andy Wroe.

Finally, this project would not have been completed without the encouragement and patience of my loving family and friends.

This work is dedicated to Beth, Oscar, and Lucy.

Introduction

". . . to promote the public health by promptly and efficiently reviewing clinical research and taking appropriate action on the marketing of regulated products in a timely manner; and with respect to human and veterinary drug, protect the public health by ensuring that those drugs are safe and effective."[1]

FDA MISSION STATEMENT

"Government exists to protect us from each other. But as the years have gone on and the bureaucracy grows, as bureaucracies do, we find that they have gone far beyond protecting us from poisonous or harmful substances, and they have now set themselves up as the doctor and decided that they will tell us what medicines are effective."[2]

RONALD REAGAN

Federal regulatory agencies, be they social or economic regulators, play essential roles in the markets and institutions they watch over and societies and consumers they protect. The U.S. Food and Drug Administration's regulation of the nation's food and drug supply in the 1970s and 1980s is no exception to this rule. The FDA, an executive branch regulatory agency, is the ultimate authority in whether or not a human drug meant for human consumption goes to market. Over its long history the agency has evolved considerably. The first incarnation of the FDA was a part of the Department of State in 1839. Then it was shifted to the Department of the Interior, the Department of Agriculture, and the Federal Security Agency, until, at last, it found its home

1

in the Department of Health, Education and Welfare, later renamed the Department of Health and Human Services. A part of the executive branch, and therefore subject to Office of Management and Budget, the FDA now stands as a crucial U.S. regulatory agency that regulates, besides drugs, the food supply, blood supply, vaccines, drugs and feed for animals, and cosmetics and medical devices. The agency's regulatory task is enormously complex and just as difficult.[3]

This book investigates the FDA during what historian Sean Wilentz has recently described as the "Age of Reagan."[4] In Wilentz's estimation, 1974-2008 was a period of political, economic, and social history given shape by Ronald Reagan and the ascension of a robust conservative movement. I too view the Reagan era as exceptional and one that consumed other presidential administrations. Reagan succeeded in shifting the policy discourse about the size and scope of federal government programs and he drove the conversation about which government program to launch or expand into how much of a program's or agency's budget *ought to be cut*. Focusing on an era similar to Wilentz's, I explore how the Reagan administration's ambition to limit the size and scope of government, reduce excessive regulation, and promote increased cooperation between businesses and U.S. regulatory agencies affected the FDA. I question the rise of deregulation in the 1970s, its establishment at the FDA in the early 1980s, and accordingly, how subtle regulatory modifications at the agency influenced the balance between consumer protection and product innovation.

Ronald Reagan, whether as a candidate or president of the United States, did not desire the dismantling of the FDA, but neither did he trust it. In his view, its authority, like that of many other regulatory agencies, needed curtailing. In 1975, he told an audience at the American Enterprise Institute that the FDA was hurting Americans, yet also made clear he did not want to totally "eliminate the responsibility of the FDA . . ."[5] The problem, as Reagan saw it, rested in the restriction of freedom of choice for American consumers, since the agency had established itself "as the doctor and decided that they will tell us what medicines are effective."[6] He felt that a degree of regulation was necessary to protect Americans from each other, but the FDA had overreached and, as bureaucracies do, went beyond "protecting us from poisonous or harmful substances . . ."[7] By the end of his two terms in office, however, his administration's strategic accomplishment was not wholesale deregulation of the FDA but instead a controlled conversion, at least compared to future Republican initiatives, combined with the preclusion of regulation-making.

To be sure, dire consequences rest in both overregulation or deregulation of any industry. Throttling the U.S. drug industry in the 1970s and 1980s was (and remains) a genuine danger for policy makers. Stifling product innovation with an excessively cautious approach to risk not only damages pharmaceutical profits, but also has the potential to deny desperate Americans revolutionary, life-saving, or life-enhancing drugs. Yet significant hazards also rest in reform—in either the rolling back or total removal of the rules and regulations that govern the conduct of drug companies, the medical establishment, and public use of drugs. According to Sally Unrang, writing in *Chemical Marketing Reporter* in December 1981, "extremely convincing arguments" were being made on both sides, but "for the moment, those who favor relaxing some of the [drug approval] requirements appear to be winning."[8]

In the turbulent political climate of the 1970s-1990s, regulatory policy makers, politicians in Washington, interest groups, and the drug industry were forced to confront and try to influence pharmaceutical regulation. The struggle always centered on product innovation, consumer protection, and choice. In the face of a stuttering economy, the stakes were high. For instance, interest groups like the Center for Science in the Public Interest and Public Citizen competed fiercely with such organizations as the Pharmaceutical Research and Manufacturers Association (PhRMA), Heritage Foundation, and American Enterprise Institute to influence favorable policies and decisions that were made by both legislators and the FDA. Since its inception the agency had attempted to guard Americans against a "plethora of products that are at best ineffective and at worst dangerous," but in the antiregulatory environment of the late 1970s the standard relationship between consumer choice and the government's obligation to offer protections was questioned.[9] With a lack of evidence, should citizens have the right to Laetrile, a dubious anti-cancer drug, even if the FDA did not deem it safe or effective? Were sick Americans entitled to underground HIV/AIDS drugs even if, again, the agency had not offered its stamp of approval? Adding to the complexity of this problem was the increased awareness of Americans about medical issues. The American tradition, according to Alan M. Rees, is one of self-reliance and proud independence, which also applied to health matters. In Rees' view, during the 1980s, the medical profession's exclusive control over specialized medical knowledge diminished and American patient-consumers closed the knowledge gap. As he described it, self-reliant consumer activity reemerged and patient-consumers recognized the "value of informed choice" and "shared decision making" in the doctor's office and hospital.[10] This reassertion of consumer rights, which cut both ways, in advocacy for greater consumer protections and less restriction on goods and services, undoubtedly influenced the FDA.

Thus, the debate about the FDA's role in society during the 1970s-1990s was often disorganized and pitted scientists against scientists, regulators against drug company representatives, and consumers against consumers. Not surprisingly, transformation of the agency's modus operandi—its traditional regulatory posture and profile—was received with mixed emotions in some cases and warmly in others. For some, the changes at the FDA marked positive growth; for others, they were a prescription for scandal. And within this milieu any modification—whether proposed or actually implemented—was almost always bound up in consumer choice, conservatism, and patient activism.

The Treacherous Tightrope

The Food and Drug Administration's role in protecting America's human drug supply requires walking a treacherous tightrope. An enduring question within the FDA has been how it should relate to the regulated industries, for the agency's mission statement emphasizes the FDA's responsibility for "protecting the public health by assuring the safety, efficacy, and security of human and veterinary drugs . . . ." The same statement, which was modified in 1997, also highlights how the agency is responsible for "advancing the public health by helping to speed innovations that make medicines and foods more effective, safer and more affordable; and helping the public get the accurate, science-based information they need to use medicines and foods to improve their health."[11] An important balance must therefore be struck between activities that promote consumer protection and product innovation. In 1981, the outgoing FDA commissioner, Dr. Jerry Goyan, articulated the FDA's perception of this delicate equilibrium, and the types of problems it necessarily created. The "FDA . . . appreciates the fact that it has a dual role, not a single one." He also highlighted the problem with too much and too little regulation: "While the safety and effectiveness of regulated products must be demonstrated, the process of demonstration must not deter innovative companies from developing new and important products."[12]

It should come as no surprise that in the face of such responsibilities the FDA has grappled with its institutional identity. At different times the FDA has characterized itself as a "regulatory agency," a "law enforcement agency," or a "science agency," depending on the political party in power and the ideology of the FDA Commissioner. Though contrary pressures push and pull the agency in different directions—such stakeholders as the regulated industry, consumers, health care professionals, trade associations, and advocacy groups—the FDA has (according to former staff members at least) maintained a specific identity based on a set of core principles. The FDA, that is, has kept a dedicated inspection cadre, kept an "arms-length" approach to the companies that made regulated products, and kept a strong commitment to consumer protection.[13] In accordance with this long-standing identity, the agency has subsequently carried out regulatory activities, including pre- and post-approval drug evaluation, drug manufacturing inspections, as well as a host of others responsibilities.[14]

Even prior to the Reaganite 1980s, however, the FDA's institutional identity was tested in the political and economic tumult of the 1970s. The New

Deal Democratic order, built by Franklin Roosevelt in the 1930s, was decaying; meanwhile, the U.S. economy was slumping and so was Americans' faith in their established institutions. High levels of inflation, a persistent problem, plagued policy makers and undermined confidence. Further compounding difficulties was rising unemployment. Liberal economists, bewildered and divided, asked what had happened to the Phillips Curve, the famous trade-off between unemployment and inflation. President Jimmy Carter, who had himself struggled mightily with setting the nation's national economic policy, was rejected in 1980. His failure to find a solution to this economic malaise made him a one-term president. His successor, the affable and optimistic Ronald Reagan, promised he would establish a new economic order and limit the size and scope of government.[15]

The FDA, an executive branch regulatory agency beholden to Carter and Reagan, was constrained and shaped by this broader economic and political milieu. Between 1974 and 1980 congressional scrutiny of the FDA reached new heights. First, the agency was investigated for what was perceived to be a hazardous and over-friendly relationship with industry. It was subsequently revealed that officials within the Bureau of Drugs "neutralized" certain drug reviewers who were unsympathetic to industry. Second, the drug lag, the name given for the unusually long time it took to approve a drug, brought the FDA a torrent of criticism. The drug lag generated a number of congressional hearings as well as significant and long-lasting debate that carried into the Reagan administration. These events demonstrated the contrary pressures affecting the FDA during the 1970s: members of Congress from both the left and right of the political spectrum probing the agency, and accusations that the FDA was both too strict and too lenient in the application of its regulatory powers.

The mid- and late-1970s were also a revolutionary time for the drug industry, and, consequently, the FDA as well. Americans, in university labs, corporate boardrooms, and government circles, became more conscious of a nascent bio-pharmaceutical industry. Drug research switched from a chemical to a biological basis, and a radical change of the technological paradigm, which would dramatically affect the pharmaceutical industry, was underway. The new biological approach rested upon rational understanding of the functioning of the human body, specifically molecular actions and pathologies, and the actions of the body and brain. This fundamental shift affected private firms of varying size, including state sponsored scientific institutions. It was a shift that also impacted the statutes and the regulatory procedures governing the pharmaceutical industry, as well as research and development (R&D) costs and the proliferation of mergers.[16]

Significant laws passed in 1980 underpinned and reinforced the new biological pharmaceutical movement. In June of that year, the Supreme Court ruled in *Diamond v. Chakrabarty* that living organisms engineered by humans were potentially patentable under existing statutes, thereby sparking a period of speculative frenzy over genetic engineering.[17] On October 14, 1980, bio-tech company Genentech went public becoming the largest initial public stock offering in history. Within minutes of the opening bell, investors on the New York Stock Exchange had purchased one million shares, pushing the stock prices from $35 to $89, raising $38.5 million.[18] Also important was the passage of the Bayh-Dole Act in 1980, named for Senator Birch Bayh (D-IN) and Robert Dole (R-KS), which transformed the legal environment for the nascent biotechnology and bio-pharmaceutical industry. The law encouraged federally funded researchers and university sponsors to license their patented discoveries by giving them clear titles to the patents, a move designed and passed to increase American competitiveness in the global pharmaceutical trade.

With Ronald Reagan's victory against incumbent Jimmy Carter, the drug industry and the press envisaged a pharmaceutical industry boom in the near future. The *New York Times* reported in 1981's "The Drug Business Sees a Golden Era Ahead" that pharmaceutical associations were positively giddy. Just a year prior, the same paper had printed: "The FDA: Too Slow." Authored by Representative James Scheuer (D-NY), the opinion-editorial denounced the agency's over-cautiousness and emphasized the need for immediate reform. Moreover, think tanks such as the Heritage Foundation and American Enterprise Institute promulgated changes to the FDA's mission as a means of unleashing the once-mighty American pharmaceutical industry. This, they thought, would fuel the U.S. industry and the greater economy.[19]

All the prognostications about U.S. pharmaceutical growth were well founded. The former editor of the *New England Journal of Medicine*, Dr. Marcia Angell, called 1980 a watershed year.[20] Over the next decade the U.S. pharmaceutical industry expanded at an immense rate. It maintained 35-40 percent of worldwide sales, more than double the next ranked foreign competitor. Research and development activities—the lifeblood of the industry—also increased at a rapid rate after 1980. The European and Japanese pharmaceutical industries, by contrast, generally exhibited declining positions throughout the 1980s.[21]

Even as the U.S. pharmaceutical industry grew in the 1980s, so too did the FDA's authority to regulate it. Congress passed twenty-four new laws that expanded the FDA's jurisdiction during the decade. For example, the 1983 Orphan Drug Act established a new program within the FDA to advance the development of drugs for rare medical conditions. The 1983 Federal Anti-Tampering Act, an outgrowth of the Tylenol poisoning incident in 1982, gave authority to investigate tampering incidents related to products the FDA regulated, including pharmaceuticals. In addition, the 1987 Drug Marketing Act required the FDA to restrict the distribution of drug samples, supervise a ban on specific resales of drugs, and police drug wholesalers.[22]

However, the most significant piece of legislation to emerge in the 1980s was the Drug Price Competition and Patent Term Restoration Act of 1984. This simultaneously restored part of the all-important patent life lost during the pre-market regulatory process and facilitated entry of generic competition *after* patent expiration by eliminating duplicative testing. [23]

Still, for all the growth in U.S. pharmaceutical industry profits and spending as well as the FDA's regulatory authority, the FDA's actual operating budget, in real dollars, remained relatively stagnant throughout the 1980s. Following the precedent set by Jimmy Carter, Ronald Reagan continued to cut FDA funds in fulfilment of his promise to reduce federal spending. [24] When controlled for inflation, the FDA's budget remained constant in the 1980s. In real dollars, the agency's budget increased just two percent over the entire decade, from $320 million in 1980 (equivalent to $482 million in 1989 dollars) to $492 million. [25] As a result, the FDA's overall workforce declined from 8,089 to 7,398. Representative John Dingell (D-MI) commented in December 1988, "This is a terrible mess, the denigration and emasculation of a fine and once-proud agency." Dr. Sidney M. Wolfe, head of the Public Citizen Health Research Group, bewailed: "We've seen a deterioration in the FDA's policing of the drug-medical device industry, and Americans are beginning to taste the fatal or health-destroying fruits of this partnership." [26]

The FDA's chief also spoke up. On May 18, 1990, the Acting Commissioner of the Food and Drug Administration, James S. Benson, testified to a Department of Health and Human Services advisory committee. "Since 1976," he said, "Congress has assigned FDA vast responsibilities under several new laws, requiring major initiatives in areas such as medical devices, generic drugs, drug diversion, orphan drugs, pesticides, AIDS and anabolic steroids." Such an expansion, he continued, had certain negative, unintended consequences for the agency. "The cumulative effect has forced FDA to *withdraw* more assets than it has in its resource bank. In effect," Benson lamented," we are *overdrawn* on virtually all accounts. FDA managers have been forced to cannibalize core functions and other programs to accommodate these new legislative activities." [27] It was evident, therefore, that the FDA was having trouble in sustaining its conventional regulatory mission by the end of the Reagan administration.

Worse still, beginning in 1988, outright scandal gripped the agency. After scores of affidavits, investigations, and hearings, it was revealed that FDA staff members had undermined the sanctity of the generic drug supply by engaging in illegal activity. The saga lasted three years and capped the end of the Reagan administration. I evaluate the generic drugs scandal at the FDA and, as such, focus on Representative John Dingell from Michigan, drug reviewer Charles Chang, and Commissioner Young. If this tale of the FDA during the Reagan presidential years articulates anything, therefore, it is a cautionary message: pitfalls surely follow from the hollowing out of a regulatory agency, by depriving it of resources, shearing it of morale, and all the while increasing its regulatory mandate.

Building Blocks and the Blueprint

Conservatism and Reaganism in the United States hold a broad fascination for not only scholars but also everyday readers. My book takes up these themes and I am indebted to a number of authors. Specifically, Jonathan Schoenwald's study of modern conservatism, Robert M. Collins's work on economic growth in the United States, and Michael Schaller's explorations of Ronald Reagan, have provided me with a robust foundation on which to build my arguments.[28] Lewis, McCraw, Neustadt, and Pertschuk provide a theoretical basis for my monograph's analysis of presidential decision-making and regulation in America, whereas the first-rate work by Patterson and others offer a larger framework of American politics and society for me to situate my work.[29]

As mentioned previously, Sean Wilentz's important book, *The Age of Reagan*, argues that Reagan ushered in an era of conservative domination, which stretched from the fall of Nixon in 1974 to the Republican electoral clattering in 2006. But in a clever and balanced thesis, Reagan is actually embraced by Wilentz as both conservative alpha dog and avatar. Indeed, the former president is given "grudging admiration for his political adroitness."[30] On the topic of Republican presidents, though, Wilentz's warm and breezy treatment of Reagan is not transferred to George H.W. Bush, the Gingrich-led Republicans in Congress during the 1990s, or George W. Bush, who is basically deemed a failed president practicing a "radicalized form of Reaganism."[31] Regarding the latter Bush, readers are told of intransigent proxies in Congress unwilling to negotiate with Democrats across the aisle, as well as the outright abandonment of compassionate conservatism for a zealous pursuit of a doctrinaire agenda. Wilentz also focuses on the promulgation of the unitary executive, which held up President Bush as absolute authority over independent federal agencies and "not bound by congressional oversight or even by law."[32] Thus, the reader is asked to accept that the Bush administration benefited from and operated in *The Age of Reagan,* yet Bush and his cronies practiced a far more ideologically charged version of conservative politics. After reading this book, one will notice that a similar dynamic is playing out with respect to conservatism and the FDA. While Reagan certainly sought to curtail the authority of the agency, it was the Gingrich-led successors in Congress that aimed to undercut the FDA and thereby similarly practicing a "radical" form of Reaganism.

In recent years, moreover, social scientists and medical practitioners have articulated clear concerns about the medicalization of human behavior, the

U.S. drug industry's excessive but disguised influence on the parameters and definitions of sickness, and the modern industry's formidable lobbying power in Washington, D.C.[33] Jeremy A. Greene has tackled disease diagnosis and definition in the United States since the 1950s and focuses on the development and prescribing of Diuril, Orinase, and Mevacor, whereas Dominique Tobbell, in arguing drug companies used the politics of the Cold War to defend itself against charges made by congressional investigations, has recast the understanding of debates about pharmaceuticals in the 1960s and beyond.[34] Also, historians and political scientists have charted the history of such drugs and narcotics as Miltown, LSD, marijuana, and heroin on the home front and abroad. What seems to be missing in recent scholarship, however, is an effort to capture the modern presidential, congressional outlook on pharmaceuticals and connect that to the regulatory apparatus.[35]

In addition, the FDA has itself served as the focus of several studies. Jerry Avorn, Herbert Burkholz, Jay Cohen, Fran Hawthorne, and Philip J. Hilts have all investigated the FDA in the specific context of the 1980s, but they largely neglect the development of conservative economics as an influencing factor on the agency and do not necessarily position their analyses within a particular political order.[36] Moreover, Dominique Tobbell and Dan Carpenter have also produced significant new scholarship. Their efforts to understand the FDA and conservatism have been extremely valuable, but also raised many new questions. Tobbell's excellent book, *Pills, Power, and Policy*, charts how the drug industry and key components of the medical profession resisted pharmaceutical reform after World War II; however, in offering an incisive and innovative view of how drug companies, physicians, and academic researchers developed a complex relationship to dominate health care policy, Tobbell's narrative does not specifically focus in on consumer choice, scandal, and patient activism. *Reputation and Power*, Carpenter's magisterial history of the FDA, addresses numerous overlapping audiences and is positioned at the nexus of social sciences, law, pharmacology, and the clinical sciences. As the title suggests, the FDA's extraordinary influence over pharmaceutical regulation is contingent on the mutually reinforcing concepts of reputation and power. According to Carpenter, "reputation built regulatory power in all its facets" and the concept is defined "as a set of symbolic beliefs about an organization, beliefs embedded in multiple audiences."[37] In his persuasive view, that reputation has always answered to the particular needs and demands of American consumers and government at different points in political, social, and technological history. At the same time, even as it proposes a new taxonomy of power to understand the agency, it also calls for additional research on relationship between the agency, interest groups, and industry as well as the implementation of user fees and FDAMA in the 1980s and 1990s.

The approach and structure of this book is relatively straightforward. Focusing on a period stretching from the 1970s to 1990s, I broadly examine the political impulses, persons, and ideas that actuated the debate about the proper amount of drug regulation in a democratic and capitalist society. Using political, cultural, and business history, I chart the personalities, fights, and concrete regulatory changes in the halls of the FDA. And to accomplish this, I highlight certain case studies, including Laetrile, Reye's Syndrome, Oraflex, patient package inserts, diet pills, and HIV/AIDS drugs. The FDA was a crucial unit in the broader political and economic milieu that included the president, Congress, industry, interest groups, and the media, along with other actors. The FDA's interactions within this milieu help us to identify and appreciate FDA behavior. At the same time, the FDA is an excellent vehicle for understanding the power of the modern pharmaceutical industry in American society and how, moving forward, citizens ought to regard the relationship among all the major players in health product regulation.

The first two chapters of this book provide a background to this relationship. Chapter 1 traces a wider history of the FDA and probes the enduring political and scientific difficulties faced by career employees at the agency. While illustrating certain theories about regulation, it also touches upon the key political actors (Presidents Teddy Roosevelt, Franklin Roosevelt, and John F. Kennedy) who actuated and shaped the FDA. Chapters 2 and 3, on the other hand, investigate disillusionment, Carter's economic policy (specifically deregulation), and the FDA. In addition, they ask whether the problems at the FDA were symptomatic of larger economic and political trends or can be attributed to Carter's leadership. However, these chapters also argue that crucial events at the FDA in the 1970s—the fights over Laetrile and Patient Package Inserts (PPIs), allegations of bias in the halls of the FDA, and the deadly drug lag—reveal much about the contentious political firmament of the times.

Chapter 4 investigates how the transitional relationship between the pharmaceutical industry, the FDA, and the Reagan administration in 1981 and 1982 altered public health. The implementation of regulatory reform policies profoundly affected the FDA's enforcement profile and I make the case that the balance between consumer protection and product innovation was tilted in favor of the latter. Chapter 4 blends an analysis of bureaucratic power plays with crafty personalities and administrative manoeuvrings.

The years of 198 and 1984 were complicated times for the FDA and chapter 5 seeks to advance an understanding of the Reagan administration and the FDA's evolving regulatory policy at the FDA. The agency had undergone a startling, dramatic shock in 1981, whereupon the bureaucracy adapted to changing circumstances. Pundits and the press, along with academics of all political stripes, began to argue whether Reagan had ushered in a fresh political and economic order. But in 198 and 1984, the agency was forced to meet manifold new challenges: the success and growth of the pharmaceutical industry, zealous congressional hearings, no commissioner for a prolonged period of time, and the new pressures of the Hatch-Waxman legislation, which increased the FDA's workload considerably.

Chapter 6 interrogates the FDA's regulatory posture amid a climate of fear over the increasing prevalence of HIV/AIDS and highlights the complex relationship between policy makers at the agency, pharmaceutical companies, and AIDS activists. In an absence of presidential leadership, the FDA took bold action to confront the epidemic. A corollary argument is that the FDA liberalized the drug approval process at the behest of significant external pressure from media and potent activist movements. That is, the agency instituted regulatory reform at the insistence of others besides the Reagan administration. Chapter 6 focuses on such health activist groups as AIDS Coalition To Unleash Power (ACT-UP) and Project Inform. It also investigates the approval of Burroughs Wellcome's AZT.

The final chapter examines the FDA at the end of the 1980s and beyond. I argue that the Reagan administration's goal to limit the size and scope of government, reduce excessive regulation, and promote increased cooperation between businesses and U.S. regulatory agencies had far reaching effects at the FDA. According to government reports and various commentators, the FDA suffered shortfalls in the 1980s and chapter 7 chronicles how the agency, during a period when the rhetoric of limited government, reduced regulation, and enhanced cooperation between businesses and U.S. regulatory agencies was on the ascent, reached the point where it could be roundly condemned for corrupt criminal behavior. Following the conclusion of the Reagan administration, though, the FDA faced even more harsh criticism in the mid-1990s. This chapter not only chronicles the denouement of the Reagan years but explores the shifting nature of conservative political thought as it pertained to drug regulation and access.

NOTES

1. Federal Food Drug and Cosmetic Act (FDCA) SEC. 903. [393] (b), quoted in Enrique C. Seoane-Vazquez, *Analysis of the Patent Life of New Molecular Entities Approved by the FDA Between 1980 and 2001*, Unpublished PhD Dissertation (University of Minnesota, 2002), 17.

For further information on the U.S. Food and Drug Administration's mandate see website: http://www.fda.gov/AboutFDA/WhatWeDo/default.htm.

2. Elizabeth Drew, *Portrait of an Election: The 1980 Presidential Campaign* (London: Routledge & Kegan Paul Ltd., 1981), 111.

3. Henry I. Miller and David R. Henderson, "The FDA's Risky Risk-Aversion," *Policy Review* 145 (2007): 3–27, consulted at http://www.hoover.org/publications/policyreview/10183506.html. As part of the executive branch its budgets, congressional testimony, and legislative and regulatory proposals are subject to approval by the Office of Management and Budget (OMB) on behalf of the President; moreover, like other executive branch agencies the FDA is subject to a variety of executive orders and general statutes that bear on its regulatory activities.

4. Sean Wilentz, *The Age of Reagan: A History, 1974–2008* (New York: HarperCollins, 2008), 1–11.

5. Reagan is quoted in speech by Commissioner Jere Goyan, "The Future of the FDA Under a New Administration," 61.

6. Elizabeth Drew, *Portrait of an Election: The 1980 Presidential Campaign*, 111.

7. Ibid.

8. Sally Unrang, "Reagan's FDA: Streamlined or Undermined?" *Chemical Marketing Reporter*, December 14, 1981, 10.

9. Ibid.

10. Alan M. Rees, "Characteristics, Content, and Significance of the Popular Health Periodicals Literature," *Bulletin of the Medical Libraries Association* 75, October 1987, 317.

11. Anthony A. Celeste and Arthur N. Levine, "The Mission and the Institution: Ever Changing Yet Eternally the Same," in *FDA: A Century of Consumer Protection*, ed. Wayne Pines (Washington: Food and Drug Law Institute, 2006), 71.

12. Jerry Goyan, "FDA Aim: Meeting the 75-Year Challenge," *U.S. Medicine*, January 15, 1981, 63-64.

13. Celeste and Levine, 71–98.

14. "A Question of Competence: The Judicial Role in the Regulation of Pharmaceuticals," *Harvard Law Review* 103 (3) (1990): 773–793. The FDA's involvement in the development of a commercial medication begins with an investigational new drug application (IND). The IND contains information about the proposed drug's chemistry, manufacturing, pharmacology and toxicology. If approved, the IND application permits the medication's sponsor to gather information on clinical safety and efficacy needed for the next stage in the process, the new drug application (NDA), the formal application.

15. David A. Stockman, *The Triumph of Politics* (New York: Coronet Books, 1987), 10–12. See also Judith Stein, *Pivotal Decade: How the United States Traded Factories for Finance in the Seventies* (New Haven: Yale University Press, 2010), xii and 258–259.

16. Alfonso Gambardella, *Science and Innovation: The U.S. Pharmaceutical Industry During the 1980s* (Cambridge: Cambridge University Press, 1995), 162.

17. Diamond v. Chakrabarty (United States Supreme Court) 447 U.S. 303, 206 USPQ 193: consulted online at http://digital-law-online.info/cases/206PQ193.htm.

18. Sally Smith Hughes, "Making Dollars Out of DNA: The First Major Patent in Biotechnology and the Commercialization of Molecular Biology, 1974–1980," *Isis* 92 (30) (2001): 569.

19. "The Drug Business Sees a Golden Era Ahead," *New York Times*, May 17, 1981, F1 and James Scheuer "The F.D.A.: Too Slow," *New York Times*, May 22, 1980, A35.

20. Marcia Angell, *The Truth About Drug Companies: How They Deceive Us and What to Do About it* (New York: Random House, 2004), 3.

21. Henry Grabowski, "An Analysis of US International Competitiveness in Pharmaceuticals," *Managerial and Decision Economics*, (1989): 31.

22. U.S. Food and Drug Administration, *Milestones in U.S. Food and Drug Law History*, consulted at www.fda.gov.opacom/backgrounders/miles.html.

23. Henry Grabowski and John Vernon, "Longer Patents For Lower Imitation Barriers: The 1984 Drug Act," *American Economic Review* 76 (1986): 197–198.

24. See Herbert Burkholz's *The FDA Follies* (New York: Basic Books, 1994), 1–20.

25. Mary K. Olson, "Substitution in Regulatory Agencies: FDA Enforcement Alternatives," *Journal of Law, Economics and Organization* 12 (2) (1996): 389.

26. Philip J. Hilts, "Ailing Agency—The FDA and Safety: A Guardian of U.S. Health is Under Stress," *New York Times* December 4, 1989, A1 and Irvin Molotsky, "Critics Say FDA in Reagan Years is Unsafe," *New York Times*, January 4, 1987, A2.

27. James S. Benson, *State of the Food and Drug Administration*, delivered May 18, 1990 [italics mine]. Posted at www.fda.gov/bbs/topics/SPEECH/SPE00004.htm, consulted 3/11/05.

28. Jonathan M. Schoenwald, *A Time For Choosing: The Rise of Modern American Conservatism* (New York: Oxford University Press, 2001); Robert M. Collins, *More: The Politics of Economic Growth in Postwar America* (Oxford: Oxford University Press, 2000); Michael Schaller, *Reckoning with Reagan: America and its President in the 1980s* (New York: Oxford

University Press, 1992), and Michael Schaller and George Rising, *The Republican Ascendancy in American Politics, 1968–2001* (Wheeling, Ill.: Harlan Davidson, 2002).

29. See David E. Lewis, *The Politics of Presidential Appointments* (Princeton, NJ: Princeton University Press, 2008); Thomas McCraw, *Prophets of Regulation* (Cambridge, Mass: Harvard University Press, 1984); Richard E. Neustadt, *Presidential Power and the Modern Presidents* (New York: Free Press, 1990); Michael Perschuk, *Revolt Against Regulation: The Rise and Pause of the Consumer Movement* (Berkeley: University of California Press, 1982); Robert M. Collins, *Transforming America: Politics and Culture in the Reagan Years* (New York: Columbia University Press, 2007); James Patterson, *Restless Giant: The United States from Watergate to Bush v. Gore* (Oxford: Oxford University Press, 2006).

30. Douglas Brinkley, "The Long Shadow," *New York Times Sunday Book Review* (May 18, 2008) consulted online at http://www.nytimes.com/2008/05/18/books/review/Brinkley-t.html.

31. Wilentz, *The Age of Reagan*, 434.

32. Ibid, 441.

33. John Abramson, *Overdo$ed America: The Broken Promise of American Medicine.* New York: HarperCollins, 2004); Marcia Angell, *The Truth About Drug Companies*; David Healy, *Pharmageddon* (Berkeley, CA: University of California Press, 2012); Merrill Goozner, *The $800 Million Pill: The Truth Behind New Drug Costs* (Berkeley: University of California Press, 2004). One has to be cautious in using texts of this kind. Often, authors will offer robust, polemical, and sometimes ahistorical, accounts of the FDA's relationship with the American pharmaceutical industry. Useful and informative, works by these authors nonetheless hinge on a clear-cut narrative often directed at a popular audience.

34. Jeremy A. Greene, *Prescribing by Numbers: Drugs and the Definition of Disease* (Baltimore: Johns Hopkins University Press, 2007); Dominique Tobbell, "'Who's Winning the Human Race?' Cold War as Pharmaceutical Political Strategy," *Journal of the History of Medicine and Allied Sciences* 64 (4) 2009: 429–473.

35. Erika Dyck, *Psychedelic Psychiatry: LSD from Campus to Clinic* (Baltimore: The Johns Hopkins University Press, 2008); David Herzberg, *Happy Pills in America: From Miltown to Prozac* (Baltimore: The John Hopkins University Press, 2008); Jeremy Kuzmarov, *The Myth of the Addicted Army: Vietnam and the Modern War on Drugs* (Boston: University of Massachusetts Press 2009); Eric Schneider, *Smack: Heroin and the American City* (Philadelphia: University of Pennsylvania Press, 2008).

36. Jerry Avorn, *Powerful Medicines: The Benefits, Risks, and Costs of Prescription Drugs* (New York: Alfred A. Knopf, 2004); Herbert Burkholz, *The FDA Follies* (New York: Basic Books, 1994); Jay Cohen, *Overdose: What's Wrong with the FDA? And What Can be Done About it?* (New York: Tarcher-Putnam, 1999); Fran Hawthorne, *Inside the FDA: The Business and Politics Behind the Drugs We Take and Food We Eat* (Hoboken, N.J.: John Wiley & Sons Inc., 2005); Philip Hilts, *Protecting America's Health: The FDA, Business, and One Hundred Years of Regulation* (New York: Alfred A. Knopf, 2003).

37. Dominique Tobbell, *Pills, Power, and Policy: The Struggle for Drug Reform in Cold War America and its Consequences* (Berkeley: University of California Press, 2012); Daniel Carpenter, *Reputation and Power: Organizational Image and Pharmaceutical Regulation at the FDA.* (Princeton, NJ: Princeton University Press, 2010), 10. Carpenter argues in his 800-page, 100-year history of the FDA that its powers, which developed in concert with its reputation, are categorized into directive power, gatekeeping power, and conceptual power. It is also worth noting that this taxonomy of power is explicitly Carpenter's and he is not simply revealing an evident historical situation.

Chapter One

The FDA in the Political and Regulatory Order, 1906–Present

The FDA, the principal regulator of the U.S. pharmaceutical industry and one-quarter of the American economy, has developed tremendously since its inception in the mid-nineteenth century, and particularly so since the early 1900s.[1] Its regulation of drug products has the potential to affect corporate behavior, personal freedom, and society at large. Yet, what is less well understood is just how much the FDA, just like the other U.S. regulatory agencies, is subject to multiple extraneous influences.[2] It must deal with numerous contrary pressures, separate useful recommendations from spurious self-serving advice, and produce policy decisions and take enforcement actions that benefit the greater public.[3] Journalist and author Fran Hawthorne explained how it fits into the political order:

> Its commissioner is appointed by the president. Its budget and commissioner have to be approved by Congress. Its officials can be hauled before a congressional committee for interrogation at any time. Its major decisions are usually vetted by the Department of Health and Human Services (DHHS), if not the White House. On top of all that, the FDA regulates the industry—pharmaceuticals—with the most powerful lobbying force in Washington, D.C. Of course all those all those players try to influence FDA decisions on issues they care about, and of course, the FDA gives in when the pressure is too great.[4]

Hawthorne's point, that the FDA has been forced to negotiate with myriad countervailing political forces and occasionally succumbs to the pressure exacted upon it, was amply demonstrated during the Reagan era.

FDA BACKGROUND: FROM 1906 TO THE REAGAN YEARS

The FDA did not begin as a "critical gatekeeper."[5] Indeed, the creation of the modern FDA surely emanated out of the reformist and progressive zeitgeist of the early twentieth century, but the agency's development, and indeed the dialogue about the proper amount of food and drug regulation in American society, was fostered by a key historical actor, Harvey Washington Wiley. Now a legend in the halls of the FDA, he championed regulation, railed against food and drug adulteration, and propelled the development of the modern FDA. Scientist, advocate, and rabble-rouser, and later appointed the FDA's first commissioner, Wiley strove to raise awareness of and lay the foundation for a greater public discussion of food and drug adulteration—one of regulation. He promoted his position before women's groups and business and trade organizations, and used such magazines as *Collier's Weekly, Good Housekeeping*, and *Ladies Home Journal*.[6]

For all Wiley's hard work, however, the issue of food and drug adulteration was only elevated to national prominence with the publication of Upton Sinclair's *The Jungle*. Describing the disturbingly unhygienic conditions under which the nation's meat supply was administered, Sinclair's book struck a visceral and resonant chord with Americans and they began to take greater stock of the issue of sullied meat and bogus drugs. Shortly thereafter, President Theodore Roosevelt (who had done some cattle ranching himself) signed the 1906 Pure Food and Drug Act and thus established the first *de jure* drug regulation. When the Act was introduced, products, including medical ones, were often incorrectly labeled, and some even contained inactive or dangerous ingredients.[7] In the words of medical doctor and author Jerry Avorn, the 1906 law signified "the first official recognition that the wholesomeness of what people put into their bodies was too important to be left exclusively up to the haphazard control of unregulated commerce."[8]

Nonetheless, this legislation generated considerable debate. According to critics, the 1906 Pure Food and Drug Act was an unnecessary, even harmful piece of legislation. First, tort actions were already available to citizens injured by mislabeled or poorly manufactured drugs, which meant Americans already possessed a legal recourse to seek financial compensation. According to this rationale, the legal system was itself a deterrent and the tort mechanism more than adequate to discourage unethical or careless business practices. Second, economic analyses also suggested that market forces themselves intrinsically provided incentives for manufacturers to create and distribute safe, trustworthy drugs of high quality, thereby rendering regulation superfluous.

The New Deal era, another epoch of reform, saw the nation's drug laws further strengthened. In 1938, President Franklin Roosevelt signed the Food, Drug, and Cosmetic Act in the wake of a drug safety scandal. The year before, in 1937, the Massengill Company had released a "sulfanilamide elixir" which contained a poisonous industrial solvent, diethylene glycol, otherwise known as anti-freeze. It killed over one hundred Americans.[9] The public was revolted by the magnitude of the tragedy and, in the aftermath of the event, John Grant published *200,000,000 Guinea Pigs* and Ruth Lamb published *American Chamber of Horrors*. Such works, similar to Sinclair's earlier politically charged book, induced further improvement of the FDA.[10] Both books indicted the drug business and the American government's complicity. In response to the furore, the U.S. Congress passed the Food, Drug, and Cosmetic Act (FDCA) and it substantively enlarged the FDA's authority to regulate the drug industry.

The FDCA held drug manufacturers to a higher standard of quality, empowered the FDA to enforce these standards through inspections and injunctions, and required pharmaceutical companies to provide evidence of safety.

Figure 1.1. Miss Ruth Lamb, Chief of Public Relations of the Department of Agriculture, Food, and Drug Administration, and her display of the worthless and harmful which she calls the "Chamber of Horrors." It is composed of before and after pictures, showing how women have been disfigured by the unknowing use of dangerous cosmetics, death certificates, and testimonials. Washington, D.C., December 20. The Library of Congress. Harris & Ewing, photographer.

According to Frank E. Young, commissioner of the Food and Drug Administration from 198 to 1989, the law was instrumental in promoting economic and scientific growth. "When President Franklin Roosevelt signed the Food, Drug, and Cosmetic Act into law on June 25, 1938," Young proclaimes, "he thus launched a half-century of scientific progress and regulatory protection for Americans."[11] A Reagan appointee, Young also touched on the U.S. pharmaceutical industry's fears of the stifling effect of regulation. In his view, the new regulatory regime established in 1938 fostered, rather than hindered, innovation. This new regime saw the genesis of the "first therapeutic revolution."[12]

Following the passage of the 1938 law, the U.S. regulatory architecture governing pharmaceutical drugs was not substantially modified again until 1962. These changes would play a significant part in the debate about FDA regulation in the 1970s and 1980s. The inspiration for the 1962 Kefauver Amendments was again tragedy. Thalidomide, a tranquilizer/sedative, had been found to cause a deformity of the limbs in newly born babies called phocomelia and though distributed largely in Europe and Canada, the dangers of the drug unsettled Americans. Photographs and television images of armless and legless babies stunned the U.S. public and left indelible, petrifying images in American hearts and minds. The liberal and ambitious Senator Estes Kefauver (D-TN), who had risen to national prominence largely on the back of his investigations into the Mafia[13] and Anti-trust and Monopoly Subcommittee hearings, quickly adopted the issue as his own. Kefauver found plenty of support in the Senate and White House for an "effectiveness" amendment. President John F. Kennedy wanted little to do with Kefauver's earlier piece of pharmaceutical pricing legislation, but the young president gladly signed the effectiveness amendments.[14]

When President Kennedy signed the amendments to the FDCA and closed the "effectiveness" loophole in the existing legislation, he gave the FDA more wide-ranging and formidable authority. In doing so, the FDA's entire *raison d'etre* was revised. A standard of effectiveness and safety had to be met prior to approval of a given drug. In the advertising and labeling of drugs, both the brand and generic name needed to be included, as well as the warnings of contraindications and possible side effects. Drug manufacturing plants were to be regularly inspected by FDA inspectors.[15] In short, the 1962 law dramatically changed the remit of the FDA, its interaction with the pharmaceutical industry, and its enforcement profile. According to one commentator, the Kefauver Act represented nothing less than a "watershed moment in the nation's approach to medications." The legislation "completely changed the way doctors and patients thought about drugs."[16]

Dissenting from this view, University of Chicago economist Milton Friedman wrote in his *Newsweek* column that the new law was dreadful and ought to be repealed. According to Friedman,

They [the amendments] are doing vastly more harm than good. To comply with them, FDA officials must condemn innocent people to death . . . Shocking it is—but that does not keep it from also being correct. Indeed, further studies may well justify the even more shocking conclusion that the FDA should be abolished.[17]

Whether one agreed with Friedman or not, and however much or little one regarded the FDA and its changing approach to drugs, the 1962 law sparked an uneven bureaucratic growth spurt at the agency. For, as the FDA was entrusted with multiple new powers (new product review, rule-making, and standard-setting obligations), the agency began to experience a significant growth in staff. From 1960 to 1970, the number of FDA employees grew from approximately 1,700 to 4,200, and by 1980, to more than 7,600. Similarly, the FDA's 1960 budget of approximately $14 million dramatically expanded to over $300 million by 1980.[18] Yet the mid- to late-1970s and 1980s was a period of static budgets and reductions in workforce levels at the FDA. According to some commentators and FDA employees, it was also a period of declining morale.

The 1970s and 1980s were indeed stirring and tumultuous times for the FDA, and though interpretations of the period vary, they are largely critical. For example, Philips Hilts, a former journalist for the *New York Times* who covered the agency observes, "the 1970s were a time of disillusionment and reaction. These forces directly affected the FDA."[19] When Reagan won the White House, "the mood in Washington suddenly changed . . . and the FDA was among the first to feel it."[20] He also asserts that New Right conservatives virulently attacked the FDA, which subsequently saw its "budgets for enforcement slashed" in an "utterly demoralizing" fashion.[21] Moreover, political scientist Stephen Ceccoli comments on the stagnation of the FDA in the 1980s. "This can be attributed largely to the efforts of the Reagan administration in reducing the size of the federal bureaucracy," he writes.[22] It was only in the late 1980s that the size of the agency began to expand. Similarly, Fran Hawthorne and Herbert Burkholz mourn the disgrace of the venerable FDA in the 1980s. Hawthorne writes, "In terms of scandals and politics, the 1980s would prove the FDA's worst decade since the passage of the 1938 law."[23] According to Herbert Burkholz, in the 1980s the FDA was transmogrified into a "symbol for bumbling bureaucracy, a byword for inefficient foot-dragging, and a fertile field for greed and corruption."[24]

Yet the FDA was also criticized for its failure to reform during the 1980s. It is crucial to note that the 1962 law had durable negative impacts on drug approval times and on drug development.[25] According to Henry I. Miller, a former FDA official, the total time required for new drug development nearly doubled after 1962—from 8.2 years to 15.2 years.[26] Since 1980, the average number of clinical trials conducted to support a new drug application more than doubled, from thirty to approximately seventy. Meanwhile, the number of patients required to support that new drug application nearly tripled, from 1,576 in the late 1970s to 4,237 in 1997. In contrast to Hilts, Ceccoli, or Hawthorne, Miller view the FDA's excessive drug regulation as harmful for Americans. "The agency," he argues, "has constantly sought new mandates and promulgated new requirements, regardless of the costs to patients and to regulated industries."[27] From his perspective, regulatory zeal has a dark side that disguises pitfalls.

As this review indicates, the contestability of drug regulation has remained a consistent feature of political debate since the enactment of the FDA in 1906. This debate has surely waxed and waned, and this pendulum swing was often directly related to catastrophes in the United States and abroad. The tenor of this contest changed in the 1970s and this was precipitated by America's economic and political fortunes, as well as a declining optimism about the future. Drug regulation was, then, a lens through which to view American society, and a subject loaded with potential political and economic pitfalls. The FDA, a bureaucracy charged with a staggeringly difficult task, reflected the times—the malaise, fear, stagnant growth, and desire for change. As a means to providing a structural and theoretical basis for this book, the following pages will be devoted to illustrating the complexity of the FDA's drug review process in reference to bureaucratic theory, the definitions of regulation, regulatory reform, and deregulation, as well as the FDA stakeholders involved in championing them.

"ALL MEDICINES ARE POISONS"

"It is easy to see why morale at the FDA is low," wrote medical doctor Jay Cohen in 2004. "FDA officers have to make difficult decisions about drugs, all of which are probably going to harm some fraction of the population."[28] When an FDA doctor must decide whether to recommend approval of a new drug, relatively little is known about the drug, and much of what is known derives from the drug company's research. Meanwhile, as the FDA deliberates, drug companies pressure the agency, their congressional supporters lobby the government, and consumer groups and the media scrutinize. The job of approving medicines is highly specialized and pressure filled, but it is also political. No wonder "many respected FDA officers have left the agency."[29]

The FDA's regulation of drugs, for the average outsider, remains a byzantine process. Many federal regulatory agencies weigh potential economic benefits in particular sectors of society against generalized risk to healthy populations of that society. Regulation of prescription drugs by the FDA involves a specialized type of risk to the individual that is never completely minimized.[30] When describing this task, it is helpful to look backward. According to Paracelsus, a sixteenth-century alchemist, "All medicines are poisons" and "the right dose differentiates a poison from a remedy."[31] His point, made during the Renaissance, highlights the intricacy of the FDA's job in evaluating medicines for both safety and efficacy.

All pharmaceutical products involve varying degrees of risk and benefit that are assumed by individual patients and consumers. No level of testing by the drug company or by the FDA can provide complete, incontrovertible information on safety and efficacy. It is near impossible for FDA regulators to accurately approve all drug products that are safe and accurately reject all drug products that are unsafe.[32] Thus, taking an FDA approved drug to mitigate health problems or enhance one's lifestyle often presents a given patient with a trade-off between possible therapeutic gains and possible adverse reactions. According to Dr. Robert Temple, FDA Director of Research and Review, no drug is completely safe.[33] In fact, FDA decisions pose risks for the agency itself, and one of four outcomes can result from an FDA drug review. First, regulators can approve a safe and effective drug product. Second, drug regulators can reject an unsafe drug product. Third, regulators can approve an unsafe drug product (Type II error). Fourth, regulators can reject a safe and effective drug product (Type I error). Since the agency's inception, FDA regulators have historically been more concerned with avoiding Type II errors because they involve the most negative feedback from policy makers, the legislature, and the public at large.[34]

Sometimes, as in the case of AIDS in the 1980s, the disease and drugs even reshape the patient's and agency's conception—the very definition—of risk and benefit. The trade-off is actually recalibrated by stakeholders, and by the perniciousness and prevalence of the given disease. With death imminent, greater risk is not just acceptable, but preferable, sometimes absolutely necessary. Hence, regulations are passed which symbolize this changing conception—this is what occurred in the 1980s, when an "angry, aware, and articulate" AIDS movement, in collaboration with Congress and pharmaceutical companies, helped refashion public perception of HIV/AIDS and influenced the FDA to change existing regulations.[35]

The marketing of a new drug, from its birth in the research lab to FDA approval, is a long, arduous, expensive process, and is another crucial element of this book. In 1987, one source estimated that the process cost an average of $231 million per drug, whereas in 2002 another source estimated $800 million.[36] Unsurprisingly, the methods of calculation vary and it is vital to note the cost of development is used to legitimate drug prices and underpin claims for more or less regulation. According to historian Barry Werth, "new drugs are exceedingly rare; novel ones still rarer." This is due to the cost and risk associated with the R&D cycle as well as the approval process.[37] Companies must perform preclinical testing in the lab and on animals. This usually takes three to four years. A company then files an investigational new drug application (IND) with the FDA and, if not disapproved in thirty days, the company may move forward with testing the compound in human subjects. This occurs in three stages: Phase I, which takes about a year, involves under one hundred healthy volunteers, and determines the compound's pharmacokinetics and correct dosage level—how the drug is absorbed, distributed, metabolized, and excreted, as well as how much of the drug is safe to administer. Phase II trials evaluate the efficacy of the drug in a larger group of volunteer patients suffering from the targeted illness or disease; these tests often take two years. Lastly, Phase III clinical trials, conducted using thousands of patients across the United States (and sometimes abroad[38]), take three years and are designed to pinpoint contraindications, also known as adverse reactions. Once the phases are completed the drug company may file for a new drug application (NDA) with the FDA.

The FDA's review process has been aided greatly by the advent of the clinical trial. A major breakthrough in its own right, the modern randomized and controlled clinical trial (RCT) was developed to determine whether a drug actually works for that which it is intended. The RCT has, at the very least, made the FDA's job easier—since the new and improved drug trial eliminated some of the problems that hitherto confused the interpretation of a trial's outcome.[39] The RCT randomly assigned patients to different treatment groups, and no human choice was involved in such action. All subjects were given an inert pill to control for the placebo and nocebo responses and physicians in some cases also operated in a "blinded" or "double-blinded" fashion, so that the experimenter's knowledge would not distort results; these changes invariably improved the validity of trial data.

As dependable as the RCT is, however, the FDA, like any business or bureaucracy, must make well-informed and safe decisions to protect the American public but also its reputation and future budget prospects. Thus, to approve a new drug application the agency must employ a benchmark to ensure the (relative) certainty of that drug trial's outcome. A given drug company, as noted earlier, must prove safety and effectiveness: it must be demonstrated "by all methods reasonably applicable" as "safe for use under the conditions prescribed, recommended or suggested in the proposed labeling." Also required, as outlined in Section 355(d) of the FD&CA, is "substantial evidence" of the drug's effectiveness.[40]

REGULATION AND DEREGULATION

Regulation in the most general sense may be considered the intentional restriction of a subject's choice of activity by an entity not directly involved in performance of the activity. It abridges a personal freedom and the scope of personal options. Some academics, for example, inject the source of authority into the definition, describing regulation as a *government's* direct influence on the social and economic activity of a society through its ability to pass rules and make laws. Certain groups, such as physicians' groups, have complained in the past that the FDA infringes on their therapeutic territory in the practice of medicine. Such complaints included calls for regulatory reform or deregulation. A broad definition of *deregulation* may therefore be simply the removal of such a choice restriction.[41]

The distinction between deregulation and regulatory reform is nuanced but important. In the broadest sense, the latter represents minimization of regulation through amendments,

> whereas the former represents a targeted measure aimed at a specific industry statute. Richard M. Cooper, formerly chief counsel for the Food and Drug Administration, explains *regulatory reform* as an effort to reduce regulation in an "across-the-board" fashion rather than "sector-by-sector."[42] The mechanisms used to achieve reform include: amendments to the Administrative Procedures Act, requirements of impact statements, sunset legislation, legislative veto, and legislative budget. In short, the goal of such mechanisms is to curtail new regulations by increasing the difficulty to regulate or by forcing reconsideration of the need for regulatory programs.[43]

Regulation is frequently separated into social and economic categories. And the Food and Drug Administration's regulation of the pharmaceutical industry falls into the former category. Clifford Winston and Robert W. Crandall, for instance, define economic regulation as the control of rates and entry conditions in a given market, whereas they define social regulation as those activities of the federal government designed to control externalities or exposures that imperil human health and safety.[44] Political ideology, moreover, is also central to understanding regulation and deregulation. According to Robert Horowitz, a given political ideology—for instance, a liberal, libertarian, or conservative model—remains a significant factor in how the value of regulation is assessed. The liberal perspective, he argues, underpins the creation of regulatory agencies. In Horowitz's estimation, they represent the concrete expression of the spirit of democratic reform; that is, they represent institutional manifestations of the victory of "the people" in their struggle against various corporate special interests.[45] In his view, the clamor for regulation is induced by market failures and monopolistic abuse by corporations and industries. By contrast, the conservative perspective criticizes regulation as counterproductive. It charges that regulation produces inefficiencies and political corruption, and that state intervention, being inimical to individual liberty, irreparably skews the proper functioning of markets. For conservatives, regulatory agencies thus constitute autonomous, self-serving, and continually expanding bureaucracies that have the potential and incentives to waste public monies and foil private initiative.[46]

According to Guthrie Birkhead, author of *Reagan's First Term,* "economic regulation is carried on by older agencies, usually with jurisdiction over specific industries, and by law independent of the executive branch. Social regulatory agencies are generally newer, have jurisdiction across industries, over substances or processes, and are parts of the executive branch."[47] Donald P. Berk breaks down social and economic regulation categorizing regulation by function. He cites four typologies: policing functions, interest-representation functions, rationalization functions, and standard-setting functions. First, policing functions flow from the public interest image of regulation occurring when a sovereign (for example, a president, commissioner, or secretary) either gives power to business or takes it away. Second, interest-representation functions hold that leisure and intangible consumption have brought individuals together into recreation organizations, which have then turned to political activity. Third, rationalization functions of regulation refer to the process of bringing rationality to business. Fourth, the standard-setting function interpretation of regulation holds that regulations are enacted to increase reliability and certainty. Standards, in other words, serve both competitive and anticompetitive purposes in relations between producers.[48] In one form or another, the FDA's regulation of the drug industry has carried out all four functions.

Scholars of bureaucracy and government also speculate and hypothesize about how deregulation tangibly affects agencies such as the FDA. Barry M. Mitnick, for example, has posited four operational forms of deregulation:

1. Catastrophic ending
2. Wind-down (guided or unguided)
3. Stripping
4. Disintegration with transfer of programs.

Each form of deregulation, according to Mitnick, occurs under different circumstances. First, catastrophic ending sees a program or agency cease without an appreciable wind-down. The result is high rate of unemployment. Second, in a wind-down (guided or unguided) form, all functions are retained for a brief period, but worker commitment dwindles and key, able personnel seek alternative jobs, which may or may not lead to seriously degraded performance. Third, in the stripping form, functions, activities, and subprograms are dropped one by one. Finally, in the last form—the disintegration with transfer of programs—a program or agency is dissolved and certain constituent parts are recombined elsewhere or transferred to a new or different agency.[49] This last form in many ways resembles the 1980s trend of the leveraged buy out, wherein a company was purchased, broken apart, and sold off. If one had to take a position about how the FDA fit within these models in the 1980s, then it most closely resembled Mitnick's form two, wind-down.

Two key figures, economists Alfred Kahn and George Stigler, emerged as influential opinion leaders in the acceptance of deregulation as a rational economic policy alternative in the 1970s. A micro-economist at Cornell University, Kahn published his two-volume opus, *The Economics of Regulation*, in 1971. It documented the failures of traditional regulation, advocated a new reliance on marginal cost-pricing, and propelled him to academic stardom. Now a celebrity in the field, he was tapped by the Carter administration to assist in the deregulation of transportation industries and a reform gala was thrown at the White House to underscore its commitment to deregulation.[50]

Also in 1971, while at the University of Chicago, where a school of free-market advocacy had begun to challenge regulatory orthodoxy, George Stigler published *The Theory of Economic Regulation*.[51] Stigler surmised that regulation could only be created for the benefit of the regulated industry and politically significant demands, in his reckoning, emerge only from producer groups, such as firms, labor unions, and trade associations. These groups have high stakes and low information costs and they are organized to pursue collective interests. Stigler theorized, moreover, that regulation "is intended merely to transfer wealth to the industry by protecting it from competition," as opposed to "being designed to cure market failures and improve allocative efficiency."[52] Significant demands are made only by the regulated industry itself and, in effect, "capture" the regulators.[53]

PRESIDENTS AND REGULATORY AGENCIES IN THE 1960S AND 1970S

In the 1960s and 1970s, a regulatory explosion occurred when a number of agencies were established by Congress to protect the environment and promote health and safety. First, the National Highway Safety Traffic Administration was created in 1966 to encourage motor vehicle safety. Then, in the early 1970s, during the Nixon administration, three important agencies were created. The Environmental Protection Agency (EPA) set standards for toxic waste and for air and water pollution control; the Occupational Safety and Health Administration (OSHA) was charged with setting safety and health standards in the workplace; and last, the Consumer Product Safety Commission (CPSC) was established to protect consumers from hazardous products. It is noteworthy that these agencies were authorized with strong bipartisan support.

Few Americans now question the need to safeguard health, safety, and the environment, but program implementation nevertheless requires a difficult balancing act. The enduring challenge—faced by the FDA and other such agencies—is to achieve the intended purpose of legislative enactments without imposing unreasonable standards and avoidable burdens on the nation's productive capacity. However, media reports of unreasonable, costly rulings by regulatory bureaucracies often appeared in the news press in the late 1960s and 1970s, forcing successive presidents to take substantive action.

Even as the regulatory state was expanded in the 1960s and 1970s, every president since Nixon has attempted, in one form or another, to exert a measure of control over the expansion of the bureaucracy. Though the peak post-war level of total bureaucratic employment was in 1968—2.9 million civilian employees and 3.6 million military personnel—Presidents Nixon, Ford, Carter, and Reagan sought to constrain the growth of bureaucratic power.[54] According to political scientist David E. Lewis, "the amount of authority delegated to bureaucratic officials has only grown over time" and, as this has occurred, Congress and presidents must increasingly rely on the expertise and capacity of government workers, particularly in areas where elected officials lack experience or knowledge." It follows "that whoever controls the bureaucracy controls a key part of the policy process."[55]

Compared to the legislative branch, presidents only have meager formal powers in the Constitution and they are forced to rely on their informal powers to achieve the political goal of reining in a U.S. bureaucracy. Congress writes specific statutes, mandates deadlines, imposes performance standards, cuts or increases budgets, and conducts investigations to rein in cabinet departments, independent agencies, clientel agencies, revenue agencies, and independent regulatory commissions. Presidents, by contrast, can use bargaining, public appeals, moral leadership, and their appointment power as sources of political influence.[56]

According to historian Edward Berkowitz, "the seventies was a time in which people rediscovered the power of the marketplace and individual responsibility and raised questions about the effectiveness of regulation to change behavior in a desired way."[57] Political scientist Marc Eisner, for his part, asserts that the dominant regulatory regime shifted from a "societal regime" to an "efficiency regime" wherein the mitigation of unpleasant health and environmental side-effects gave way to an emphasis on remedying the nation's poor macroeconomic performance.[58] And the initial effort to strengthen presidential control over the federal regulatory agencies in this time frame began with Nixon. Disturbed by the number of regulations being generated by the Environmental Protection Agency, he established the Quality of Life Review process and forced the EPA to evaluate its regulation-making. President Ford emulated his predecessor. After holding a number of economic summit meetings addressing the inflationary impact of regulations, Ford announced that his WIN (Whip Inflation Now) program would incorporate regulatory reform. On November 27, 1974, he issued Executive Order 11821, or "Inflation Impact Statements." It provided that all major legislative proposals, including regulations, certify "that the inflationary impact of such actions on the nation [had] been carefully considered."[59]

President Carter also sought to increase presidential control of the federal regulatory agencies and reduce expensive regulation. In January 1978, Carter established the Regulatory Analysis Review Group (RARG), an interagency group headed by Council of Economic Advisors Chair Charles Schultze, which was tasked with reviewing annually between ten and twenty major regulations and assessing their inflationary impact.[60] Thereafter, in March 1978, Carter issued Executive Order 12044, "Improving Government Regulations," which directed regulatory bureaucracies to prepare analyses for proposed rules that might have a price impact of $100 million. In his own defense, Carter asserted its purpose was to "ensure that Federal regulations are cost-effective and impose minimum economic burdens on the private sector."[61] Carter's actions subsequently aroused significant dissatisfaction on the part of the regulatory agencies and, in response, the president created in November 1978 the Regulatory Council, a unit composed of all heads of the executive-branch regulatory agencies. Carter ultimately proved successful in promulgating economic regulatory reform—in the trucking and airline industries—but he largely failed to make meaningful, long-lasting changes to social regulatory agencies like the FDA or EPA. According to historian Carl Biven,

> . . . economic deregulation was a matter of direct legislative action at a time when a consensus for reform existed, whereas social regulatory reform required continuing administrative battles. The president's freedom to act was limited by statutory requirements enacted by Congress, by the intense feelings of the various constituencies, and by sharp differences within the administration.[62]

Regulatory reform and relief were central goals of the Reagan administration's economic agenda and in February 1981, President Reagan's economic advisers immediately embarked on a comprehensive program to effect change.[63] The administration established a Task Force on Regulatory Relief (chaired by Vice President Bush) and issued Executive Order 12291 (which expanded Carter's previous order on cost-benefit analysis). Of course, President Reagan was not innovative in advocating regulatory relief. In fact, by 1981 it had become common practice for the chief executive to seek to limit the power of regulatory bureaucracies. Reagan's policy, however, was marked by an intensified pursuit of deregulation and heightened rhetoric about bureaucratic waste, but it was still one of continuity rather than originality.

Reagan's program of deregulation was underpinned by a robust public relations campaign that combined the language of individualism, principle, and consumption. In particular, he argued convincingly that deregulation was grounded in principled behavior and would prove good for the nation. At the same time, freedom and individualism were underlined as core values in Republican orthodoxy. Thus, any extreme limits on growth and choice in the marketplace were viewed as anathema to liberty. Reagan's administration, while not "adopting outright a libertarian position, nevertheless campaigned continuously for significant movement of the nation toward the individualism end of the continuum."[64] In historian Phillip Cooper's estimation, the campaign to win American hearts and minds struck a responsive chord in the public.[65]

REGULATORY AGENCY INFLUENCES AND STAKEHOLDERS

In the 1970s and 1980s, the agency's stakeholders attempted to influence the FDA to carry out its regulatory mandate in a certain fashion. Such stakeholders for the most part agreed upon the principle that expedient access to new drugs was needed as long as those drugs were deemed safe within the parameters of the law.

The most significant and intense pressure on the FDA to approve drugs at quicker rate, according to political scientist Paul Quirk, has traditionally emanated from industry lobbying. In 2008, George W. Bush's administration was criticized seriously for the failure to recognize and limit that industry's influence.[66] During the evaluation process there are frequent contacts between agency officials and representatives of drug companies. Paid to promote a certain drug, the latter rely on substantive clinical trial data when pitching their products; but there is evidence that they also employ hard-sell tactics, threats, and bribes. In addition, an industry trade organization, the Pharmaceutical Research and Manufacturers Association (PhRMA), wields significant clout.[67]

Adding to industry pressure in the 1980s were the American Medical Association (AMA) and American Pharmaceutical Association (APHA), medical professionals' groups which exerted tremendous influence on the FDA. In some cases, the AMA's and APHA's disaffection with the drug evaluation process lent legitimacy to industry claims of FDA over-regulation. The former argued in the mid-1970s that individual physicians were better equipped to determine patient needs than a distant and slow-moving bureaucracy. According to Paul Quirk, this organization in fact entered a new era in its history, by allying itself with the drug industry to defend the physicians' prerogatives against the growth of the FDA's authority. In his assessment, "The AMA is often the FDA's staunchest opponent."[68] Still, medical practitioners and pharmacists were by no means uniform or unwavering in their support of the pharmaceutical industry's position regarding drug regulation, but the AMA and APHA did represent a significant influential pressure on FDA employees.

At the same time, a "radical consumer movement flourished" in the early 1970s. According to historian Jeremy A. Greene, this movement, an agent of "progressive political change," proved incredibly diverse.[69] The Public Citizen's Health Research Group, for instance, which established itself as one of the more influencial groups representing patient-consumers, condemned the FDA in the 1970s and 1980s for failing to fulfill the agency's mandate and protect Americans.[70] Ralph Nader, one of America's most recognizable consumer activists, helped found the Public Citizen, a consumer group concerned with the pharmaceutical industry and its lobbying practices. Of the Public Citizen's many hard-charging health advocates, Dr. Sidney Wolfe established himself in the 1980s as the most influential and vociferous. Whether the topic was Reyes Syndrome, budget cuts, or the generic drug scandal, he challenged the FDA to tighten its regulatory standards and practices, and generally opposed the anti-regulatory advocates in business and industry. Consumer groups such as Public Citizen, it should be noted, possessed relatively paltry financial resources compared to the drug industry, but have "a generally favorable public image and can often count on rallying significant public support for their actions, and they have powerful allies in Congress."[71]

While many patient-consumers felt adequately represented by Wolfe and Public Citizen, many others believed that his protectionism and paternalism ultimately limited consumer choice. In Greene's historical treatment of the diabetes drug Orinase, he discovered that "the majority of letters from consumers found in the hearings docket appear to be concerned that the FDA might *overly restrict* consumer freedoms, not that the agency needed to increase its regulatory activities . . ."[72] The struggle over the safety of Orinase underlined, first, that no single group represented patient-consumer interests in the early 1970s and, second, the political value inherent in a timely response to patient demands.

Other patient-consumer groups, as in the case of HIV/AIDS victims, also applied considerable pressure on the FDA in the 1980s. AIDS activists and the leaders of the AIDS treatment underground, for instance, eventually helped trigger significant policy changes.[73] The treatment underground was home to a group of sympathetic doctors and scientists who were dissatisfied with the quantity and quality of new chemical entities being tested which could potentially be added to the HIV/AIDS drug armamentarium. Consequently, these displeased individuals took drastic actions, and developed clinical testing protocols and conducted unsanctioned trials. The effort was a success, of sorts, in that the FDA adapted its standard regulatory behavior and consulted with these "renegade" drug testers. For the first time, FDA officials established a liaison with leaders of a drug study that had not been

issued an investigational new drug (IND) permit and in which no institutional review board (IRB) passed judgment on the protocol. [74]

Other AIDS activists and activist groups also played significant roles in
changing FDA's standard operating procedures. The activist group that established itself as the most potent was ACT-UP (the AIDS Coalition To
Unleash Power), founded by playwright and author Larry Kramer. ACT-UP
held as its mission the urgent release of promising experimental drugs for
AIDS and it soon became highly influential. By means of civil disobedience,
protests, and meetings with high-level FDA and NIH officials the group
essentially forced the FDA to selectively rethink and redesign its traditional
regulatory and enforcement activities. [75]

Congress, for its part, has traditionally had two functions with respect to a
regulatory agency such as the FDA. It not only creates the agency, but it
conducts oversight to determine any weakness or limitations. Thereafter,
Congress recommends changes in both legislative and administrative policy.
During the 1970s and 1980s the rate at which legislators sought to investigate
and influence agency behavior increased. [76] In the 1980s, House and Senate
Subcommittees on Agriculture, Rural Development, and Related Agencies
investigated the FDA's behavior, as each had appropriations authority. The
House Committees on Government Reform, Energy and Commerce, Science, Resources, among others, investigated the agency's enforcement profile and drug approval process. Senate Committees on Agriculture, Nutrition,
and Forestry and Governmental Affairs did the same. In the Senate, John
Glenn (D-OH), Ted Kennedy (D-MA), Richard Schweiker (R-PA), among
others, championed issues related to the FDA. In the House of Representatives, John Dingell (D-MI), Al Gore (D-TN), Lawrence Fountain (D-NC),
Paul Rogers (D-FL), James Scheuer (D-NY), and Ted Weiss (D-NY), also
utilized the mechanism of congressional oversight to explore what they considered major issues of the day.

John Dingell, for example, used his position as chairman of the House
Committee on Energy and Commerce to examine the FDA's conduct. According to Herbert Burkholz, Dingell's critical letters to two successive FDA
commissioners gave birth to the pejorative term "Dingellgram." [77] Dingell
thus emerged as a *bête noire* inside the halls of the FDA in 1988, but he
proved crucial. His hearings on the FDA Division of Generic Drugs revealed
distressing flaws within the agency—in essence, a rigged approval process. It
was discovered, at his instigation, that certain drug officials had taken
bribes—holidays and hookers—to aid some companies, while hurting others.

THE CARROT OR THE STICK?

Regulatory agency behavior is far from easily explainable. The number of models designed to understand agency behavior testifies to this fact and what follows, which is by no means comprehensive, is a broad selection of theories pertinent to agency behavior. To begin, political scientist Marc Eisner, in his comprehensive examination of the various regulatory regimes in American history, places a premium on the "synthesis of policy change and institutional reform." As he sees it, "regulatory change often occurs in response to economic change and the uncertainty that such change creates. Groups mobilize in hopes of preserving or promoting certain values and interests." Thus, in his multi-causal analysis, Eisner would place the FDA within a complex milieu in which interests, political-economic ideas, and administrative reform doctrines influenced agency behavior.[78]

Moran's and Weingast's "congressional dominance theory" contends that Congress holds both the carrot and sticks necessary to control agency behavior and suggests that the FDA's actions are therefore conditioned by the preferences of the corresponding congressional oversight committees.[79] Terry Moe, however, posits the opposite; instead, he argues that given the complex hierarchy and internal organization within bureaucratic agencies such as the FDA, many career bureaucrats—who have "superior information regarding regulatory activities"—are less responsive to pressures from Congress. William Niskanen contends that an agency acts to maximize its expected budget from Congress, whereas Paul Joskow's external-signals theory holds that agencies such as the FDA try to maximize not their budget but positive feedback from outside groups. Negative feedback naturally leads to congressional oversight, internal investigations, or other attempts to intervene in agency operations, so pursuing the objective that is positive feedback ensures that the agency possesses a degree of autonomy and a foundation of political support. Political scientist Barry Friedman uses exchange theory to study why Congress, the courts, interest groups, and regulatory agencies such as the FDA comply with an anti-regulatory agenda. Exchange theory posits that a powerful actor will exact compliance from a less powerful actor as long as the powerful actor "offers his good will, his approval, or some other resource in return."[80] The less powerful actors, in short, are accommodating as long as they perceive themselves as gaining something from the exchange.[81]

Richard H.K. Vietor's organizational theory is the most multi-causal and sustainable approach currently available. It views regulatory agency policymaking as a process of constant negotiation between myriad actors and institutional structures. According to Vietor, ideology has informed the traditional regulatory models, the public-interest theory and the private-interest theory. The "public interest theory" holds regulation to be an altruistic government response to undesirable business conduct based on market failures, known as "externalities," whereas the "private-interest theory" holds that regulation works against precisely the people it is meant to protect: the public. Yet, to Vietor's mind, these approaches lack the ability to describe the FDA during the Reagan era; for the first is too naïve and the second too cynical. The answer, he suggests, rests in a combination of the two approaches and, moreover, in assigning emphasis to individual actors in addition to such aspects of the bureaucratic process as information dependency, informal procedures, organizational culture, and budgetary restraint. "We need," Vietor writes, "a broad and dynamic framework that will accommodate all four of our regulatory histories, from start to finish" and "none of those models is broad enough to explain regulation as a dynamic political-economic system, embracing causation, consequences, and the impact on business organizations." He also values this third way because it purports that the evolution of regulatory policy can only be understood industry by industry and agency by agency.[82]

Over its long history, disaster has triggered pivotal legislative changes that fundamentally altered the FDA's regulatory portfolio and its relationship with American consumers and the U.S. pharmaceutical industry. Meanwhile, the agency has negotiated with manifold stakeholders, including doctors, consumers, industry lobbyists, and politicians in Washington. These actors, going back as far as 1906, possessed contrary interests and attempted to alter the FDA's mission. The 1970s and 1980s, which saw the beginning of the Reagan era, were no different.

NOTES

1. Other agencies do have a degree of regulatory jurisdiction over the pharmaceutical industry: the Consumer Product Safety Commission, the Department of Transportation, Environmental Protection Agency, and Drug Enforcement Agency. The FDA nonetheless retains the bulk of the regulatory authority.

2. Jean-Claude Bosch and Insup Lee, "Wealth Effects of Food and Drug Administration (FDA) Decisions," *Managerial and Decision Economics* 15 (6) (1994): 589.

3. For a broader history of American regulation, see Marc Eisner, *Regulatory Politics in Transition* (Baltimore: Johns Hopkins University Press, 2000). Eisner's book does a masterful job of tracing the evolution of federal regulatory politics from the Progressive era through the New Deal and then after.

4. Fran Hawthorne, *Inside the FDA: The Business and Politics Behind the Drugs We Take and Food We Eat* (Hoboken, N.J.: John Wiley & Sons Inc., 2005), xi.

5. Henry I. Miller and David R. Henderson, "The FDA's Risky Risk-Aversion," *Policy Review* 145 (2007): 3–27, consulted at http://www.hoover.org/publications/policyreview/10183506.html.

6. Oscar E. Anderson Jr., *The Health of a Nation: Harvey W. Wiley and the Fight for Pure Food* (Chicago: University of Chicago Press, 1958) and Harvey W. Wiley, *Harvey W. Wiley, An Autobiography* (Indianapolis: Bobbs-Merril, 1930).

7. Peter Temin, *Taking Your Medicine: Drug Regulation in the United States* (Cambridge, Mass: Harvard University Press, 1980).

8. Jerry Avorn, *Powerful Medicines: The Benefits, Risks and Costs of Prescription Drugs* (New York: Alfred A. Knopf, 2004), 43.

9. Mickey Smith et al., *Pharmaceutical Marketing: Principles, Environment and Practice*, (New York: Haworth Press, 2002), 56.

10. Ibid.

11. FDA Website. Frank E. Young, *Remarks to the Association of Food and Drug Officials*, June 14, 1988, posted at www.fda.gov/bbs/topics/SPEECH/SPE00008.htm and consulted on November 22, 2005.

12. Ibid.

13. The investigations into organized crime were conducted through a Senate Special Committee to Investigate Crime in Interstate Commerce.

14. Throughout 1959–1962, Kefauver, the Democratic vice presidential candidate in 1956, raised public awareness of the pharmaceutical industry's pricing policy. He was not focusing explicitly on an efficacy amendment, rather how the industry gouged the American consumer with inordinately high prices. The thalidomide tragedy quickly changed Senator Kefauver's priorities.

15. Quoted in W. Carl Biven, *Jimmy Carter's Economy: Policy in an Age of Limits* (Chapel Hill. The University of North Carolina Press, 2002), 222. According to Biven, the law made the FDA unique. "Prior to 1964, only one regulatory agency, the FDA, had been established with the primary goal of protecting the well-being—as opposed to the economic interests—of consumers, workers, or the public. Between 1964 and 1977, eleven regulatory agencies were created to meet these goals."

16. Avorn, *Powerful Medicines*, 44.

17. Quoted in *Congressional Quarterly Almanac 1973*, 93rd Congress, 1st Session, 1973, 520–522. See also M. Silverman and Philip R. Lee, *Pills, Profits, and Politics* (Berkeley, CA: University of California Press, 1974), 244–245.

18. Anthony A. Celeste and Arthur N. Levine "The Mission and the Institution: Ever Changing Yet Eternally the Same," *FDA: A Century of Consumer Protection*, ed. Wayne Pines (Washington: Food and Drug Law Institute, 2006), 79.

19. Philip J. Hilts, *Protecting America's Health: The FDA, Business, and One Hundred Years of Regulation*, (New York: Alfred A. Knopf, 2003), 179.

20. Hilts, 209.

21. Hilts, 214–215.

22. Stephen J. Ceccoli, *Pill Politics: Drugs and the FDA* (New York: Lynne Rienner Publishers, 2004), 38–39.

23. Hawthorne, *Inside the FDA*, 48–50.

24. Herbert Burkholz, *The FDA Follies* (New York: Basic Books, 1994), 13.

25. Eli Ginzberg, *The Medical Triangle: Physicians, Politicians, and the Public* (London: Harvard University Press, 1990), 260.

26. Miller and Henderson, 5–7.

27. Henry I. Miller, "Failed FDA Reform," *Regulation* 21 (3) (1998): 24.

28. Jay Cohen, *Overdose: What's Wrong with the FDA? And What Can be Done About it?* (New York: Tarcher-Putnam, 1999), 192.

29. Ibid.

30. "FDA Reform and the European Medicines Evaluation Agency," *Harvard Law Review* 108 (8) (1995): 2010.

31. Quoted in Avorn, 72.

32. Angela Beth Ritzert, *Essays on the Development and FDA Approval of Pharmaceutical Drugs*, Unpublished PhD Dissertation (University of Kentucky, 1999), 8.

33. Committee on Government Operations, *Oversight of the New Drug Review Process and FDA's Regulation of Merital: Hearing Before the Intergovernmental and Human Resources Subcommittee of the Committee on Government Relations*, 99th Congress, May 22, 1986, 15.

34. Kip W. Visuci et al., *Economics of Regulation and Antitrust, 2nd ed.* (Cambridge, MA: MIT Press, 1998).

35. Merrill Goozner, *The $800 Million Pill: The Truth Behind New Drug Costs* (Berkeley: University of California Press, 2004), 88.

36. Goozner, 215.

37. Barry Werth, *The Billion Dollar Molecule: One Company's Quest for the Perfect Drug* (New York: Touchstone, 1995), 216.

38. Dave Collins, "Lawyer challenging reported Pfizer settlement," *Washington Post*, May 26, 2009, http://www.washingtonpost.com/wp-dyn/content/article/2009/05/26/AR20090526 01303.html.

39. Doubts about a given drug had existed for a number of reasons. The *placebo effect* in some cases caused symptomatic improvement in patients. Based on the brain's release of endogenous morphine, the placebo effect skewed trial results because of patients' innate tendencies to see causal relationships where they do not exist (this is called the recall fallacy, or post hoc, ergo propter hoc). The *nocebo response*, by contrast, induces noxious new symptoms in a given patient. The RCT eliminated confusion by systematizing the evaluation of a given treatment, and this conceptual shift, though astonishingly obvious now, symbolized nothing less than a revolution.

40. The FDA's all-important index of proof in these matters is the p-value. Though a tiny number, it is a fundamental determinant of the FDA's stamp of approval. The randomized clinical trial, while a breakthrough, rarely provides incontrovertible, clear-cut evidence that a drug is in fact effective—only that it is probably effective. In this way, the FDA's drug regulation is wedded to Sir Isaac Newton, quantum mechanics, and probabilistic reasoning. The p-value, set at .06, signifies a 6 percent chance that the observed finding in a given clinical trial can be chalked up to coincidence and 94 percent chance that the drug's effects were in fact "real." The FDA's use of the p-value thus reduces the agency's risk—and therefore the president's risk—in making a mistake regarding "substantial evidence"; it weeds out accidental results, randomness, and fluke. In a mathematical way, it lends legitimacy to trial data and allows FDA officials to make an informed decision about the risk/benefit tradeoff of a given drug.

41. Paul J. Quirk, "In Defense of the Politics of Ideas," *The Journal of Politics* (1) 50 (1980): 32–33. See also Jonathan Liebenau, "Review of Peter Temin's Taking Your Medicine: Drug Regulation in the United States," *The Economic History Review* 35 (1) (1982): 350 and Barry M. Mitnick, "Deregulation as a Process of Organizational Reduction," *Public Administration Review* 38 (4) (1978): 351.

42. Richard M. Cooper, "Regulation: Looking to the Future," *FDA Consumer* 14 (5) (1981): 52–53.

43. However, the policy of regulatory reform often has nominal effects on long-standing regulatory agencies. Major change—deregulation—will occur in regulation reduction, according to Cooper, only when the substance of regulatory standards is addressed sector by sector and statute by statute.

44. Clifford Winston and Robert Crandall, "Explaining Regulatory Policy," *Brookings Papers on Economic Activity, Microeconomics* (1994): 1–49. They define economic regulation as the control of rates and entry conditions in a given market, whereas they define social regulation as those activities of the federal government designed to control externalities or exposures that imperil human health and safety.

45. Robert B. Horowitz, "Understanding Deregulation," *Theory and Society* 15 (1986): 139–140.

46. Ibid.

47. Guthrie S. Birkhead, "Reagan's First Term," *Public Administration Review* 45 (6) (1985): 872.

48. Donald P. Berk, "Approaches to the History of Regulation," in *Regulation in Perspective: Historical Essays*, ed. Thomas K. McCraw (Cambridge: Harvard University Press, 1981), 196–200.

49. Mitnick, 351.

50. Thomas K. McCraw, *Prophets of Regulation* (Cambridge, Mass: Harvard University Press, 1981), 268.

51. Quirk, "In Defense of the Politics of Ideas," 32–33.

52. Ibid.

53. See also Gabriel Kolko's *The Triumph of Conservatism* (London: The Free Press of Glencoe, 1963) and Gabriel Kolko, *Railroads and Regulation, 1877–1916* (Princeton: Princeton University Press, 1965).

54. Bureaucrats implement, rule-make, and adjudicate. First, bureaucrats, in various departments and agencies, translate laws into specific bureaucratic routines. Second, they create quasi-legislative administrative processes that produce regulations by government agencies. Third, they apply those rules and precedents to specific cases to settle disputes with regulated parties.

55. David E. Lewis, *The Politics of Presidential Appointments* (Princeton, NJ: Princeton University Press, 2008), 6–7.

56. Ibid.

57. Edward D. Berkowitz, *Something Happened A Political and Cultural Overview of the Seventies* (New York: Columbia University Press, 2006), 10.

58. Eisner, *Regulatory Politics in Transition*, x.

59. Edward P. Fuchs and James E. Anderson, "The Institutionalization of Cost-Benefit Analysis," *Public Productivity Review* 10 (4) (1987): 29–30.

60. Susan J. Tolchin, "Presidential Power and the Politics of RARG," *Regulation* 2 (4).

61. Biven, 227–228.

62. Ibid.

63. Fuchs and Anderson, 30–31.

64. Cooper, *The War on Regulation*, 46.

65. Ibid.

66. Harold Meyerson, "Bewilder Thy Father and Mother," *Washington Post,* November 30, 2005, A23.

67. In 1994, the Pharmaceutical Manufacturers Association changed its name to Pharmaceutical Research and Manufacturers Association. The group was founded in 1958.

68. Paul Quirk, "The FDA," in *The Politics of Regulation*, ed. James Q. Wilson (New York: Basic Books, 1980), 199–200.

69. Jeremy A. Greene, *Prescribing by Numbers: Drugs and the Definitions of Disease* (Baltimore: Johns Hopkins University Press, 2007), 139–140.

70. It is important to note that not all consumer groups support upholding the existing regulatory structure. The homosexual AZT drug movement in the 1980s, for example, lobbied for a fast track system to combat the perceived drug lag so that new auto-immune deficiency syndrome cocktail drugs were more readily available for usage.

71. Quirk, 215.

72. Greene, *Prescribing by Numbers*, 141.

73. Paul A. Sergios, "The AIDS Underground, AIDS Activists, and the FDA—A Historical Overview," in *Stop the FDA: Save Your Health Freedom*, eds. John Morgenthaler and Steven Wm. Fowkes (Menlo Park, California: Health Freedoms Publications, 1992), 105–111.

74. IRB is a committee of physicians, lay people, clergy, and attorneys that approves and periodically reviews experimental protocols to ensure that the rights of human subjects are protected. Although no IRB reviewed the Q protocol, the study was adjudicated by a committee of medical and legal professionals assembled by the principal investigators themselves.

75. "AIDS Activists Stage Day-Long Demonstration at FDA," *FDA Today,* November 1988, 1.

76. Celeste and Levine, "The Mission and the Institution," 71–98. In a general sense, the intensity of congressional hearings often depends on a number of variables, namely the political leanings of certain committee chairmen and the kinds of issues about which they care.

77. Burkholz, 13.

78. Eisner, *Regulatory Politics in Transition*, xiv.

79. Barry R. Weingast and Mark Moran, "Bureaucratic Discretion or Congressional Control: Regulatory Policymaking by the Federal Trade Commission," *The Journal of Political Economy* 91 (5)(1983): 765–800; Terry Moe, "Control and Feedback in Economic Regulation: The Case of the NLRB," *American Journal of Political Science* 79 (4) (1985): 1094–1117; William Niskanen, *Bureaucracy and Representative Government* (Chicago: Aldine-Atherton, 1971); Paul Joskow, "Inflation and Environmental Concern: Structural Change in the Process

of Public Utility Regulation," *Journal of Law and Economics* 17 (2) (1974): 291–327; and Mary K. Olson, "Regulatory Agency Discretion Among Competing Industries: Inside the FDA," *Journal of Law, Economics and Organization* 11 (2) (1995): 383.

80. Barry Friedman, *Regulation in the Reagan-Bush Era: The Eruption of Presidential Influence* (Pittsburgh: University of Pittsburgh Press, 1995).

81. See also Matthew McCubbins, "The Legislative Design of Regulatory Structure," *American Journal of Political Science* 29 (4) (1985): 721–48 and Roger Noll, "Government Regulatory Behavior," in *Regulatory Policy and the Social Sciences* (Berkeley: University of California Press, 1985): 1253–1282.

82. Richard H.K. Vietor, *Contrived Competition: Regulation and Deregulation in America* (Cambridge: Harvard University Press, 1994), 311–12. Vietor outlines these models by way of introduction to his examination of the transportation (American Airlines), the energy sector (El Paso Natural Gas), telecommunications (AT&T), and financial services (BankAmerica) industries.

Chapter Two

Disenchantment and Drug Regulation during the Seventies

"The 1970s were a time of disillusionment and reaction . . . these forces directly affected the FDA." [1]

PHILLIP J. HILTS, *PROTECTING AMERICA'S HEALTH*, 2003

"The character of a nation changes with time just as an individual's character changes as he matures." [2]

STEVEN HAYWARD, *THE AGE OF REAGAN*, 2001

In the 1970s, congressional, industry, and consumer activist pressure mounted on the FDA to fulfill its mandate. For multiple, sometimes contradictory, reasons there was sustained criticism of the agency. Looking back, the period from the late 1940s to the 1960s had seen the pharmaceutical industry go through a "Golden Age" of remarkable growth and scientific achievement associated with spending during World War II. According to FDA Commissioner Frank Young, this era marked the first therapeutic revolution that spawned such momentous drugs as Cortisone in 1949, the first tranquilizer in 1952, anti-fungal antibiotics in 1954, an oral anti-diabetic agent in 1955, and an anti-viral drug in 1963. By the mid-1970s, however, talk of the "Golden Age" had passed. Instead, many critics decried an onerous drug lag that had its roots in the 1962 Kefauver-Harris "efficacy" amendments to the original 1938 Food Drug and Cosmetics Act. Yet other FDA stakeholders endorsed a sobering alternative viewpoint that would resonate

37

throughout the 1980s: the FDA was beholden to industry and it was exceedingly paternalistic toward American patient-consumers.[3]

The FDA in the mid-1970s was wedged in a middle ground between warring factions and diverse stakeholders. A number of actors and groups on both the left and right of the political spectrum—consumer advocates, regulatory reformers, academicians, industry representatives, and administration officials—sought to advance the idea that regulations governing the nation's drug supply were being applied too strictly or too leniently. Various groups saw the agency as an inefficient entity and a burdensome obstacle to growth. By contrast, others viewed the agency as either coddling or kowtowing to industry. The FDA was compelled to negotiate with these contrary pressures, even as the number of congressional hearings increased. An acrimonious and lengthy investigation of the drug approval process ramped up the agency's public profile and the debate over the Carter administration's Drug Reform Act intensified. Accordingly, the Bureau of Drugs became no less than a policy battle ground, a test-tube, in which oppositional conceptions of the proper role of regulation in society faced off.

Hot Dogs, Baseball, and Apple Pie

In the fall of 1975, the Democratic leaders of the Senate and House Commerce Committees sent a strong but fallacious message to President Ford addressing what they perceived to be a destructive wave of regulatory reform initiatives. They interpreted the legislative proposals made earlier in the year to deregulate the Securities and Exchange Commission and the trucking, banking, and airline industries as contradicting traditional American ideals. "Regulation," the message read, "is as American as hot dogs, baseball, apple pie and Chevrolet."[4]

In fact, this was not quite right. The late 1960s and early 1970s had indeed seen the expansion of the regulatory state during the Nixon presidency, but the public's feelings toward regulation in 1975 were, contrary to the wording of the message, far from static.[5] If anything, American citizens were beginning to question the necessity of regulation in general, prompting both Republicans *and* Democrats to eventually champion regulatory issues. According to political scientist Stephen Skowronek, "By 1976, the liberalism of Roosevelt had become vulnerable . . . to political charges of burdening a troubled economy with bureaucratic overhead."[6] Historian Edward Berkowitz has argued that deregulation in the 1970s transcended the nation's ideological divide. "Deregulation represented one of the era's few successful liberal-conservative collaborations."[7] Similarly, historian Robert M. Collins contended, "The drive toward deregulation was bipartisan in nature . . . Reagan was a latecomer to the deregulatory push."[8] Richard H.K. Vietor, another business historian of the period, agreed:

... the recision of regulation across a dozen industries in the [late 1970s and early 1980s] was no more a coincidence than the imposition of regulation was during the crisis of the Depression . . . sudden economy-wide performance problems undermined political faith in the prevailing systems of economic management—competition in the first instance, regulation in the second.[9]

These scholars commonly regard the 1970s as a turning point for regulation. The drivers behind that turning point, most agree, were widespread dissatisfaction with the governmental institutions, an apparent decline in American prestige on the world stage, and a sluggish U.S. economy.[10] This further bolstered the debate about the proper amount of regulation in society.[11]

Looking backward, dissatisfaction with government began with odious behavior in the executive branch and was exacerbated by a perception that America was losing the Cold War. After Nixon resigned in August 1974 and was pardoned by his successor President Gerald Ford, some Americans concluded a Faustian bargain had been struck. Ford subsequently proclaimed that the national nightmare was over, but erosion of faith in the presidency and of the U.S. government continued unabated. Abroad, U.S. supremacy was challenged. Though the reality was far more complex, it appeared that the United States was losing the global struggle against Communism—in such far off places as Mozambique, Angola, Ethiopia, Laos, and Vietnam. The future did not seem as bright and "Americans," according to Robert Collins, "came increasingly to lose their traditional faith in the future. . . ."[12]

The foundering American economy was a significant factor in the emergence of regulatory reform as a viable policy alternative. The recession of 1974–1975 (precipitated by reductions in oil exports from the Organization of Petroleum Exporting Countries) caused Americans to howl "in economic pain and anxiety."[13] Between the years 1947–1973, the average annual increase of output per worker had been 3 percent. From 1973–1979, it dropped to 0.8 percent.

By the presidential election in 1980, inflation had reached 12 percent, and would reach an inconceivably high 18.5 percent. One outcome of this combination of high unemployment and inflation, what economist Arthur Okun dubbed stagflation, was widespread disillusionment with the established Keynesian doctrine. While confused economists squabbled about the micro-level causes of stagflation (and there were myriad reasons[14]), older economic debates such as the amount proper amount of social and economic regulation gained traction.[15]

Theories of deregulation and regulatory reform materialized in the 1970s as solutions to the nation's economic woes, including the pharmaceutical industry's slowdown. While the Club of Rome and E.F. Schumacher advocated restraint and proposed that a threshold had been reached, theories of deregulation instead offered hope of a rosier, richer future. [16] Certain analyses found, for instance, that the total resources devoted annually to regulatory enforcement and compliance during the 1970s ranged from 2 to 4 percent of GNP. Evidence suggested, furthermore, that as much as 10 to 25 percent of the slowdown in productivity growth in the late 1970s might have been attributable to regulation. [17] An American Enterprise Institute book series on prescription drug regulation, for example, noted that adjustments to the FDA's drug approval process would not only stimulate U.S. pharmaceutical industry growth but also create the conditions for U.S. companies to supplant emerging Japanese and Western European competition, and once again achieve unrivaled preeminence in the global pharmaceuticals market. Deregulation was thus touted as a solution to the slow economy.

Regulatory theories of this sort had remarkable appeal. In the Democratic Party, for example, President Jimmy Carter made common cause with Senator Edward Kennedy, his foremost liberal critic on many other socioeconomic issues, on regulatory reform. Despite minor opposition from the left of the Democratic Party base, President Carter and Kennedy held a joint press conference to announce trucking deregulation. [18] They also stood side by side during the ceremonial signing of the airline deregulation bill. [19] In doing so, President Carter kept his campaign promise to reform government in a moderate, deliberate manner but he also, inadvertently or not, legitimized deregulatory ideas and policies for his eventual successor. He established the conditions and thereby enabled Ronald Reagan to further an economic program of this type. Carter later commented of his deregulatory program, "[it is] the greatest change in the relationship between business and government since the New Deal." [20]

You Can't Trust the Government in Washington

Americans were generally receptive to this change in the late 1970s and there may even have been a shift toward greater acceptance of regulatory review and reform. Polling data backs this up. Reagan was elected in 1980 at the lowest point of a sixteen-year trend of declining confidence in government. In 1980, the view that government wastes "a lot of the money we pay in taxes" reached a peak of 78 percent. It fell to 63 percent in a post-election survey taken in 1984 by CBS News and the *New York Times*. The view that "you can't trust the government in Washington to do right most of the time" was held by 73 percent in 1980 and 51 percent in 1984. [21]

The upward trend of disenchantment with government influence unmistakably affected the electorate's perception of regulatory reform. A *New York Times*/CBS poll reported in 1978 that 58 percent of respondents agreed that the government had gone too far in regulating business. In November 1980, that number was 65 percent. Five months later the same percentage agreed.

The National Opinion Research Center, in a similar survey, found in August 1979 that 47 percent of people felt there should be less government regulation of business. In December 1980, 54 percent felt this way. According to certain Harris polls, 60 percent of respondents agreed when asked in October 1979 that Ronald Reagan was right to get government out of business. In April 1980, 69 percent agreed. Was the FDA's regulation of pharmaceuticals affected by such opinion trends? In 1980, 37 percent said there was not enough social regulation, namely, government regulation of "the health and safety of working conditions"; in 1984, the figure was 48 percent.

The regulation of pharmaceuticals was not thought special by Americans. That is, the regulation of pharmaceuticals *did not* stand out. A Harris poll conducted in the late 1970s found in March 1976 and May 1977 that 48 percent of respondents favored "breaking up" the drug industry. This percentage was not statistically different from any other American industry, meaning Americans did not assign any greater significance or value to the pharmaceutical industry.

Contrary to this overall assessment, however, Seymour Martin Lipset and William Schneider have argued, "A majority has always said they opposed greater regulation, but over the years—as more and more regulation has been enacted—a majority has also voiced approval of existing regulation and indicated that it did not want to roll back the tide."[22] A *National Journal Opinion Outlook* "briefing paper" found "little or no evidence to suggest that disaffection with the regulatory activities has made more people willing to transfer power to business."[23] It is thus prudent to conclude that among the electorate there was no uniform consensus concerning either deregulation or regulatory reform. If anything, Americans exhibited pragmatism and a "substantial ambivalence" toward regulation. They sought protection from what economists would call harmful externalities.[24] They also desired an unfettered free market system that facilitated growth and freedom.[25] Depending on how a polling question might be asked, Americans favored or did not favor regulation. In an interview with journalist David S. Broder, presidential domestic adviser Stuart Eizenstat summed up the electorate's viewpoint. "There is a basic conflict between the public's desire for greater services—especially in the areas of health, education and the quality of the physical and social environment—and its resistance to government spending and regulation."[26] America's citizens wanted government to protect them but they did not want to pay for that protection.

It is crucial to highlight that Americans were conflicted in the 1970s. Public opinion surely remained diverse, but tilted toward pessimism and disenchantment with government. Regulation was regarded by the electorate with a mixture of scepticism, support, and self-interest. In 1975, key Democratic leaders in Congress may have thought regulation was American as hot dogs, apple pie, baseball, and Chevrolet. By 1991, it was a different story.

"Gradually, there has been a realization that regulation can damage very important interests," said Senator Carl M. Levin (D-MI). "Even the more progressive members of my party understand that."[27] In short, Americans and their political representatives were uncertain about regulation—a profoundly significant fact for the chief regulator of the pharmaceutical industry, the FDA.

The Tipping Point

Politicians and voters began to see regulation in a different light in the 1970s, and business and academia participated in this process. The passage of multiple new regulatory laws that cut across a wide spectrum of American industries—those considered necessary to manage externalities which industry was either incapable of or unwilling to do—spurred business owners into action.[28] American business leaders, with the support of the academic establishment, steadily grew more attentive to the politics of regulation by 1974. According to sociologist Patrick J. Akard, "a general consensus emerged [in the mid-1970s] between big and small businesses, industrial and financial capital, over the domestic *political* sources of economic instability and the steps needed for economic revitalization."[29] One such step was the promotion and enactment of deregulatory policies. According to Akard, "the issue of regulation was especially significant in unifying business interests."[30] Historian Thomas McCraw called the overall deregulation movement a "broad and strikingly mixed coalition."[31] A tipping point had been reached and the subsequent actions taken to influence Congress to reduce or reform regulation manifested in three distinct but interlocking forms.

One form promoted political action committees (PACs). Organized labor in the United States had pioneered the PAC in the early 1970s and was well ahead of business in total numbers. In 1974, for example, labor political action committees outnumbered corporate PACs by 201 to 89. By 1978, however, business held the advantage. Over 784 corporate PACs and 500 trade association or business-oriented PACs outweighed and overshadowed the 217 labor-oriented PACs. According to political historian William Berman, in 1978 the top ten corporations in the United States donated $70,000, whereas those nearer the bottom of the top 500 largest firms gave $6,000 per firm.[32]

A second form of business political action was grassroots lobbying. Business organizations in the mid- to late-1970s established extensive lobbying networks, copying the strategies developed by others (in this case public interest activists). The best example is the Chamber of Commerce. Traditionally, this organization had spoken for the grassroots of American business, mainly small entrepreneurs, but in the climate of the mid-1970s, the Chamber of Commerce, under aggressive new leadership (the heads of Procter &

Gamble, U.S. Steel, and General Motors), became a powerful voice of big business. The Chamber of Commerce's lobbying activities involved mobilizing employees, customers, suppliers, and stockholders as well the use of direct mail and other technologically sophisticated organizing techniques. According to Thomas B. Edsall, between 1974 and 1980, the Chamber of Commerce doubled its membership to 165,000 companies and tripled its annual budget to $68 million.[33]

A third way in which American businesses involved themselves in the politics of regulation was through the creation or revitalization of business policy groups. The Business Roundtable, composed of most major U.S. companies' chief executive officers, represented the largest businesses; however, smaller businesses also united in organizations such as the National Federation of Independent Businesses, the American Council for Capital Formation, and the National Association of Manufacturers.[34] These groups, once clustered, wielded considerable influence.

The Food and Drug Administration, for its part, faced a potent business and trade lobby. First, the Pharmaceutical Manufacturers Association (PMA), now known as Pharmaceutical Research and Manufacturers Association (PhRMA), was a significant force that proved very effective in advancing its own agenda. This industry pressure was further enhanced by the medical profession's support, including the American Medical Association's (AMA) and American Pharmaceutical Association's (APHA). Intermittent disaffection on the part of the AMA and APHA lent authenticity to industry's claims of FDA over-regulation.[35]

The actions taken by businesses and trade associations exerted unmistakable pressure on policy-makers in government and officials at the FDA; yet it would be erroneous to assert that these American businesses operated independently or without guidance. That guidance—vital for the purposes of legitimacy—derived from economists, political scientists, and sociologists, who, while working in academia and think tanks, provided an intellectual foundation for certain organizations' criticism of governmental regulation. Business in turn offered recompense in the form of generous donations to libraries and university departments.[36] According to law professor Grant Gilmore,

> There has always been a symbiotic relationship between the academic establishment, which provides the theories, and the economic establishment, which appreciates being told that the relentless pursuit of private gain is the best way of serving public interest.[37]

The academic establishment, in his view, provided an objective and rational critique of regulation, a perspective that helped business leaders "transcend the apparent pursuit of narrow self-interest."[38]

Basis for the intellectual backlash against regulation had begun as early as the mid-1960s but did not gain real traction until the early 1970s. Economists Alfred Kahn and George Stigler produced substantive and critical analyses of regulation in operation, particularly in transportation.[39] In 1989, economist Sam Peltzman offered a reflective assessment of the field of economics in the 1970s and early 1980s. Professional economists, in his estimation, were nearly homogeneous in their support of wholesale deregulation of business. "Probably not since the rise of free trade in the nineteenth century has so broad a professional consensus been so reflected in policy" and "the reason for this consensus is economist's belief that deregulation enhances efficiency."[40] Former Chairman of President Nixon's Council of Economic Advisers Herbert Stein agrees with the assessment of homogeneity. "For a long time," he writes, "almost all American economists—conservatives and liberals, Keynesians and monetarists—have agreed that deregulation of the economy, or at least of some aspects of it, would be a good thing . . . after all, the virtue of the market is one of the first things every American economist learns."[41]

Yet Kahn's and Stigler's original theories were disseminated into the political dialogue of the times more quickly than heretofore largely because of the advent of the think tank, a forum independent of the university which also facilitated academic research and a discussion of regulation. The Heritage Foundation and its sister organization, the Committee for the Survival of a Free Congress, were established in 1973 with the help of a $250,000 grant from Colorado beer baron Joseph Coors. That same year billionaire Richard Mellon Scaife gave the Heritage Foundation $900,000. Oil and gas millionaires David and Charles Koch co-founded the Cato Institute in 1977. Other major institutions include the Lynde and Harry Bradley Foundation, the John M. Olin, Foundation and the Smith Richardson Foundation.[42] With the resources provided by such donors, the relationship between academia and business was fortified.

Targeting the Food and Drug Administration

Amid this climate of increased business activity and disillusionment, the FDA was specifically targeted for attack. According to historian Dominique Tobbell, "the industry and its allies situated their opposition to greater pharmaceutical regulation with the broader debate about the appropriate level of government oversight of the American economy."[43] The American Enterprise Institute (AEI), for example, sponsored a book series called AEI Studies on the Impact of Regulation on Drug Regulation. In 1974, Sam Peltzman published *Regulation of Pharmaceutical Innovation: The 1962 Amendments*, which articulated the problems inherent to the 1962 law signed by President Kennedy. The next year, in 1975, William Wardell and Louis Lasagna co-authored *Regulation and Drug Developments*. In 1976, Henry Grabowski published *Drug Regulation and Innovation: Empirical Evidence and Policy Options.* The fourth in the AEI series, Robert Helms' *Drugs and Health* was published in 1981.

In addition to the book series, the American Enterprise Institute hosted events that questioned the FDA's regulation. A 1975 roundtable featured Ronald Reagan, who claimed that the FDA was needlessly killing Americans. Referring to the tuberculosis drug Rifampin, he declared, "I think something more than 40,000 tuberculars alone have died in this country who conceivably could have been saved by a drug that has been widely used the past few years throughout Europe."[44] In this case, Reagan was woefully inaccurate. Rifampin had already been on the U.S. market for four years and been approved by the FDA five months after the manufacturer submitted the application. Such book series and the public events, if nothing else, fostered greater consciousness of drug regulation in the United States. According to journalist Greg Anrig, groups like AEI continued to "hammer away" on the topic of "unreasonable delays in approving drugs and medical devices." The evidence marshaled against the FDA, states Anrig, was often as fallacious as Reagan's Rifampin claim. Nevertheless, the sheer repetition of the argument—the FDA as executioner—helped it gain traction.[45]

There was by no means total academic uniformity vis-à-vis FDA regulation. In fact, there were strong undercurrents of radical consumer activism during the 1970s.[46] Dr. Sidney Wolfe created the Health Research Group, which has continually monitored the government's health regulatory activities with a dogged and perceptive eye. Moreover, the noted consumer advocate Ralph Nader helped found the Public Citizen, an intellectual watchdog organization that condemned the FDA and pharmaceutical industry lobbying practices during the 1970s and 1980s.[47] These consumer groups, as well as others like the Consumer Federation of Americas, acted as counterpoints to the anti-regulatory advocates, pharmaceutical industry lobbyists, the AMA, and APHA.

The Negative Influence of Congress in the 1970s and Beyond

The U.S. Congress was another essential influence on the Food and Drug Administration in the 1970s, and it would remain so in the 1980s. During the first half of its existence, the FDA was subject to relatively little oversight from congressional committees and essentially left to its own devices. During the 1950s, however, Congress put a spotlight on the FDA and the agency's actions were increasingly politicized. Especially after 1960, the number of oversight hearings was ratcheted up even further. This phenomenon increased to an even greater extent in the 1970s and beyond. Leaders in the pharmaceutical industry agreed. According to Robert P. Luciano, one-time president and chief executive officer of Schering-Plough, the "show" hear-

ings in the 1970s "occupied a lot of time" and the increased political pressure
was not always helpful in resolving the issues of the day.[48]

In 1974, FDA Commissioner Alexander M. Schmidt commented on the
frequency and persistent negativity of the congressional oversight hearings:

> By far the greatest pressure that the Bureau of Drugs or the Food and Drug
> Administration receives with respect to the new drug approval process is
> brought to bear through Congressional hearings. In all of our history, we are
> unable to find one instance where a Congressional hearing investigated the
> failure of FDA to approve a new drug.[49]

In his estimation, Congress was invariably negative. The commissioner
also added:

> The occasions on which hearings have been held to criticize approval of a new
> drug have been so frequent in the past ten years that we have not even at-
> tempted to count them. At both the staff level and the managerial level, the
> message conveyed by this situation could not be clearer. Whenever a difficult
> or a controversial issue is resolved by approval, the Agency and the individu-
> als involved will be publicly investigated. Whenever it is resolved by disap-
> proval, no inquiry will be made.[50]

He concluded, "The congressional pressure for *negative* action is therefore intense, and ever increasing."[51] The merits of Schmidt's statement were
questionable but his remarks nonetheless revealed the defensiveness of the
FDA's leadership as Congress enlarged the scope of its oversight.

As the 1970s reached their end, the FDA undertook an evaluation of its
relationship with the legislative branch of government and it concluded that
it indeed had just cause to be defensive, for the agency was surely under
threat. According to the FDA's internal report on the 96th Congress of
1979–1980, it anticipated increased congressional pressure in the 1980s. The
report also discussed the ascendance of regulatory reform as a major policy
issue in Washington. Also, three other interlocking trends had their genesis
in this growth and acceptance of regulatory reform. One was Congress's
growing tendency to restrict FDA actions and reduce its authority. A second
was strong and continuing emphasis on broad scale regulatory reform measures. A third trend, according to the FDA report, foresaw Congress applying
greater pressure on the FDA to approve or speed approval of products or
categories of products.

The report concluded, lastly, that the reform effort was uncharacteristical-
ly robust and would remain so after the Republican victory in 1980. Whereas
Congress had periodically sought to constrain the FDA, ". . . the 96th Congress was unusual in that it imposed or attempted to impose a large number
of restrictions, utilising a variety of methods, including legislation, appropri-

ation report language and oversight hearings."[52] There had been a move to abolish the 1962 efficacy requirement, for example, and individuals had introduced bills in the House to mandate approval of such drugs as Laetrile. The immediate future, according to the FDA's report, held much of the same. "The November 1980 election resulted in Republican control of the Senate for the first time in 25 years and substantial GOP gains in the House." This would encourage "conservative Members to continue to exert greater control over regulatory agencies such as FDA" and it was thus "not unreasonable to anticipate a continuation or even expansion of anti-regulatory restrictions."[53]

The report, as it happened, was prescient. Congress surely placed pressure on the FDA to justify certain decisions. Emboldened by the AIDS epidemic, Congress also advocated a speedier, more streamlined FDA. That would be years ahead, however. What follows is an analysis of the contrary pressures that drew the Carter administration and Congress into the FDA's day-to-day operations in the 1970s—and how this, in turn, set the stage for the FDA during the Reagan years.

FDA Bias, the Drug Lag, and the Drug Regulation Reform Act

The FDA in the 1970s was clearly caught between regulatory reformers and consumer activists in the Carter administrations as well in Congress. The following pages will examine the allegations of bias, the drug lag, and the failure of the Drug Regulation Reform Act. These vignettes are enlightening because they illustrate how the agency was attacked for its sympathetic treatment of the drug industry, but also how it was derided for its inability to approve enough new drugs. The Drug Regulation Reform Act, for example, a massive bill designed to ameliorate both issues—by simultaneously strengthening the FDA's regulatory powers and streamlining the drug review process—could not find enough support in Congress. These stories encapsulate how the FDA interacted with Congress, the Carter administration, regulatory reformers, and consumer activists in the 1970s; but they also encapsulate the complexity of the political firmament of the times.

In 1974, the FDA was shaken by allegations of bias. The key congressional figure investigating the agency at that point was Senator Edward Kennedy, a politician who possessed both consumer activist and regulatory reform instincts. But in 1974 it was his consumer activist side that was on full display as he commenced Health and Judiciary committee hearings directed at the relationship between drug companies and the FDA. A number of witnesses, physicians, and drug reviewers subsequently told Congress that recommendations for drug approvals were often accepted quickly, while recommendations for non-approvals were met with antagonism and were sometimes contested, or even overruled.[54] These witnesses, who had overseen new drug applications, alleged that they were transferred, harassed, or simply excluded from further important meetings for insisting that the evidence supporting the drug approval was, if not false, certainly inadequate to justify approval.[55] In one case, a reviewer was transferred to a new division within the Bureau of Drugs. In a number of other cases, reviewers were transferred to work on a project or field not even related to their principle area of expertise. This amounted to a widespread policy of neutralization that undermined the spirit of the regulatory statutes—in short, a bias in favor of industry.[56]

In response to the alarming allegations, Commissioner Alexander Schmidt took immediate action to appease Congress, consumer activists, and the general public. Any question about the FDA's integrity had to be examined promptly and the agency's stakeholders needed mollification; therefore, the commissioner, even as he defended the agency energetically, promised to establish an internal task force to investigate the validity of the claims. For the sake of objectivity and propriety, on August 21, 1974, he also requested that the Assistant Secretary for Health Charles C. Edwards create an independent and concurrent panel to investigate the FDA's policies and procedures relating to new drugs. The overall goal of the investigations, both internal and external, was to scrutinize the FDA's protocols and personnel, foster public confidence in the FDA, and prove or disprove whether the agency was a bona fide regulatory agency rather than a slavish puppet of industry.[57]

Commissioner Schmidt thus took the necessary and prudent steps to investigate the claims of industry favoritism, but he also publicly defended the agency in a vigorous fashion. As demonstrated earlier, Schmidt articulated a widespread feeling within the FDA, justified or not, that Congress's oversight function had become excessively and improperly politicized. This meant the Health subcommittee itself, as well as countless other congressional hearings, was partly culpable for the drug review slowing down. "Until perspective is brought to the legislative oversight function," Schmidt argued, "the pressure from Congress for FDA to disapprove new drugs will continue to be felt, and could be a major factor in health care in this country."[58] Schmidt was, as he made such comments, voicing the belief that the FDA was under numerous pressures in a political environment in transition.

On February 21, 1975, the scandal over potential bias at the FDA mounted when the Secretary of Health, Education, and Welfare Caspar Weinberger established the Review Panel on New Drug Regulation. He charged it with a number of tasks: (1) review current policies and procedures of the FDA relating to the approval and disapproval of new drug; (2) evaluate the implementation of these policies and procedures by the Food and Drug Administration; and (3) ascertain the nature, extent, and adequacy of public, industry, and professional participation in the new drug review process. Besides such duties, the Panel was also asked to review Commissioner Schmidt's internal investigation, determine its authenticity, and assess whether the evidence justified the conclusions.[59] With detachment and a desire for truth, HEW thereby set in motion a process that would hopefully produce an unequivocal and reliable assessment of the FDA, the implication being that this was something the FDA itself could not provide.

First, Commissioner Schmidt reported the findings of his own internal audit to Congress in October 1975 and the results *did not* accord with the testimony of the former Bureau of Drugs officials. Schmidt contended that there was *no bias*. His report contained five key points:

1. No drugs had been approved improperly
2. Bias during the drug approval process was nonexistent
3. Industry domination of the Bureau of Drugs was nonexistent
4. Harassment of employees or pressure to approve drugs through transfer was nonexistent
5. No official had been overruled without the justifiable evidentiary basis.

The five points of Schmidt's report directly contradicted the assertion about a policy of neutralization. Nevertheless, the commissioner did admit that certain drug review officials had been, as was alleged, overruled and transferred during the drug approval process; but such incidents were precipitated by "administrative and personnel deficiencies," and did not involve "the integrity of the review process or its managers."[60] These findings, not surprisingly, failed to quell the scandal; allegations of bias during the drug approval process were far too important to be papered over hastily.

By March 1977, Schmidt's report, which exonerated the agency, was found to be flawed. The Review Panel had investigated the accusations of bias independent of the FDA and it arrived at a different conclusion; it asserted that allegations of "undue industry influence," "improper transfers, details or removals," "improper use of advisory committees," and "improper use of medical officer recommendations,"[61] had not been correctly addressed by Schmidt's FDA report.

To make matters even more complicated, the Chairman of the Review Panel Dr. Thomas Chalmers quit his job amid serious disagreements about the direction of the Panel. He argued that the Review Panel's report overemphasized the inadequacies of the initial FDA report and too much was being made of the bias allegations by the HEW Panel. Enough analysis had already been done, he felt, and more than enough money had already been spent; thus, Chalmers concluded that a reinvestigation of the FDA—one of the Review Panel's primary recommendations in 1976—was unwarranted and unnecessary. To make his point, Chalmers, already a pariah on the panel, resigned as chairman in June 1976, and his vice-chairman, Norman Dorsen of Columbia University, was elected chairman on July 18, 1976.[62]

The second investigation, led by Dorsen, again found the FDA report unsound. On March 21, 1977, after conducting an exhaustive investigation, the Review Panel's Special Counsel submitted a finding.[63] Published in its entirety in May 1977, the report was critical of the FDA. It held:

1. FDA has not been dominated by the pharmaceutical industry and during the years in question the agency often took a firm regulatory posture, although individual cases of inappropriate contacts with drug companies occurred.
2. Beginning in 1970, FDA management, while not dominated by industry, made a conscious effort to make the agency less adversarial toward and more cooperative with drug manufacturers and to neutralize reviewing medical officers who followed a different philosophy.
3. The program to neutralize the more adversarial reviewers was carried out by various devices, including a systematic pattern of involuntary transfers. Some of these transfers were probably unlawful in that they constituted "adverse reactions," without the transferees being offered a hearing as required by Civil Service regulations, and some actions, while not unlawful, were carried out in an unprofessional and discourteous manner.[64]

The Review Panel thus disagreed with the Commissioner Schmidt's internal report. In fact, the FDA was condemned for its spurious behavior and entrenched values, if not its outright bias favoring industry; and the Bureau of Drugs, as a regulator, as a safeguard, and protector of America's health, was found unreliable.

The perception of the FDA in the mid-1970s mirrored broader disenchantment with government and its institutions. This vignette suggests the FDA was considered untrustworthy. Many consumer activists believed the FDA favored industry, and if the new Review Panel report was believed (for it, too, was disputed), BOD was not a model of bureaucratic virtue, neither wholly efficient, nor above reproach. The drug approval process, rather, was shaped and influenced by industry preferences, and to a disconcertingly high degree. Of course it was always known that industry plays a role in the drug approval process, for such input was and remains vitally necessary; however, the revelations elicited by the original Edward Kennedy hearings emphasized that the regulator/industry relationship was far from equitable.

NOTES

1. Philip J. Hilts, *Protecting America's Health: The FDA, Business, and One Hundred Years of Regulation* (New York: Alfred A. Knopf, 2003), 179.

2. Steven Hayward, *The Age of Reagan: The Fall of the Old Liberal Order, 1964–1980* (Roseville, CA: Prima Publishing, 2001), 612.

3. Frank E. Young, *Remarks to the Association of Food and Drug Officials,* June 14, 1988. Posted at www.fda.gov/bbs/topics/SPEECH/SPE00008.htm, consulted on November 22, 2005. With respect to regulatory capture and how an agency can beome beholden, consult Stigler and Kahn. Also, see Sam Peltzman, Michael E. Levine, and Roger Noll, "The Economic Theory of Regulation After a Decade of Deregulation," *Brookings Papers on Economic Activity, Micro-economics* (1989): 1–59.

4. Quoted in Michael Pertschuk, *Revolt Against Regulation: The Rise and Pause of the Consumer Movement* (Berkeley: University of California Press, 1982), 50. This message was, according to Pertschuk, a Congressional Democratic Policy Statement on Regulatory Reform paper and was presented to the White House on June 25, 1975.

5. More than twenty-five federal laws were enacted between 1967 and 1973, the most important of which were the National Environmental Policy Act (1969), the Occupational Health and Safety Act (1970), the Consumer Product Safety Act (1972), and the Clear Air Act Amendments (1970).

6. Quoted in John W. Sloan, *The Reagan Effect: Economics and Presidential Leadership* (Lawrence: University Press of Kansas, 1999), 34.

7. Edward D. Berkowitz, *Something Happened A Political and Cultural Overview of the Seventies* (New York: Columbia University Press, 2006), 166.

8. Robert M. Collins, *Transforming America: Politics and Culture in the Reagan Years* (New York: Columbia University Press, 2007), 82.

9. Richard H.K. Vietor, *Contrived Competition: Regulation and Deregulation in America* (Cambridge: Harvard University Press, 1994), 2.

10. A number of key events fused with business, academic, and political phenomena on the home front to animate anti-regulatory ideas in the 1970s: the assassinations of high-profile public figures like Bobby Kennedy and Martin Luther King, Jr. in the late 1960s, the contestation surrounding the war in Vietnam, the Watergate scandal, the oil crisis, the Ford pardon of Nixon, and Communist gains in Africa and Southeast Asia combined with the Soviet invasion of Afghanistan created a perception the United States was losing the Cold War as did the kidnapping of American diplomats at their Tehran embassy by Islamic fundamentalists.

11. William Leuchtenburg, "Jimmy Carter and the Post-New Deal Presidency," in *The Carter Presidency: Policy Choices in the Post- New Deal Era,* eds., Gary M. Fink and Hugh Davis Graham, *The Reagan Effect,* (Lawrence: University Press of Kansas, 1998) 7–29. See also Sloan, 33–34 and Dan T. Carter, *From George Wallace to Newt Gingrich: Race in the Conservative Counterrevolution, 1963–1994* (Baton Rouge: Louisiana State University Press, 1996), Gary Gerstle and Steve Fraser, eds. *The Rise and Fall of the New Order, 1930–1980* (Princeton, NJ: Princeton University Press, 1989). Politicians like Richard Nixon and George Wallace had managed to exploit cleavages in this coalition through the use of wedge issues such as law and order, busing, abortion, and prayer in schools.

12. Collins, *Transforming America,* 14.

13. Pertschuk, *Revolt Against Regulation,* 50.

14. The most persuasive and resonant *general* reason behind the economic turmoil during the decade was the ongoing transition from a stable, manufacture-based post-war economy to a volatile service-based global economy.

15. For a fuller, more comprehensive account of the political economy during the 1970s see Robert M. Collins's *More: The Politics of Economic Growth in Postwar America* (Oxford: Oxford University Press, 2000); James Patterson's *Restless Giant: The United States from Watergate to Bush v. Gore* (Oxford: Oxford University Press, 2006); Sloan's *The Reagan Effect*; and Michael J. Boskin's *Reagan and the Economy: The Successes, Failures, and Unfinished Agenda* (San Francisco: Institute for Contemporary Studies, 1987).

16. Donella H. Meadows, et al., *The Limits to Growth: A Report for the Club of Rome's Project on the Predicament of Mankind* (London: Pan Books, 1974) and E.F. Schumacher, *Small is Beautiful: A Study of Economics as if People Mattered* (London: Blond and Briggs, 1973).

17. Perry Quick, "Businesses, Reagan's Industrial Policy," in *The Reagan Record*, John L. Palmer and Isabel V. Sawhill, eds. (Cambridge: Ballinger, 1984), 307.

18. Iwan Morgan, "Jimmy Carter, Bill Clinton, and the New Democratic Economics," *The Historical Journal* 47 (4) (2004): 1023 and Roger Noll and Paul L. Joskow, "Deregulation and Regulatory Reform during the 1980s," *American Economic Policy in the 1980s, in* Martin Feldstein, ed. (Chicago: University of Chicago Press, 1994), 376.

19. Leuchtenburg, "Jimmy Carter and the Post-New Deal Presidency," 15.

20. Quoted in Leuchtenburg, 14.

21. William Schneider, "The November 6 Vote for President: What Did It Mean?" in *The American Elections of 1984,* Austin Ranney, ed. (United States of America: Duke University Press), 228–229.

22. Seymour Martin Lipset and William Schneider, "The Public View of Regulation," *Public Opinion* (January-February 1979), 6.

23. *National Journal Opinion Outlook Briefing Paper* (Washington: Government Research Corporation, 1982), 3–5.

24. Robert Y. Shapiro and John M. Gilroy, "The Polls-Regulation I," *Public Opinion Quarterly* 48 (2) (1984): 532.

25. Ibid.

26. David Broder, *Changing of the Guard* (New York: Simon and Schuster, 1980), 122.

27. "Deregulation: A Fast Start for the Reagan Strategy," *Business Week*, March 9, 1981, 64.

28. Jerome L. Himmelstein, *To the Right: The Transformation of American Conservatism* (Berkeley: University of California Press, 1990), 144–145.

29. Patrick J. Akard, "Corporate Mobilization and Political Power: The Transformation of U.S. Economic Policy in the 1970s," *American Sociological Review* 57 (5) (1992): 601.

30. Ibid.

31. Thomas K. McCraw, *Prophets of Regulation* (Cambridge, MA: Harvard University Press, 1981), 268.

32. John Micklethwait and Adrian Wooldridge, *The Right Nation: Why America is Different* (London: Penguin Books, 2004), 79–80 and William C. Berman, *America's Right Turn: From Nixon to Reagan, 2nd ed.*(Baltimore: Johns Hopkins University Press, 1998), 71.

33. Thomas B. Edsall, "Business Coalitions Form to Win Congressional Clout," *Baltimore Sun,* February 27, 1980, A6.

34. Akard, "Corporate Mobilization and Political Action," 601.

35. John Abraham, *Science, Politics, and the Pharmaceutical Industry: Controversy and Bias in Drug Regulation* (New York: St. Martin's Press, 1995), 61.

36. Lewis Lapham, "Tentacles of Rage," *Harper's,* November, 2004, 34.

37. Grant Gilmore, *The Ages of American Law* (New Haven, CT: Yale University Press, 1977), 66.

38. Pertschuk, 62.

39. Paul Quirk, "In Defense of the Politics of Ideas," *The Journal of Politics* 50 (1) (1988): 32–33.

40. Peltzman "The Economic Theory of Regulation After a Decade of Deregulation," *Brookings Papers on Economic Activity, Microeconomics* (1989):18.

41. Herbert Stein, *Presidential Economics: The Making of Economic Policy From Roosevelt to Clinton,* 3rd ed. (Washington D.C.: The American Enterprise Institute Press, 1994), 405.

42. Micklethwait and Wooldridge, *The Right Nation,* 78–79.

43. Dominique Tobbell, *Pills, Power, and Policy: The Struggle for Drug Reform in Cold War America and Its Consequences* (Berkeley: University of California Press, 2012), 184–186.

44. Quoted in Greg Anrig, "Who Strangled the FDA?" *The American Prospect*, December 12, (2007): Web Version Only. Consulted online at http://www.prospect.org//cs/articles;jsessionid=aS2rKBbxapH53-DB0h?article=who_strangled_the_fda.

45. Ibid.

46. Greene, *Prescribing by Numbers*, 140–442.

47. Samuel Loewenberg, "Sidney Wolfe," *Lancet* 373 (2009), 537. See also Alicia Mundy, "A Wolfe in Regulator's Clothing: Drug Industry Critic Joins the FDA," *Wall Street Journal*, January 9, 2009: A10.

48. Robert P. Luciano Interview, Chemical Heritage Foundation Oral History Collection, 8.

49. Committee on the Judiciary and Committee on Labor and Public Welfare. *Regulation of New Drug R&D by the Food and Drug Administration*, 93rd Congress, 1974, 207. Italics mine.

50. Ibid.

51. Ibid.

52. *FDA and the 96th Congress* (Washington, D.C.: Food and Drug Administration, 1980).

53. Ibid.

54. Committee on Labor and Public Welfare. *Examination of the Pharmaceutical Industry (Part 7)*, 93rd Congress, August 1974, 28–30.

55. Ibid.

56. John Abraham, *Science, Politics and the Pharmaceutical Industry: Controversy and Bias in Drug Regulation* (New York: St. Martin's Press, 1995), 78.

57. *Final Report Review Panel on New Drug Regulation*, Department of Health, Education, and Welfare, May 1977, 12–13.

58. Committee on the Judiciary and Committee on Labor and Public Welfare. *Regulation of New Drug R&D by the Food and Drug Administration*, 93rd Congress, 1974, 207.

59. Ibid.

60. Quoted in Abraham, *Science, Politics and the Pharmaceutical Industry*, 77–79.

61. Ibid.

62. *Final Report Review Panel on New Drug Regulation*, Department of Health, Education, and Welfare, May 1977, 16–17.

63. A month later, on April 20, 1977, the Panel expressed broad agreement with the principal findings and recommendations in the report.

64. Ibid.

Chapter Three

President Carter and the FDA

"I agree with the freedom of choice but not with the freedom to exploit desperate cancer patients."[1]

DR. CHARLES MOERTEL, 1981

After the 1976 presidential election, President Carter adopted Gerald Ford's policy of regulatory reform, especially in transportation; but the Carter administration, like the Democratic Party itself, was home to a collection of varied, often disputatious, opinions and interests, which of course included a potent consumer activist wing. "Established Democratic liberalism," according to historian Sean Wilentz, suffered through numerous shocks, but in the 1970s "it was philosophically at loose ends."[2]

The Carter administration showed signs of discord when it came to creating health policy and establishing a clear direction for the FDA. A coterie of consumer activist-oriented Democrats, including Secretary of Health, Education, and Welfare (HEW) Joseph Califano, presidential consumer advisor Esther Peterson, and Federal Trade Commission Chairman Michael Pertschuk, invariably weighed in on the side of strengthening the agency and bolstering product safety protocols. However, strained relations and factionalism also wracked Carter's administration; FDA Commissioner Donald Kennedy, for instance, Carter's first appointment to head the agency, sparred constantly with Secretary Califano. Often the source of their disagreement was the agency's responsiveness to consumer activist complaints.[3] Califano, according to reporter James Dickinson, was a demanding consumer activist-oriented official who was occasionally "volatile and erratic."[4] Whatever the nature or driver of this bureaucratic infighting, it surely did not help the FDA discharge its duties.

Similarly, Commissioner Jere Goyan, Kennedy's successor, found himself at loggerheads with Califano's successor, Patricia Roberts Harris. She, too, was a demanding consumer activist cabinet member—in an administration that was championing deregulation in other areas of the economy. Harris ordered Goyan to report to her each week on consumer-oriented matters of potential significance. Kennedy and Goyan tried as best they could to shelter their subordinates from the politics and pressures of the larger Carter administration, though neither was completely successful. As part of the executive branch and thus not wholly independent, the average FDA staffer could not help but be affected by the conflict in the Carter administration officials. According to Dickinson, "dread" and "irritation" marked the period.[5]

However much or little FDA officials were influenced by, or even aware of, the conflict between cabinet secretaries and FDA commissioners is unknown, but there were also power struggles in the halls of the FDA. A prime example is that of the stormy relationship between Commissioner Goyan and FDA general counsel Nancy Buc. Buc, like many in the Carter administration, was a consumer activist. A feminist, assertive and outgoing by nature, she was for a time the *éminence grise* at the FDA; according to one account,

Figure 3.1.   FROM LEFT TO RIGHT – Jere Goyan (Commissioner of the FDA) and President Jimmy Carter June 13, 1980. President Jimmy Carter greets FDA Commissioner Jere Goyan at a Regulatory Council Meeting at the White House. Courtesy of the Jimmy Carter Presidential Library

she was in fact at the heart of the FDA's policy-making, not Commissioner Goyan. Some officials occasionally likened Nancy Buc to Harris, individuals who they felt represented the worst aspects of the Carter administration— "misdirected enthusiasm, disdain for reality, and an inability to inspire confidence."[6]

These strained relationships within the FDA mirrored larger struggles in the Carter administration—indeed they mirrored the turmoil within the Democratic Party and society at large. Such struggles also added to the FDA's troubles in dealing with persistent criticism of the drug lag and the FDA's cosy relationship with the drug industry. What follows is more in depth assessment of the Carter administration's policy toward the FDA to help answer the broader question of how the 1970s established conditions for the FDA during the Reagan years.

The Moral Outsider from Plains and Reform of the FDA

President Carter, like the FDA itself, was trapped between consumer activists and regulatory reformers in the 1970s, and his administration's FDA policy reflected this tension. Not only would he seek to strengthen the FDA's regulatory power over the pharmaceutical industry and ensure greater safety for American consumers, he wanted to defeat the drug lag and streamline the drug approval process.

It was certainly a bold dual thrust, but it was a target that would not be met. Compounding the complexity of achieving his objective were the political exigencies of the 1980 presidential election; in fact as the November election crept closer and closer, Carter's FDA policies appeared increasingly bipolar and he sent mixed messages about policy through his political appointments and his speeches.[7] Part of this had to do with the appeal of Senator Edward Kennedy, who possessed a strong record on consumer protection and the FDA and was challenging the president; part of this had to do with the broader struggle over economic and regulatory policy within the administration and within the larger Democratic Party; and, lastly, part of this had to do with President Carter himself.

President Carter was a multi-faceted, complex individual. Journalist James Fallows remarked that President Carter was "perhaps as admirable a human being as has ever held the job."[8] Nonetheless, he was also a man who, like many of his Georgian compatriots, exhibited an arrogance, aloofness, complacence, and provincialism that ill served the country.[9] According to Philip J. Hilts, Carter was a political hybrid, the precursor to President William Jefferson Clinton's centrist Democratic model, because he possessed strong democratic tendencies and fierce anti-government attitudes simultaneously.[10] He was an economic conservative in that he promised to balance the budget in four years and do away with unnecessary bureaucracy and government regulations.[11] Much like President Barack Obama, Carter also vowed to fix Washington and provide change—and the electorate either people believed them or gave them the benefit of the doubt. In Carter's case, he was not a product of the tightly interwoven Washington establishment and when he narrowly won the presidency, many pundits and commentators argued his victory was based on the merits of his outsider status, his distrust of government, and his castigation of the status quo in Washington. The sentiment predictably left a sour taste in the mouths of many career regulators at the FDA and elsewhere in the nation's capital.

President Carter's palpable distrust of Washington and his pledge to reform government regulations were soon manifested in policy. First, Carter's across-the-board regulatory reform initiatives included the establishment of the Regulatory Analysis Review Group (RARG), in January 1978; it was comprised of members of major executive agencies as presidential economic advisers.[12] According to Stuart Eizenstat, RARG served "as a good example of the constructive role economists can play in governmental decision-making. . . ." Second, later that year, in March 1978, Carter issued Executive Order 12044 and effectively strengthened existing regulatory analysis requirements by demanding that proposed regulations be assessed in the context of their overall economic impact. Under E.O. 12044, agencies were to reflect on the lower-cost alternatives for achieving regulatory objectives. However, this provision was vague and individual agencies retained the authority to determine which of their regulations were subject to economic impact analysis. This meant the provision was unclear about who had the ultimate responsibility for resolving conflicts between presidential advisory bodies and the agencies and because of this in-built imprecision E.O. 12044 had few long-lasting effects. Third, Carter also advanced his pledge with the Paperwork Reduction Act in 1980. The act established an Office of Information and Regulatory Affairs (OIRA) in the Office of Management and Budget (OMB); OIRA was charged with the responsibility to reduce the amount of information required of citizens and businesses by creating a paperwork budget and clearing agency information-collection requests.[13]

The Carter administration, in pursuing its regulatory reform program, did not attack the regulation of the nation's drug supply outright. But President Carter's tightening of the FDA budget would undoubtedly create change and Director of Planning and Management Communications Charles Gorton thought zero-based budgeting was essential to this tightening.[14] Constriction of the FDA's budget in the mid- to late-1970s had other ramifications. The FDA established a policy of voluntary compliance (requiring more cooperation with industry) and the agency shifted away from resource-intensive individual law enforcement actions. Voluntary compliance would eventually become a hotly debated issue in the 1980s, and it will be accorded due attention.[15]

The Carter administration was, if anything, indirectly hostile to the nation's public servants, including FDA staff members. Much of President Carter's initial popularity and political capital derived from his outsider status. He was supposed to embody a new model of truthful, trustworthy, and clever politician who stood in opposition to the Washington establishment. Joseph Paul Hile, the Associate Commissioner for Regulatory Affairs, remarked:

> Mr. Carter came into the presidency running, at least in my view, on a very strong anti-federal-government platform. . . . You'll recall that this was the post-Nixon era; there was still a major concern over the possibility of wrongdoing within government. [16]

Carter's anti-government sentiment, as the FDA insider Paul Hile phrased it above, was made manifest at the FDA through the power of appointment. Dr. Donald Kennedy, for example, appointed FDA Commissioner in 1977, emulated Carter's general suspiciousness of the Washington establishment and the status quo. Kennedy brought to the position of commissioner, according to colleagues, "an apparent concern—and I'm reluctant to use the word 'distrust,' but perhaps there's not a better term for the present time—of the persons who had been in positions of responsibility within the federal government and within the FDA prior to the Carter administration."[17]

The choice of Kennedy as commissioner was criticized for a number of other reasons at the time. Like the president, Dr. Kennedy was also an outsider; he apparently knew little of drug policy, the drug industry, or the agency he was to oversee. Said one colleague, Kennedy instilled at the FDA, "just an entire atmosphere of aloofness."[18] Philip J. Hilts has written that Kennedy's selection was a political blunder.[19] While it may or may not have been a blunder, the decision to make Kennedy commissioner was characteristic of Carter's binary approach to the FDA: he not only sought to strengthen it with additional powers, but he sought to minimize its regulation-making. Kennedy, for his part, was unlucky to take over the agency when he did, for it was a period of time in which the FDA was besieged.

Formal Rules, a New Commissioner, and Patient Package Inserts

In 1977, the FDA's Bureau of Drugs was plagued by the negative perception that the agency's drug regulators had failed the American public and had transformed into a de facto subsidiary of industry.[20] Responding to this unhelpful publicity, Commissioner Kennedy initiated the development of formalized policies on how the FDA ought to interact with the regulated industries. The objective was to ameliorate the harmful perception of the Bureau of Drugs and also prevent any further inappropriate relations between drug industry officials and members of drug reviewing teams.

Unfortunately, the formal rules were also cumbersome and antiquated. They were "much, much more conservative—not in the political sense, but in the sense of allowing for interaction between government and industry—than had been the policies leading up to that time."[21] Kennedy's initiative required every contact between a drug industry representative and FDA official to be in writing and he even sought to expand the requirement so that contacts were made part of the public calendar of the agency. Such stipulations, while a sensible response to the agency's critics, invariably slowed the drug review process down. And this was at a time when social and economic deregulation appeared to be gaining momentum and when the drug lag restricted access to important new drugs. These rules were abandoned and never formalized.

Commissioner Jere Goyan also embarked on a journey to pass more formal rules and regulations at a precarious time. In June 1980, five months before the presidential and congressional elections, Kennedy left the FDA for a position at Stanford University and was replaced by Goyan, formerly of the University of California at San Francisco. Bearded, grey, and somewhat feisty, Goyan soon established a reputation for his unremitting frankness.[22] He, too, was suspicious of close ties between the drug industry and its regulator; yet Goyan was decidedly more vocal on this subject than Kennedy, often to the consternation of administration officials.[23]

Shortly after becoming Commissioner, Goyan was candidly critical of the pharmaceutical industry and the U.S. medical establishment in general. In an era when numerous politicians and economists fretted over flagging pharmaceutical industry growth, Goyan aired his concerns about the overuse of prescription and over-the-counter drugs:

> Our society has become overmedicated. We have become too casual about the use of drugs, and I'm referring to legitimate prescription and nonprescription drugs, not illicit drugs. . . . Too many people are taking too many drugs without proper understanding of their potential harmful effects. . . . I'm a therapeutic nihilist. My philosophy is the fewer drugs people take, the better off they are.[24]

At another meeting, Goyan told doctors that the medical establishment or industry did not impress him:

> I staunchly refuse to accept the notion that any physician, merely because he graduated from medical school and is currently a card-carrying member of his county medical society, is great, or good, or even tolerably competent. Too much of drug therapy has been atrociously irrational.[25]

The veracity of Goyan's statements remains contested. Nevertheless, his sympathy for regulation and antipathy toward industry soon set him at odds with the very individual who had appointed him; in fact, Goyan's beliefs seemed to cut against the grain of regulatory reform and a renewed faith in American industry. As the 1980 election approached, the Carter administration sought to keep Goyan's verbosity and consumer activist regulation-making in check. For the most part, Goyan was constrained.

In one area, patient packaging information (PPI), Goyan's consumer activism predilections would not be stymied and he would not be controlled; indeed, the story of PPIs informs how the FDA was caught between consumer activists and budget-minded regulatory reformers, how Carter was forced to make certain difficult choices, and how the Reagan administration diverged from Carter's.

Patient package information had originated with Donald Kennedy's promotion of consumer information initiatives. Before leaving for Stanford, he had developed a regulation that called for a patient package insert (outlining proper use and side effects) in every prescription drug. Goyan, agreeing with the thrust of the regulation, took up Kennedy's plan in May 1980. Explaining the measure, he said he sought "to provide greater insight to the general public and to the consumer about what the agency was doing." He also promised the measure would "provide greater understanding about the products that [the agency] regulated."[26] It was also an important issue for him, personally, because it represented openness, transparency, personal sovereignty—all intrinsic goods. According to Goyan, providing patients with greater information liberated them from the burdensome shackles of the medical profession, from doctors the commissioner had previously made clear he did not even regard as competent. Patient package inserts, moreover, were democratic and they informed consumer decision-making. Consumer activists outside the agency felt this was a crucial step in the right direction, since the information in the inserts outlined the proper use and side effects of a given drug, which meant Americans were empowered and, consequently, could take greater participation in their healthcare decisions.[27]

In what was another example of bureaucratic infighting, Carter administration officials strove to limit the number of regulations enacted in 1980, and specifically sought to undermine patient package inserts. Thus Goyan's new regulation soon found itself the target of the Regulatory Analysis Review Group (RARG), which condemned the cost of the PPI project. The regulation would be too pricey, too burdensome, too meddling, and it was felt the FDA ought to seek a less expensive manner of disseminating a drug's information to the consumer, especially at a time when the economy itself was contracting and Carter's budgets were being squeezed.[28] RARG nevertheless offered a number of proposals to lower the costs of the regulation:

1. A reference book available in pharmacies containing needed drug information.
2. Patient labelling only for the seventy-five most prescribed drugs

3. PPIs given out only with new prescriptions.

Throughout 1980, RARG, which stood against the regulation, found an ally in the American Pharmaceutical Association (APhA). The APhA, a trade association lobby group, was opposed to the enactment of the regulation and it argued, using data cobbled together to fight the PPI provision of the failed Drug Regulation Reform Act, that the outlay for the regulation was simply too high. American pharmacies would have to be redesigned, at a significant financial loss, in order to accommodate the many thousands of inserts and the costs, in turn, would be passed on to the consumer.[29] Yet the APhA also contended that Americans given patient package inserts (PPIs) were actually less knowledgeable about their prescription drugs; that is, they complied less with therapy than those who were counseled by pharmacists on a personal basis. According to this drug industry argument, American consumers were too daft to understand the wording or the language used in the package inserts, and, for this reason, they sometimes did not take their medication rather than ask further questions. Patient package inserts, noted the APhA, thereby acted as an informational deterrent; they discouraged patients from asking questions, even when they did not understand the PPI. This meant that the regulation, meant to democratize drug information, actually hindered knowledge transfer.[30]

The FDA under Commissioner Goyan (who had the support of HHS Secretary Patricia Harris) resisted the pressure from Carter's RARG and the drug industry. With a great flurry of activity at the FDA to complete the PPI regulation it was officially finished and published in final form in early January 1981. It was a victory for the agency over the drug industry and the regulatory reform zeitgeist that predominated in Washington. The new regulation, as finally constituted, forced drug makers to provide patients with greater amounts of information.[31] It was a fleeting victory, however.

After the election in early 1981 Reagan's newly appointed FDA Commissioner, Dr. Arthur Hull Hayes Jr., quickly rescinded this regulation. According to then Associate Commissioner for Policy and Planning, Office of the Commissioner, William Hubbard, "I was in a little meeting once when we were going through the rules withdrawal process in which Art Hayes essentially said to me that revocation of the PPI rule was one of his mandates when he got the job. When he was hired by Secretary Schweiker, he was told, 'You've got to revoke the PPI regulation.'" Hubbard added, "We were forced to go through this process that 'examined' the issue, but, in fact, it was a preordained thing. It was just an exercise that we had to go through to meet the legal requirements for revoking a regulation."[32] This was only one of the many changes to be made at the FDA's Bureau of Drugs in 1981.

The PPI regulation stands as an accurate illustration of the Carter administration's mixed relationship with the FDA. Carter did not deliberately or actively seek to hurt the FDA. What he achieved, though, was to send mixed messages to the agency. Commissioner Kennedy manifested aloofness and distrust to career FDA employees, while Commissioner Goyan rebelled against the president's own agenda. Furthermore, Carter's unwillingness to push a consumer activist agenda underscored how his administration established the conditions for President Reagan. Carter, that is, helped enable, even legitimate, Reagan's program of regulatory reform.

The Deadly Drug Lag

Even as the FDA absorbed the criticism about its putative friendliness with the drug industry and fended off allegations of bias, the agency found itself under attack for its failure to approve drugs speedily enough. This attack came from government-sanctioned reports and outside academic experts, and the drug lag, as it was dubbed, served as the FDA's incubus throughout the mid-1970s and then 1980s.

During this period, questions arose periodically, centering on life and death matters: Were there fewer significant life-saving and life-enhancing drugs available in the U.S. market compared to its foreign competitors? Were Americans were being denied access to essential pharmaceutical products because of bureaucratic inertia? Was the FDA culpable for such evils?[33] Advocates for the FDA suggested that the trade-off for high standards of safety was a minimal, necessary period of waiting, whereas drug industry lobbyists, critically ill patients, libertarians, and regulatory reformers assailed the FDA for the overly rigorous application of the statutes and its bureaucratic sluggishness. "There didn't seem to be a hell of a lot coming out of research pipelines at the time," declared the president and CEO of Schering-Plough, Robert Luciano. In his view, this fact prompted many questions and congressional hearings about the diminishing productivity of the drug industry.[34]

The regulatory reformers in the 1970s blamed government. They saw the FDA as a hidebound, bureaucratic morass. Dr. Louis Lasagna, of Rochester University's Medical School, an expert on the drug approval process who tilted toward less regulation, told Congress in 1978:

"... I have been increasingly alarmed over the past several years at the disastrous effects FDA regulations and their administration have had on drug research and development in this country."[35] Another regulatory reformer, Congressman James Scheuer (D-NY), chairman of the Oversight Committee of the Committee on Science and Technology, a politician not at all disquieted by the prospects of either a neutralisation policy or an entrenched bias toward industry, believed the regulatory pendulum had swung too far in favour of consumer activists. "... How far behind we were in the sophisticated expeditious approval of a new drug,"[36] he contended, was a serious problem that needed immediate investigation. Other like-minded individuals, such as Dr. William Wardell, a noted critic of the FDA who actually coined the phrase "drug lag," wanted a *streamlined* and *speedier* drug approval process.

In response to such critiques, Schmidt's successor (and Carter's first appointment), Dr. Donald Kennedy, called the term "drug lag" ambiguous and ultimately worthless in resolving the agency's perceived drug approval problem. Name-calling, he argued, was unhelpful; thinking about the totality of the system was, instead, far more important. Accordingly, in July 1979, Kennedy delineated a number of factors that contributed to the length of time to approve a drug which factors included the public's role in the process, the stringent requirements for human subjects, as well as many others. What was of real importance, Kennedy emphasized, was to think about "whether we in the United States have been approving drugs as rapidly as we can, given the system of regulation established by law." Whereupon the commissioner admitted, "the answer to that question, is that we are now approaching the maximum rate possible commensurate with the design of the system itself."[37]

The new commissioner was correct. The 1962 Kefauver-Harris amendment to the 1938 Food Drug and Cosmetics Act, signed by President Kennedy in the wake of the Thalidomide tragedy, was largely considered to have had discernible negative results for the pharmaceutical industry and for product innovation. This was the system of law to which the FDA commissioner was referring. As noted earlier in this book, the 1962 Kefauver amendments increased the requirements for drug products and established the U.S. regulatory architecture as the world's most robust. Pursuant to the statute, drugs now needed to be tested for safety *and* effectiveness (a condition not established in other nation's regulatory framework).

Yet critics pointed to the lack of industry growth and the lack of profits comparable to other industrialized countries; this was due to the complex nature of the American drug approval process and the resulting delay in the introduction of new drugs to the U.S. marketplace. There were other negative results as well. First, the effective patent life of new chemical entities (NCEs) decreased. Second, the U.S. industry's share of the multi-national pharmaceutical market showed little real growth throughout the 1970s.[38] And third, premarket expenditures rose. Of the $123 million increase in research and development costs, critics argued that roughly half was attributable to tougher regulation.[39] These arguments bolstered claims for reform at the FDA.

A study by the National Academy of Engineering reaffirmed fears about the declining position of the U.S. pharmaceutical industry and offered some other conclusions. The NAE's report asserted that pharmaceutical R&D expenditures in Europe and Japan had been growing faster than in the United States; the Japanese industry, which had evolved rapidly from the 1960s, was considered a significant threat and thought to pose a challenge to U.S. leadership in the late 1970s and 1980s.[40] In summation, the report estimated "future competitive performance in a dynamic Schumpeterian industry like pharmaceuticals will be significantly affected by national policies influencing the technological and economic opportunities for drug innovation."[41] According to Lasagna, Scheuer, and Wardell, such new policies—less restrictive policies—were totally warranted to reverse the U.S. industry's slowdown.

Another government report, *FDA Drug Approval—A Lengthy Process that Delays the Availability of Important New Drugs,* further contributed to the dialogue. Conducted by the General Accounting Office and released in 1980, *FDA Drug Approval* attempted to quantify the drug lag and assess its antecedents.[42] In stark contrast to the Dorsen report, it found that the drug approval process was too exacting and too strict and consequently, it was detrimental to both business and patients. The balance between safety and innovation was skewed in favor of the former, to the disadvantage of the latter.

In addition, the General Accounting Office also described the standing of the American pharmaceutical industry in the late 1970s. The GAO found the industry's position had been steadily deteriorating since 1965. The FDA had approved 69 of 132 NDAs (52 percent). The average time to approval for these 69 NDAs, which included 11 important new drugs, was about 20 months. This represented 17 months of FDA time and 3 months of industry time. Six of the 11 important new drugs took 20 months or more.[43] The report further noted the FDA could improve in every area.

The overall findings of the GAO report thus ran counter to the findings of the earlier Review Panel and Special Counsel's report. Whereas the FDA had been criticized in 1977 for its improper pro-industry conduct during the drug approval process, *FDA Drug Approval—A Lengthy Process that Delays the Availability of Important New Drugs* declared quite the opposite was true. The GAO also spread the blame in an even-handed fashion. Culpability for the lack of new drugs ultimately rested with both the FDA's Bureau of Drugs and the pharmaceutical industry. The principal findings of the GAO report are as follows:

1. FDA guidelines are not precise and, therefore, are subject to varying interpretations.
2. Reviewers change during the NDA review, which slows the process.
3. Scientific and professional disagreements between the FDA and industry are not resolved quickly.
4. FDA feedback to industry is slow or inadequate, and drug firms are not promptly notified of deficiencies.
5. Chemistry and manufacturing control reviews delay processing.

6. Limited time spent reviewing NDAs and uneven workloads slow the process.
7. Industry submits incomplete NDAs and is slow to resolve deficiencies.

The FDA's institutional identity itself was also deemed a major cause of the drug lag. According to pharmaceutical expert Louis Lasagna, the culture at the FDA, not just the existing regulatory statutes such as the 1962 efficacy amendments, resulted in delays. A dominant consumer activist ethos at the agency combined with the play-it-safe attitude of FDA personnel, thus creating the drug lag. "It is not the law that is at fault," Lasagna testified before Congress. "Most of the drug regulatory policy followed by the FDA today is the result of administrative decision rather than specific statutory mandate." New efficient procedures could not work because of "the attitudes within the agency." These were "factors not amenable to legislative correction."[44]

Crout

Richard J. Crout served as the head of the Bureau of Drugs at the FDA during this period and he was acutely aware of the debate about the drug lag. Discussion between FDA historian John Swann and Crout demonstrates what his bureau was considering:

> John Swann: You know . . . another issue today that Congress is continually harping on about is getting drugs out to the patients faster, fast-tracking drug approval. . . . Were there means of getting drugs approved on a faster track during your tenure?
>
> Richard Crout: Absolutely.
>
> JS: Would you say a little bit about that?
>
> RC: One of the things we discovered then was that the really important new drugs took longer to review than the me-toos. And we said, "Wait a minute, that shouldn't be. I mean, it should be the reverse from a public health standpoint."
>
> So we talked about how to fix that. We invented . . . the ABC system. "A" was a very important therapeutic advance, and "B" was a modest advance, and "C" was no advance therapeutically. Then "1" was a new molecule, and "2" was a new salt or ester, and so on. That system lasted from 74 until not too long ago, and the edict was to pay more attention to and put more effort into, at the division level, of course, the A-1s.

One of the things I learned between 74 and the time I left in 1982 was that it still took just as long to approve the "A" drugs; we didn't really get the fastest review times for the "A" drugs and the "B" drugs. What we did do was to keep them from getting longer and longer. We began to get their review times to turn a corner and come down, but never did the data show that reviews of "A" and "B" drugs were faster than "C" drugs, the me-toos. . . . I always used to tell Wayne Pines, "Don't call this fast track. Call it priority review or call it a banana. Call it anything, but don't call it fast track, because somebody's going to look at the data and say, 'Well, you guys can't make the "A" and "B" drugs go faster,' which is true." So I never called the ABC system a fast track system.[45]

Crout wanted to balance consumer protection and product innovation but the perception of the FDA was also at the forefront of his thinking. In his mind, it was essential not to create more problems for the agency in already difficult times by using misleading labels.

In June 1980, amid the presidential and congressional election campaigns, Crout was called to testify before Chairman Henry Waxman's (D-CA) Committee on Health and Environment. Waxman, an established proponent of consumer safety in the House of Representatives, began the proceedings by noting, "we must assure that every drug is safe and effective." "The public expects and deserves nothing less." In charge of the Bureau of Drugs, Crout agreed with the chairman in principle, but he also harkened back to Commissioner Kennedy's statement about the 1962 Kefauver amendments. "The current standard for effectiveness in the law," said Crout, "is substantial evidence of effectiveness as shown by adequate and well-controlled investigations." "Many countries have an effectiveness requirement in their drugs," he added, but "none other, to my knowledge, has the rigorous standard of adequate and well-controlled trials. . . ."[46]

Representative Phil Gramm (D-TX), a member of Waxman's committee and a moderate regulatory reformer, challenged Crout. "I am sure you are familiar with the work that has been done by an economist at the University of Chicago, Dr. Milton Friedman." He continued, "I would like to ask what are you doing to come to a balance between the potential cost to a society of allowing drugs prematurely to come on the market that do no harm, versus the benefits that are lost by not allowing on the market drugs that could help people, save lives, that could add to people's productivity and happiness?"[47] Crout responded sympathetically. He emphasized how invaluable cooperation was to reconciling the drug lag problem. "That is a very important question," he noted, "and one that we are terribly interested in. We live with it everyday." He added:

. . . I think that the matter of improving the speed of drug development is a very complex issue and it involves industry doing its job faster, FDA assisting

in that process, and then FDA administering our review process as quickly as
that can be done. There is a whole series of little things I think one has to do.
There is no single large answer or no easy fix to speeding up the drug review
and approval process. [48]

Nevertheless, the BOD had indeed taken serious efforts to expedite drug
development. "We have tried," said Crout, "to meet with manufacturers on
problems that are developing during the course of the development of a drug.
We will review protocols on request so that we can reassure manufacturers
that they have designed their studies well. And I think that those are the
major strategies for improving the rapidity of drug development . . ."[49] Looking ahead, Crout outlined how, at the behest of the Reagan administration,
the FDA and industry would work together more seamlessly and collabora-
tively in the mid- to late-1980s.

In response to further questions from Gramm, Dr. Crout noted that the
average new drug application (NDA) review time had, since 1974, decreased
markedly. "We have," he held, "reduced the time for the review of new drugs
quite substantially since about 1974–75, when it was at its worst."[50] In 1980,
it stood at nearly two years, whereas six years earlier it was three years.
Progress on this front had indeed been made.

Laetrile

In the 1970s, a broad swath of stakeholders considered the application of
deregulatory principles to the FDA as being both natural and essential. That a
despot like Marshal Tito should have access to life-saving and life-enhancing
new drugs before American consumers was truly distasteful to many free-
dom-loving Americans, whether they cared about regulation or not. Libertarians, for their part, asserted that individuals in a free society should be empowered—allowed—to take any medicine they wished. Government, according to this perspective, had no business regulating drugs in the first place. [51]

The larger debate about consumer choice, government intrusion, and the
availability of drugs crystallized in the controversy over Laetrile, which was
promoted as a cancer treatment in the 1970s. Laetrile can be found all over
the globe, in such foods as chick-peas, lentils, lima beans, cashews, barley,
and brown rice. While part of medical practice since at least the first–second
century A.D., the ascendance of alternative healing and holistic medicine
during the 1960s, increased Laetrile's use in the United States. [52] During the
1950s–1960s, physicians employed Laetrile in combination therapies for
cancer, even as it faced resistance from the mainstream medical establishment and struggled with "an aura of illegality."[53] Yet, by the mid-1970s, the
safety and efficacy of Laetrile grew into a larger point of contestation among
Congress, the U.S. Food and Drug Administration (FDA), physician organizations, medical institutes, and patient-consumer groups. In many ways, the

debate over this treatment embodied questions of scientific and medical authority that had troubled the FDA since its inception.

The dispute began as early as 1970. That year, a non-profit scientific research organization in California, the McNaughton Foundation, submitted to the FDA an Investigational New Drug (IND) application to study Laetrile. It was ultimately rejected, since it was determined that the preclinical evidence failed to demonstrate Laetrile might be effective as an anti-cancer agent. Supporters of Laetrile, according to a review by the National Cancer Institute (NCI), "viewed this as an attempt by the U.S. government to block access to new and promising cancer therapies and pressure mounted to make laetrile available to the public." Thereafter, multiple court cases across the United States challenged the FDA's authority in determining which drugs should be available to cancer patient-consumers and the result was that Laetrile was legalized in more than twenty states during the 1970s.[54] According to *Time* magazine, by 1976 Laetrile had attracted "an avid, almost evangelical band of followers," a group that included members of the "right-wing John Birch society. . . ."[55] These supporters viewed the FDA's ban on Laetrile as "a restraint on individual freedom."[56]

From the FDA's perspective, only minimal anecdotal evidence supported the use of Laetrile and after an extensive five-month review the agency deemed there was insufficient scientific proof to justify its use at all. The agency called it "worthless and illegal as a cancer remedy."[57] In the November-December 1977 issue of the agency's *Drug Bulletin*, which was distributed to over a million health care workers in the United States, the outright rejection of Laetrile was unmistakable. It had the potential to "cause poisoning and death when taken by mouth," the article read, and was not subject to FDA inspections.[58] Moreover, in a relatively unusual move, the agency sent 10,000 posters across the United States to spread awareness about Laetrile's toxicity and unregulated nature.

Yet, legal wrangling, consumer activism, and the lack of scientific data and consensus prolonged the debate over Laetrile. In 1977, for instance, a federal district judge in Oklahoma, named Luther Bohanon, ruled that terminally ill cancer patients could obtain a personal supply of Laetrile as long they signed an affadavit.[59] Senator Edward Kennedy (D-MA) held hearings in 1977 in which Laetrile promoters declared that a collection of organizations, including the FDA, AMA, NCI, American Cancer Society (as well as the Rockefeller family) conspired against Laetrile. Kennedy, who said he would champion Laetrile in the Senate if a positive and reproducible clinical trial was concluded, nevertheless regarded the Laetrile advocates "with a blend of amusement and contempt." He also worried they offered cancer patients "a false sense of hope."[60] By 1978, it was estimated that between 50,000–100,000 people were taking over 1 million milligrams a month.[61] In 1979, the FDA's resistance to the drug was vindicated when the Supreme

Court rejected the arguments made by the proponents of Laetrile and upheld existing food and drug statutes, including the 1962 law. The unanimous decision stated:

> Since the turn of the century, resourceful entrepreneurs have advertised a wide variety of purportedly simple and painless cures for cancer, including lineaments of turpentine, mustard, oil, eggs, and ammonia; peat moss; arrangements of colored floodlights; pastes made from glycerin and limburger cheese; mineral tablets; and "Fountain of Youth" mixtures of spices, oil and suet. . . . Congress could reasonably have determined to protect the terminally ill, no less that other patients, from the vast range of self-styled panaceas that inventive minds can devise.[62]

Even with this decision, researchers and medical doctors operated in an environment in which definitive studies and answers about Laetrile were largely absent. In other words, doubts remained. To rectify this, the National Cancer Institute grew more involved. The director of NCI, Frank Rauscher had stated rather definitively in 1976, "I wish it worked, but . . . it simply is not active against cancer."[63] In 1978, though, the NCI initiated a retrospective case review (a study of past cases) and sent over 400,000 letters to doctors and other practitioners, asking them to submit positive results from cases involving Laetrile. In response, the NCI received only ninety-three "positive" evaluations—and only six of those had evidence of significant tumor shrinkage.[64]

Thereafter, NCI, given the widespread interest and the long, bitter dispute within the scientific community and activist community, further tested Laetrile in 1980. The tests, which included 178 patients with advanced cancer, were conducted in four major medical centers (the Mayo Clinic, University of California Los Angeles, University of Arizona Health Sciences Center, and Memorial Sloan-Kettering) and the unfavorable results were presented in April 1981. At that year's annual meeting of the American Society for Clinical Oncology, the Director of NCI, Dr. Vincent DeVita Jr., pronounced, "The findings present public evidence of Laetrile's failure as a cancer treatment,"[65] while Dr. Charles Moertel, who led the Mayo Clinic part of the trial, concluded Laetrile was "ineffective."[66] He reported that 50 percent of patients demonstrated evidence of cancer progression, 90 percent progressed after three months, and fifty percent died before five months. While 19 percent showed improvement in how they felt during the study, the authors attributed this to the placebo effect.[67] The results were resoundingly critical.

Patient-consumer groups reacted very differently to the news. Despite the unfavorable results, in both philosophical and practical terms groups such as the International Association of Cancer Victims and Friends, the Committee for Freedom of Choice in Cancer Therapy, and American Biologics Inc. continued to support the availability and use of Laetrile for cancer. Their rights as patient-consumers, they argued, were being violated and, more specifically, leveled criticisms at the NCI trials. For example, Robert Bradford, founder of the Committee for Freedom of Choice, stated unequivocally that the entire episode was an effort to discredit Laetrile. In his estimation, NCI "sabotaged the trials to save face" and thus the negative results meant "nothing."[68] Michael Culbert, editor of *Choice*, believed genuine Laetrile was never used during the trials. Both Bradford and Culbert launched three separate lawsuits against NCI, but all three were subsequently dismissed. By contrast, other health interest groups, including the Health Research Group, were critical of the government's response to Laetrile supporters. NCI's tests, according to Dr. Sidney Wolfe, set "an unfortunate precedent" and, at a cost of $400,000–$500,000 dollars, was "a waste of money." While the trials may have helped create consensus on Laetrile's effectiveness, Wolfe argued, "patients might have benefited from other experimental drugs."[69] Quackery, according to his logic, was provided a public forum by the NCI.

Pro-Laetrile groups, in particular, were antagonized by the FDA's approach to Laetrile and regarded the decision to oppose its use as emblematic of a broadly intrusive and imperious government. Even though there was no substantive proof underpinning Laetrile's claim of effectiveness, its proponents still sought to legalize it. Advocates for Laetrile, including Bradford and Culbert, argued that sick Americans had the freedom to choose any therapy they wanted—be it in the United States, Mexico, or Morocco. These advocates lobbied politicians hard to this end. Representatives in the House, responding to their constituents, introduced H.R. 4045, which would have legalized Laetrile, but the bill subsequently failed to generate votes. Similarly, Laetrile's supporters challenged the constitutionality of the 1962 effectiveness requirement on the basis of personal freedom. Lawyers contended during proceedings that the Kefauver efficacy amendment should not apply to drugs for persons with a fatal illness for which there was no conventional cure, even if the evidence in support of that drug was anecdotal; ultimately this line of reasoning was not successful. The FDA, for its part, fought against pro-Laetrile advocates vigorously.[70]

The Laetrile episode underscored valuable lessons that would have great import during the AIDS epidemic in the 1980s; indeed, it was a forerunner of events in the 1980s, when individuals like Lewis Engman, head of the Pharmaceutical Manufacturers Association, enunciated a faith in the sanctity of free-choice, personal freedom, and the patient's right to choose a medication. The Laetrile debate centered on the same fundamental principle: free choice in the marketplace.

First, it brought into sharp focus the need for the FDA's managerial staff, its key decision makers, to understand the persuasiveness and power of a persistent freedom-of-choice argument amid a climate of uncertainty. The agency's political appointments and—more importantly—its career employees had to ask themselves tough questions about its institutional identity and its modus operandi in the face of an epidemic of widespread public pressure. Should average Americans, be they terminal cancer patients or AIDS patients, have the right to spend their money any way they want? On any drug they want, however spurious, however hazardous? At what stage should such persons be allowed access to experimental, yet unapproved, drugs? This was surely a political pitfall for the FDA.

Second, in the wake of the Laetrile episode, the FDA also learned that it was essential to robustly defend the agency's use of the scientific method, and its regulatory standard practices, and thereby protect vulnerable patients from ineffective drugs. To this end, the FDA aggressively shored up its regulatory requirements and standards, as it instituted new benchmarks aimed at better protecting the nation's drug supply. Called good clinical practices (GCPs), the requirements included: informed consent of participants in a clinical trial, ethical evaluation by local institutional review boards, monitoring of clinical studies for adherence to protocol and data integrity, timely reporting of adverse events, and periodic reports to the FDA. These GCPs, when combined with the FDA's good laboratory practices (GLPs) standards to assure the integrity of toxicology data, established principles now accepted throughout the developed world.

In sum, the debate over Laetrile challenged the FDA's remit. It forced the FDA to define its institutional identity to both regulatory reformers and consumer activists during a time of unrest about government and institutions. The decision about Laetrile was ultimately left to the Supreme Court and though it found that the FDA was not overreaching or acting beyond its remit, Laetrile made the FDA reevaluate its own protocols. The event epitomized the growing complexity of the FDA's task in establishing the correct equilibrium between consumer protection, innovation, and access.

A 200-Page Drug Reform Bill

The FDA's Bureau of Drugs, as demonstrated earlier, faced myriad criticisms in the 1970s and such attacks emerged from disparate points on the political spectrum. President Carter, in fairness, was responsive to the issue of drug regulation, even if he was somewhat protean in that response. His broader regulatory reform and deregulatory actions, for example, would not have long-term ramifications on the Bureau of Drugs and he unquestionably acted as a deregulatory entrepreneur, establishing E.O. 12044, RARG, and the Paperwork Act. But Carter did not attack the FDA; instead, the initiatives recounted above, in addition to the appointments of Drs. Kennedy and Goyan, sent mixed messages as he tried to mollify both consumer activist and regulatory reformer factions. Nothing represented this approach more fittingly than the 200-page long, overly complex, Drug Regulation Reform bill of 1978.

Designed to achieve multiple, conflicting purposes, the Carter administration's Drug Reform bill attempted to operationalize the disparate goals of the FDA's many critics. If passed, the bill would have changed the basic structure of drug law established during the Roosevelt administration in 1938.[71] Not only did it aim to beat the drug lag but it imbued the FDA with additional regulatory powers—at a time when the political tide seemed to preclude such provisions. The bill failed in 1978 and 1979 and was never passed.

A postmortem reveals that the bill was simply too esoteric and paradoxical. On the one hand, the Drug Reform bill aimed to mitigate the lag, promote industry R&D, and liberalize access to drugs.[72] On the other hand, the Act also *strengthened* existing FDA drug regulatory authority. The agency was given increased authority to require post-marketing surveillance of and research on approved drugs, but it was also given more authority to remove such drugs from the market prior to a safety and efficacy hearing.[73] Moreover, the FDA's power to control the prescribing of drugs was enhanced and it was given statutory authority to control the distribution of a drug.[74]

The failed bill was thus a collection of incongruous parts ultimately lacking cohesion. At that point, the major trend appeared to favor deregulation of industry, not re-regulation. Every major piece of drug legislation had heretofore been enacted in eras of substantial social and governmental activism—the 1906 Food and Drug Act in the Progressive Era, the 1938 Food, Drug and Cosmetics Act, in the New Deal, and the 1962 Kefauver Amendments during the 1960s. Scandal and atrocity had precipitated the necessity for sound regulation, as in the cases of sulfanilamide in 1938 and thalidomide in 1962. Thus, seemingly necessary historical preconditions for passage of the bill were noticeably absent.

NOTES

1. Marjorie Sun, "Laetrile Brush Fire Is Out, Scientists Hope," *Science* 212, May 15, 1981, 758–759.

2. Sean Wilentz, *The Age of Reagan: A History, 1974–2008* (New York, NY: HarperCollins, 2008), 23.

3. R. Jeffrey Smith, "Califano Tells Tales of the Top Post at HEW," *Science* 212 (April 1981): 142–144.

4. James Dickinson, "Washington Report," *Pharmaceutical Technology*, February, 1981, 24.

5. Ibid.

6. Ibid.

7. A prime example of Carter's muddled approach was his desire to limit any new, major regulations emerging from the FDA. Problematically, he had appointed an activist, opinionated, consumer-oriented FDA Commissioner, Dr. Jere Goyan.

8. James Fallows, "The Passionless Presidency: The Trouble with Jimmy Carter's Administration," *Atlantic Monthly*, 243 (5) (1979): 33–48.

9. James Fallows, "The Passionless Presidency II: More from Inside Jimmy Carter's White House," *Atlantic Monthly*, 263 (6) (1979): 75–81.

10. Philip J. Hilts, *Protecting America's Health: The FDA, Business, and One Hundred Years of Regulation* (New York: Alfred A. Knopf, 2003), 207.

11. John W. Sloan, *The Reagan Effect: Economics and Presidential Leadership* (Lawrence: University Press of Kansas, 1999), 37.

12. Stuart Eizenstat, "Economists and White House Decisions," *The Journal of Economic Perspectives* 6 (3) (1992): 67.

13. Edward P. Fuchs and James E. Anderson, "The Institutionalization of Cost-Benefit Analysis," *Public Productivity Review* 10 (Summer 1987): 29–30.

14. Charles Gorton Interview, FDA Oral History Collection, 5.

15. Anthony A. Celeste and Arthur N. Levine "The Mission and the Institution: Ever Changing Yet Eternally the Same," in *FDA: A Century of Consumer Protection*, ed. Wayne Pines (Washington: Food and Drug Law Institute, 2006), 80. This change in enforcement policy (i.e., the shift toward voluntary compliance) could not have occurred without the development of the FDA as a legitimate maker of rules. Initially, the FDA's rule-making authority, based on its "authority to promulgate regulations for the efficient enforcement" of the law, was regarded as conferring only the power to issue interpretative rules subject to judicial review in enforcement actions. Later, however, the courts came to regard rules established under the Act as legally binding requirements with force and effect of law. The FDA's rule-making, furthermore, was based on the philosophy that the regulated industry would comply with FDA's interpretation of the law if that interpretation was clearly articulated, and an opportunity for comment had been provided before proposed rules were made final. By the late 1970s, the FDA began utilizing its rule-making authority to support a substantial amount of the agency's significant compliance efforts.

16. Joseph Paul Hile Interview, FDA Oral History Collection, 52–53.

17. Ibid.

18. Ibid.

19. Philip J. Hilts, *Protecting America's Health*, 207.

20. Alice Mundy, "Risk Management: The FDA's Deference to Drug Companies is Bad for America's Health," *Harper's*, September 2004, 83–84.

21. Joseph Paul Hile Interview, FDA Oral History Collection, 52–53.

22. James G. Dickinson, "Goodbye, Goyan! Some parting shots and pleasant memories," *Drug Topics*, March 1981, 84–86.

23. Quoted in Hilts *Protecting America's Health*, 207.

24. Ibid.

25. Ibid.

26. Fred Lofsvold Interview, Oral History Collection, 75.

27. Dickinson, "Goodbye, Goyan!," 84–86.

28. "The FDA Hits a Snag over Issuing Drug Data," *Business Week*, December 3, 1979, 48.

29. "PPI Users Know Less Than Nonusers, APhA Says," *Drug Topics*, June 15, 1979, 12.

30. Barbara Resnick Troetel, *Three Part Disharmony: The Transformation of the Food and Drug Administration in the 1970s*, Unpublished PhD dissertation (City Univeristy of New York, 1996), 328–329.

31. Fred Lofsvold Interview, FDA Oral History Collection, 75.

32. William Hubbard Interview, FDA Oral History Collection, 61.

33. The American Enterprise Institute, for example, sponsored a series of economic analyses in the 1970s concluding that excessive regulation indeed inhibited American competitiveness. AEI economists Richard Helms, Sam Peltzman, Henry Grabowski, John Vernon, William Wardell and Louis Lasagna surmised that Americans were suffering because of the FDA officials' unreasonable regulatory cautiousness.

34. Robert P. Luciano Interview, Chemical Heritage Foundation Oral History Collection, 8.

35. Testimony of Louis Lasagna, M.D. on Drug Regulation Reform Act of 1978 before the Subcommittee on Health and Scientific Research and Committee on Human Resources (Rochester, New York: The Center for the Study of Drug Development, April 12, 1978), 2.

36. Committee on Science and Technology, *Drug Lag*, 97th Congress, 1st Session, September 16, 1981, 2.

37. *FDA and the 96th Congress*, 135–136.

38. Henry Grabowski, "An Analysis of US International Competitiveness in Pharmaceuticals," *Managerial and Decision Economics* 10 (Spring 1989): 27–33.

39. Henry G. Grabowski, John M Vernon, and L.G. Thomas, "Estimating the Effects of Regulation on Innovation: An International Comparative Analysis of the Pharmaceutical Industry," *Journal of Law & Economics* 31 (1) (1978): 133–163.

40. Ibid.

41. Ibid.

42. Committee on Science and Technology, *FDA Drug Approval—A Lengthy Process that Delays the Availability of Important New Drugs: Report to the Subcommittee on Science, Research, and Technology, House Committee on Science and Technology*, May 28, 1980.

43. *FDA Drug Approval—A Lengthy Process that Delays the Availability of Important New Drugs*, Comptroller General's Report, 5.

44. Committee on Human Resources, *Testimony of Louis Lasagna, M.D. on Drug Regulation Reform Act of 1978: hearings before the Subcommittee on Health and Scientific Research* (Rochester, New York: The Center for the Study of Drug Development, April 12, 1978), 2.

45. Richard J. Crout Interview, FDA Oral History Collection, 29–30.

46. Committee on Interstate and Foreign Commerce, *Drug Regulation Reform—Oversight, New Drug Approval Process: Hearings Before the Subcommittee on Health and the Environment of the, House of Representatives*, 96th Congress, June 25, 1980, 1–20.

47. Ibid.

48. Ibid.

49. Ibid.

50. Ibid.

51. James H. Scheuer, "The F.D.A.: Too Slow," *New York Times*, May 22, 1980, A35.

52. Laetrile was first isolated and purified in the late 1940s by biochemist Ernst T. Krebs Jr; for commercial purposes, Laetrile was often extracted from apricot and peach pits.

53. Ralph W. Moss, *The Cancer Industry* (New York: Equinox Press, 1980), 147.

54. "Laetrile/Amygdalin," National Cancer Institute, August 10, 2012. Consulted at http://www.cancer.gov/cancertopics/pdq/cam/laetrile/HealthProfessional/page1/AllPages/Print.

55. "Laetrile Crackdown," *Time* 107, 1976, 84.

56. Ibid.

57. *FDA Quarterly Activities Report*, FY 1978, 1st Quarter, 53.

58. John Walsh, "Laetrile Tops FDA's Most Unwanted List," *Science* 199 (1978): 158–159.

59. "Court Ruling on Laetrile Seen by F.D.A. as Curb," *New York Times*, February 27, 1980, A19.

60. "Challenging the Apricot-Pit Gang," *Time* 110, July 25, 1977, 64. See also Benjamin Wilson, "The Rise and Fall of Laetrile." Consulted at http://www.quackwatch.org/01QuackeryRelatedTopics/Cancer/laetrile.html.

61. C.G. Moertel, "A Trial of Laetrile Now," *New England Journal of Medicine* 298, January 26, 1978, 218–219.

62. Wayne Pines, "Fighting Laetrile," in *FDA: A Century of Consumer Protection*, ed. Wayne Pines (Washington: Food and Drug Law Institute, 2006), 176–177. See United States v. Rutherford, 442 U.S. 544 (1979).

63. "Laetrile Crackdown," *Time* 107, 1976, 84.

64. "Laetrile/Amygdalin," National Cancer Institute, August 10, 2012. See also A. Relman, "Closing the Books on Laetrile," *New England Journal of Medicine* 306 (1982), 236.

65. "Laetrile Flunks," *Time* 117, May 11, 1981, 63.

66. Quoted in Moss, *The Cancer Industry*, 151.

67. National Cancer Institute. "Clinical Study of Laetrile in Cancer Patients, Investigators' Report: A Summary." April 30, 1981.

68. Sun, "Laetrile Brush Fire Is Out, Scientists Hope," 758–759.

69. Ibid.

70. Barbara Resnick Troetel, *Three Part Disharmony: The Transformation of the Food and Drug Administration in the 1970s.*

71. See Daniel O'Keefe Jr., "Technical Problems With the Drug Regulation Reform Act of 1978," *Food Drug and Cosmetic Law Journal* 33 (1978): 674; William W. Vodra, "The Drug Regulation Reform Act of 1978: Putting Some Economic Issues into Context," *Managerial and Decision Economics* 1 (4) (1980): 184–196.

72. *Drug Regulation Reform Act of 1978: The Administration Proposal, Section-by-Section Analysis,* Department of Health, Education and Welfare, 1978, 24–25.

73. Ibid.

74. Quirk, "The FDA," 232.

Chapter Four

Opening Moves: Reagan and the FDA in 1980–1982

". . . Reagan's attack on government deliberately made Carter look like a raging liberal and a rabid regulator."[1]

HISTORIAN PHILLIP J. COOPER

"FDA is part of the Reagan revolution, like every other agency . . ."[2]

HHS CHIEF-OF-STAFF MCCLAIN HADDOW

In 1980, the Republican presidential ticket of Ronald Reagan and George H. W. Bush promised to change Washington. President Jimmy Carter represented failure, Republicans argued, be it botched rescue attempts and helicopter crashes in the desert, the loss of the Panama Canal, or an impotent economy. According to rhetorician Paul D. Erickson, Reagan articulated how "American history went awry; along with the almost physical obstacles and hindrances of federal paperwork and bureaucracy, the country suffered deeply from a crisis of faith."[3] Historians largely agree that there were three principal reasons for his defeat: the Iranian hostage ordeal, which initially aided his approval rating but eventually sucked the energy out of the administration; division within the Democratic Party, between liberals and moderates, the Kennedy wing and Carter; finally, the flagging U.S. economy.

Reagan, by contrast, offered a tolerable alternative to Carter and he cleverly extolled patriotism, individual freedom, and a potential renewal of American glory—economic and military. At the same time, he "always appeared genial, friendly, and warm."[4] As hard as the Democrats tried to characterize Reagan as an extremist, Reagan seemed neither a doddering incompetent nor a dangerous reactionary. In fact, during the solitary presidential debate, Reagan appeared calm and measured as he parried Carter's attacks. His sincere question to the American people at the conclusion of that single debate—"Are you better off than you were four years ago?"—moved the polls in his favor with just little precious time left to campaign.[5] According to Hamilton Jordan, Carter's campaign manager and close confidante:

> . . . in retrospect, we never had a chance of winning that campaign. . . . It was only ultimately a nagging doubt about Ronald Reagan that kept that race close up until the final days.[6]

In the end, Reagan's victory was substantial. He defeated President Jimmy Carter, with 43,899,248 popular votes (50.8 percent) to Carter's 35,481,435 votes (or 41 percent). Reagan carried forty-four states, for a total of 489 electoral votes; while Carter carried six states, for a total of 49 electoral votes. Independent candidate John Anderson won 5,719,437 votes (6.6 percent) whereas Libertarian party candidate Ed Clark received 920,859 votes (1.1 percent). The other 474,699 votes were cast for seventeen different candidates. Even though Reagan's victory was not marked by increased voter turnout, he nevertheless made gains in every demographic "slice of the pollsters' pie, except blacks."[7] He won convincingly in the West, took the North and Midwest, but barely won the South. In doing so, he made inroads with blue-collar workers, Catholics, Hispanics, Jews, and women. These results were significant in several respects. First, 1980 was the second straight election in which an incumbent president was defeated for reelection. Second, Reagan's victory continued the trend that no president since Dwight D. Eisenhower had served two full terms.[8]

Republicans also made gains in Congress. The Senate, for its part, saw tremendous change: thirty-four seats were contested and the Republicans gained twelve seats (the largest increase since 1946), which meant they now had fifty-three seats to the Democrats' forty-six. These Republic gains came at the expense of long-time Democratic senators, such as George McGovern, Birch Bayh, and Frank Church. Similarly, in the House of Representatives, Republicans won a net gain of thirty-three seats, and this represented the largest increase for the Republicans in any election since 1966.[9] While the Democrats retained control of the House, according to historian Judith Stein "some of the losers were process and foreign policy liberals who were from conservative states . . ."[10]

Reagan's victory can be read as an indictment of Carter rather than wholesale of acceptance of Reagan. However, in addition to electing Reagan as commander in chief, American voters gave the Republican Party a majority in the Senate for the first time since 1954. The Democrats kept the House, but were a wounded party and lost thirty-three seats. Afterward, commentators of all stripes—historians, political scientists, and countless others—began to debate whether Reagan's victory heralded the establishment of a new conservative political and economic order.

President Reagan's Team and His Style of Leadership

As Reagan assumed the presidency and assembled his inner circle and team of closest advisors, he reached beyond his conservative base and appointed many moderate Republicans who had served Presidents Nixon and Ford. At the very top of the administration, he relied on a triumvirate of policy advis-

Figure 4.1. President Ronald Reagan at his desk in the Oval Office, Washington, D.C. From the Library of Congress. Carol M. Highsmith photographer.

ers who served him effectively. Reagan appointed James A. Baker III, a close confidante and adviser to George H.W. Bush, as White House chief of staff. According to historian Edmund Morris, Baker was impressive. "He combined the poise of Princeton with, on calculated occasions, the *huevos*-grabbing aggression of a Houston oil lawyer." These traits, wrote Morris, enabled him to "secure the second biggest office in the West Wing, plus control over every document intended for the President's eyes."[11] This was to the disappointment of the more conservative and abrasive Edwin Meese, an associate from Reagan's time as governor of California, who expected the job of chief of staff, and had to settle for the position of presidential counselor and a spot in the cabinet. Michael Deaver, another member of Reagan's California staff, was named deputy chief of staff. He was an accomplished public relations specialist, coordinated much of the president's schedule, controlled media access to him, and had a strong personal relationship with both Reagan and wife Nancy.[12] This group, though not consistently friendly or ideologically compatible, played a significant role in the success of Reagan's first term in office.

Reagan's first cabinet was composed of, for the most part, white, male Republicans, many of whom had served under Nixon or Ford. Only two positions, Interior and Energy, were given to members of the New Right, James Watt and James Edwards respectively. No women served in the first cabinet,[13] but after the 1982 midterm elections, in which the Republican Party fared poorly with female voters, Reagan appointed Margaret Heckler as secretary of health and human services and Elizabeth Dole as secretary of transportation. The president appointed Samuel Pierce, an African American, as secretary of housing and urban development, but one occasion that has been recapitulated various times saw the president fail to recognize Pierce and he greeted his HUD secretary with, "Hello, Mr. Mayor."[14]

In the early years of the Reagan administration, and in the years to follow, the president was accused of passivity and a kind of intellectual torpor. Political scientist Richard Neustadt argued that Reagan lacked many of the skills a successful president requires: "He seems to have combined less intellectual curiosity, less interest in detail, than any President at least since Calvin Coolidge . . ."[15] Secretary of State Alexander Haig was particularly critical of Reagan's leadership ability. "To me," he wrote in his memoirs, "the White House was as mysterious as a ghost ship; you heard the creaking of the rigging and the groan of the timbers and sometimes even glimpsed the crew on deck. But which of the crew was at the helm? Was it Meese, was it Baker, was it someone else? It was impossible to know for sure."[16] According to journalist and Reagan scholar Lou Cannon, "Reagan's aides became accustomed to figuring out things for themselves, for he managed by indirection when he managed at all."[17] "He made no demands, and gave almost no instructions," noted Martin Anderson, a member of the economic team. "We just accepted Reagan as he was and adjusted ourselves to his manner."[18] Larry Speakes, President Reagan's press secretary, noted: "if you worked for Ronald Reagan, you had better be good at your job. Reagan's operating style, delegating many of his oversight duties to his subordinates, gave his aides more power, for better or worse, than they would have had under any other President in memory."[19]

However, Edwin Meese, former counselor to the president, rebuts that claim. "One of the most astonishing things to me is to read the numerous accounts of the Reagan era that portray the President as an essentially passive figure, somehow disengaged, ignorant of the facts, or incapable of leading." Instead, Reagan was a "tough and decisive leader" and he had a "friendly and nonconfrontational manner." In short, "the Reagan-as-empty-vessel theory is somewhat ludicrous."[20] Reagan, discussing his own management style, noted: "The Cabinet is like a board of directors and I'm the chief executive officer, except that I'm the only one who has a vote at the end."[21]

Whatever the exact nature of Reagan's style of leadership, historians of the era generally agree that he delegated a tremendous amount of responsibility to his team and he rarely involved himself in the finer details of policymaking. This applies to the FDA, as much as it does to Iran-Contra. But there is also a consensus among Reagan scholars that the administration ran much more smoothly and efficiently when the triumvirate of Baker, Meese, and Deaver were firmly in control of the White House and controlling the paper flow and access to the president. Indeed, "Baker and Deaver had been protective of Reagan to a fault, always sensitive to the possibility of self-inflicted wounds."[22] Reagan's style of leadership, in short, was best suited to their capabilities and ideological temperaments.[23]

The War on Regulation and on the FDA

Immediately following his inauguration, Reagan set in motion a profound overhaul of the existing regulatory regime. The national press called it a "war on regulation,"[24] whereas conservatives called it sensible. The program, according to historian Phillip J. Cooper, included direct and indirect attacks on the bureaucracy and affected myriad regulatory agencies and executive branch offices. In his estimation, "the intensity of the Reagan antiregulation warriors was greater than their predecessors in significant part at least because, for these players, the battle was ideological . . ."[25] The depth and strength of the commitment to deregulation resulted in a host of victories and derived from Reagan's beliefs.

In the briefing room at the White House, President Reagan spoke of his intentions:

The regulatory reform, as you know, we've been talking about for a long time is one of the keystones in our programs to return the nation to prosperity and to set loose again the ingenuity and energy of the American people. Government regulations impose an enormous burden on large and small businesses in America, discourage productivity, and contribute substantially to our current economic woes. To cut away the thicket of irrational and senseless regulations requires careful study, close coordination between the agencies and bureaus in the Federal structure. . . . And our goal is going to be to see if we cannot reverse the trend of recent years and see at the end of the year a reduction in the number of pages in the Federal Register instead of an increase.[26]

On January 29, 1981, Reagan began the overhaul by ordering a 60-day freeze on all pending regulations, including the 119 regulations approved by Carter in his last month in office; thereafter Reagan established the Regulatory Task Force, headed by Vice President George Bush. The task force was managed by James C. Miller III, the administrator of regulatory affairs in the Office of Management and Budget; Richard Williamson, assistant to the president for intergovernmental and regulatory affairs; and C. Boyden Gray, who was the task force's counsel.

In relatively short order, the task force contacted thousands of businesses, civic leaders, governors, and others, urging them to report their most grievous regulatory stories and then submit recommendations for reform. In a speech before the U.S. Chamber of Commerce on April 10, 1981, Gray informed business leaders that they should in fact take their concerns directly to the White House instead of the heads of regulatory agencies. "If you go to the agency first," he declared, "don't be too pessimistic if they can't solve the problem there. That's what the task force is for."[27] Gray also made it clear that his job was to eliminate the conflicts between business and government and it was not essential for that consultation process to be in the public domain. "The public has no more right to know what a member of the president's staff says to an agency than a Congressman who communicates privately with his staff."[28]

In addition to this task force, President Reagan changed the nature of regulation-making with the February 17, 1981 signing of Executive Order 12291, which centralized final regulatory authority in David Stockman's Office of Management and Budget.[29] The president also appointed aggressive deregulators to leadership positions at a number of major institutions, as recent studies of the Reagan administration have illustrated.[30] Such appointments were made, in particular, at the Consumer Product Safety Commission, the Federal Communications Commission, the Federal Trade Commission, the Federal Energy Regulatory Commission, the Occupational Safety and Health Administration, the Environmental Protection Agency, and the National Highway Traffic Safety Administration. Similarly inclined appointees were named to head the Council of Economic Advisors, the Office of Management and Budget, and the Department of the Interior.

The FDA was also targeted for reform. Prior to the election, Reagan had received such specific policy advice. Months before the presidential election, on May 28, 1980, the General Accounting Office's Comptroller General released a report called "FDA Drug Approval—A Lengthy Process that Delays the Availability of Important New Drugs."[31] The Bureau of Drugs, the report charged, required streamlining because the process for approving new drug applications (NDAs) was unnecessarily long relative to other countries. The process not only delayed the life-saving and life-enhancing benefits which important drugs conferred on the public, but the relationship between BOD and the pharmaceutical industry also required improvements.

Representative James Scheuer (D-NY), a member of the House Committee on Science and Technology which requisitioned the GAO study, wrote in the *New York Times* on May 22, 1980, "Many of the [FDA's] guidelines and regulations are arbitrary, redundant and subject to frequent change or varied interpretation."[32] According to Scheuer, the FDA emphasized assiduousness and rigor in the approval process; however, this practice, which reflected an institutional fear of taking risks on potentially safe and effective medicines, was to the detriment of sick Americans. To illustrate his point, he wrote of how the drug Moxalactum an American-made antibiotic for pneumonia was being used by Marshal Tito in Yugoslavia—yet it was not available in the United States. The FDA, he suggested, was protecting Americans to death.

Days after Reagan won the presidency criticism of the agency heightened further.[33] On November 15, an 18-person Republican healthcare advisory transition committee recommended liberalizing "the regulatory efforts of the Food and Drug Administration to allow drugs to remain longer on patent, thus giving investors greater profit."[34] Dr. William Walsh, the group's chairman, said our "general approach was to relax the Federal regulation of healthcare . . ." and "the one thing we sought to bring about was an attitudinal change that Washington and indeed the Federal Government know best what to do . . . in many cases it doesn't."[35] Just like Scheuer, Walsh wanted to rattle the institutional status quo, affect change, and perhaps cure the FDA's myopia.

Prominent think tanks provided President Reagan with even more advice concerning the FDA and BOD. The American Enterprise Institute offered a substantial theoretical and empirical basis for reducing FDA authority to regulate the pharmaceutical industry. In 1981, the fourth in the AEI-sponsored book series on the FDA and drug regulation was published, and the AEI was not alone in advocating reform of the FDA; in early 1981, the right-leaning Heritage Foundation published a 3,000-page how-to-govern tome called *Mandate for Leadership,* which echoed Reagan's campaign slogan—the nation was in a crisis of overregulation and excessive legislation which was leading to mounting costs in society. The FDA, according to *Mandate for Leadership,* was part of the problem and required reform.[36]

Debating FDA Regulation and Forecasting Industry Growth

In 1981, the debate about drug regulation continued to polarize people; finding a middle ground was often difficult, and as the new administration took power, the outgoing FDA commissioner Goyan articulated a consensus-oriented, centrist approach to drug regulation. In his estimation, the FDA transcended presidential politics and ideology, since it was an essential part of the fabric of America that protected all Americans—conservative and liberal—as it carried out its duties:

> My view is that government regulation needs to strike a balance between preserving the maximum freedom for individuals while at the same time establishing the rules that are needed for us to live together, to survive as a society. Any close examination of FDA programs would reveal an agency that understands that delicate balance—an agency that is fair-minded, that has acted in the best interests of the public health, and that confines its activities to areas where people cannot adequately protect themselves. [37]

More often than not, Goyan's sensible approach went unheeded, overwhelmed by disputes about individualism and consumer choice and bureaucratic incompetence. Journalist David Perlman neatly sketched the contours of the debate. First he cited Peter Barton Hutt, former chief counsel for the FDA, who said that too many people regarded FDA staff members "as a bunch of demented bureaucrats running amok," even though the agency's "balanced" regulation of drugs was both "socially valid and moral." Perlman then used Lewis Engman, president of the Pharmaceutical Manufacturers Association, to illustrate a conflicting position. Engman felt that taking medicines, like smoking cigarettes, was a matter of personal choice. "Any time you interfere with the basic market system," he said in 1981, "you're in trouble . . . the consumer is his own best guardian."[38] Hugh D'Andrade, formerly vice president of both Ciba-Geigy and Schering-Plough corporations, helped establish the Industrial Biotechnology Association (IBA) in the early 1980s and he implied that Reagan ought to promote friendly relations between government and industry. A cooperative path, in his view, was the best way forward: "That the best way to avoid an adversarial relationship was to avoid an adversarial relationship."[39]

Though it could not be known just how the new president would transform the FDA in early 1981, political pundits, economic analysts, and pharmaceutical industry insiders suggested that Reagan as president meant less regulation, which meant industry growth.[40] The president of the National Association of Retail Druggists (NARD), Jesse M. Pike, sent a congratulatory letter to President-elect Ronald Reagan that emphasized just how delighted NARD was to see Reagan in the White House and just how much the Reagan administration's regulatory reform beliefs would be good for business.[41] In *Pharmaceutical Technology,* James Dickinson wrote, "everyone expects life to be easier for industry under the new Reagan Administration."[42] During the Reagan transition, Dickinson added, the Washington cocktail circuit was rife with speculation about the new administration repealing the Kefauver-Harris 1962 drug efficacy requirements—a move that would further enhance prospects for industry growth. This was nonsense, according to Dickinson. Yet, looking back, the fact that the notion was even bandied about, however fancifully, represented a substantial change in the debate about drug regulation.

The major U.S. newspapers reinforced the mounting enthusiasm about pharmaceutical growth in the wake of the Reagan election. The *Wall Street Journal* reported that "Pfizer Sees 15% Rise in Net and Revenue From New-Drug Sales" in March 1981. "Analysts," the article said, predicted that Pfizer Inc.'s stock could jump "by as much as $500 million to $1 billion a year by 1985."[43] Reports in the *New York Times* such as the "The Drug Business Sees a Golden Era Ahead" and "Betting the Store on Another Tagamet" noted that the pharmaceutical industry was confident about the future in this new regulatory climate.[44] D. Larry Smith, a drug analyst at Smith Barney, Harris Upham & Company was bullish about drug stocks in general, while another money manager, John R. Groome, predicted that pharmaceutical companies would start to generate more and more earning, in 1981 and 1982.[45]

The outgoing FDA commissioner Goyan interpreted the election of President Reagan as a significant shift among the electorate—a shift that was profoundly important for the FDA. Goyan believed American voters were signaling that, yes, they indeed wanted government "off their backs." "There is," Goyan remarked, "a clear mandate for less government involvement at least at the Federal level, in certain aspects of society."[46] Yet he also believed that Americans possessed a nuanced perspective on drug regulation; this meant it was necessary for his successor as FDA commisioner, Arthur Hull Hayes, to adopt a judicious approach to regulatory reform. By voting for Reagan, Goyan said Americans were communicating they wanted "reasonable regulation," "a common sense approach," "limits on economic regulation that tended to inflate prices," and "costs considered in regulatory decisions."[47] Americans did not want wholesale abolishment of regulations; rather, they simply wanted "modifications" to the current models—reform rather than removal. "It would be a mistake," Goyan concluded, "a tragic one, to interpret the election results to mean that the public wants a lessening of the standards that provide the foundation for the food and drug industries in this country, standards that make our food and drug supply the best in the world."[48]

For all the speculation about regulatory reform of the FDA, the possible repeal of the 1962 Kefauver Amendment, and the potential growth of the pharmaceutical industry, the unwaveringly optimistic Ronald Reagan had promised in 1980, with trademark sincerity, not to terminate the FDA. Instead, he made oblique references to the agency's storied history, the importance of some regulation in society, and he resorted to prosaic comments about the danger of hidebound power-hungry bureaucracies. "There's a certain amount of regulation that is always necessary to protect us from each other," he told Walter Cronkite. "And that I recognize. We don't want to, for example, eliminate the responsibility of the FDA . . . ."[49] In addition, Reagan told journalist and historian Elizabeth Drew on the campaign trail in 1980, "I have no quarrel with the federal Food and Drug Administration." He then continued to explain why he would significantly modify rather than dismantle it:

> It [FDA] began around the turn of the century, when we lost a great many people—as a matter of fact, soldiers in the Spanish-American War—through poisoned canned meat. That's fine. Government exists to protect us from each other. But as the years have gone on and the bureaucracy grows, as bureaucracies do, we find that they have gone far beyond protecting us from poisonous or harmful substances, and they have now set themselves up as the doctor and decided that they will tell us what medicines are effective.[50]

Much can be gleaned from his public statements about the Food and Drug Administration, though they do not reveal the entire picture. On a personal level, Reagan did not desire the elimination of the FDA, but he did not trust it—in his estimation, its authority needed curtailing. For example, he had made it clear in 1975, while before an audience at the American Enterprise Institute, the FDA was hurting Americans. Privately, Reagan believed this was often the case as well. His diary entry on May 20, 1986, described a meeting between Paul Laxalt, Jack Dreyfus, and himself. Dreyfus, who had "spent $50 mil. of his own money" was attempting to have the epilepsy drug Dilantin approved for various other health problems and found a roadblock in the form of the FDA approval process. According to Reagan's personal diary: "The villain in the case is the Fed. Drug Admin & they are a villain."[51]

A Bang, Not a Whimper—The Reagan Administration's Immediate Impact at the FDA

President Reagan's new policy, to reduce the size and scope of government and curtail regulation, was abundantly clear at the FDA and it soon had effects. "The Republicans came into power with a bang in 1981," according to Paul Hile, the FDA's Associate Commissioner for Regulatory Affairs. "Those were very, very difficult times . . . we knew there would be a major change in the way we conducted our affairs."[52]

Gerald Barkdoll, the Associate Commissioner for Planning and Evaluation in 1980–1981, described how the FDA's upper management dealt with the new administration's policy. During one particular planning session, FDA employees brainstormed and reevaluated their own positions. They asked, he recalled, introspective and important questions about the agency's role in society: " 'What kind of agency is this? Is this a public health agency, is this a consumer protection agency, or is this a regulatory agency?' We were having big debates."[53]

Ballard Graham, the director of the FDA's Atlanta District Office during the presidential transition, concurred with the assessment. The early 1980s were indeed difficult times. He added, however, that a flexible attitude characterized many FDA employees. In his view: "You elect people into office who you want to see there when you want to see things done differently. When the people speak and elect who will run the country, the FDA and all the departments are of course a part of that function and that electoral system, whether or not we as career employees agree or disagree with the process, that's the process. It's worked quite well for 200-plus years in this country, where the elected party comes in and set a new agenda. But we also have the regulations and the policies that have been established over the years and have worked quite well."[54]

The Reagan administration, for its part, was set on revising the regulations and policies of which Barkdoll spoke, of modifying the FDA's drug regulation in general.[55] To achieve this, the president named moderate Republican Senator Richard Schweiker (R-Penn) as his Secretary of Health and Human Services and Dr. Arthur Hull Hayes Jr. as FDA commissioner.

The administration made these appointments with clear goals in mind. One was to ameliorate the prevailing institutional culture at the FDA. During the hearings on the Drug Reform bill of 1978 and the drug lag, Dr. Louis Lasagna testified that an entrenched philosophy of restraint permeated the FDA. This contributed to delays and dangers for American consumers.[56] President Reagan sought to change this institutional culture through the appointments of Schweiker and Hayes.

A second goal of the administration in making these appointments was to select candidates who were independent and resistant to the politicization of a federal agency.[57] There was a great deal of apprehension in the Reagan administration about this. Cabinet officials, as well as appointed officials in the independent agencies, were instructed to swiftly move in and take control of their respective departments. On January 8, 1981, Reagan warned his cabinet that civil service careerists would resist new policies and it was crucial to avoid talking of government as "we" rather than "they."[58]

This meant Secretary Schweiker usurped a degree of Commissioner Hayes's standard authority. The relationship between the HHS and FDA appointees was thus closer than in years past, with Schweiker personally involving himself in certain operational decision-making processes—during, for example, Class 1 drug recall situations. This type of hands-on behavior by the secretary was abnormal. Conventionally, the secretary of HHS (and before that HEW) left actionable, operational decisions to the head of the FDA. In addition, Schweiker curtailed the commissioner's authority to promulgate regulations by involving his office in the process. Regulations now also had to travel through HHS and be signed by the secretary; only after he had signed off on a regulation would it be forwarded to David Stockman's OMB.

Secretary Schweiker's appointment as Secretary of Health and Human Services also reveals the Reagan administration's desire to provide regulatory relief at the FDA and eradicate the drug lag. Schweiker had compiled a record of support for change at the FDA, albeit not radical change. In 1979, during debates on the Drug Regulation Reform Act, he remarked:

> "Historically, pharmaceutical manufacturing has been a strong industry, and the U.S. pharmaceutical industry has been a leader in research and the development of important new therapies." Schweiker added, in a rather subtle manner, that reform was necessary. "In recent years . . . there has been rising concern about delays in new drug development due to the operation of the present drug approval system." "Almost everyone agrees," he emphasized, "that unnecessary delays that impede prompt approval of safe and effective drugs should be eliminated . . ."[59] In June 1982, he told *FDA Today,* "One of the top priorities of this department [HHS] is to promote the public health by encouraging the development of useful new drugs, and removing needless barriers to their swift approval by the FDA. Commissioner Hayes and I are committed to this goal."

Schweiker took a number of steps to achieve this aim. First, he appointed a senior FDA manager to oversee the progress of new drug applications throughout the review system. Second, he oversaw the redesign of the automatic data processing systems within the Bureau of Drugs to enhance the monitoring of new drug applications. Finally, Schweiker focused special attention on remedying the bureau's acute clerical staffing problems by filling vacancies, reassigning staff, and reallocating work to eliminate backlogs. Schweiker commented, "the steps we are announcing today, combined with other initiatives under development within the department, represent significant progress."[60]

The new secretary also commissioned an investigation into the drug review process. Making the announcement in January 1981, Schweiker made it abundantly plain what he intended to achieve as head of HHS and through the new study—the outright termination of "unnecessary delays" during drug approvals. Conducted under the direction of Dale Sopper, the Assistant Secretary for Management and Budget, the study concluded the NDE review process was "generally sound." However, it was further discovered that the drug review process was "not applied or managed as efficiently as possible." This, unfortunately, resulted "in delays in completing reviews and a lack of control over the workloads." Improvement was possible and necessary, and Sopper made certain proposals for the Bureau of Drugs to follow:

1. Upgrade management control.
2. Better distribute NDE division workloads.
3. More efficient use of staff resources, both professional and clerical.
4. Increase reviewer/drug company interaction to enhance communication between FDA and the drug industry.
5. Establish production goals to more efficiently manage the flow and movement of documents through the NDE process.

In response to Sopper's recommendations, Schweiker judiciously pledged that all ideas would be carefully evaluated. He also emphasized, "Those that hold out real promise for streamlining the [drug review] process will be promptly adopted."[61]

This discussion of streamlining soon intensified when the Bureau of Drugs produced its own internal study. Also commissioned in 1981, this second investigation was conducted by Dr. Peter Vaill, a professor at the School of Government and Business Administration at George Washington University. Vaill concluded that "the many facets of new drug evaluation are being conducted in as scientifically sound and expeditious a manner as possible." He underlined how complicated the NDE process was. Multiple outside stakeholders influenced BOD officials, Vaill wrote. Legislatively mandated time pressures, technological complexity, and the present political climate (the anti-government, regulatory reform ethos of the Reagan administration), further compounded the difficulty in understanding the process. Vaill thus highlighted that he had "never before encountered a more complex and challenging organizational situation" prior to making several suggestions to improve the NDE review process.[62] These included: rewarding effective performance, using experimental administrative processes, creating new ways to handle professional development, and providing staff seminars in the administrative aspects of the NDE process.[63]

The results of the Sopper and Vaill studies were similar in that they identified the NDE review process as fundamentally functional and sound. The studies varied, however, in their levels of criticism and proposed measures to alleviate the inherent problems of the drug review process. The Schweiker-commissioned study, which was more critical, suggested better use of resources, controls, and a goal-oriented approach, whereas the BOD's study was, by contrast, more sympathetic. The latter underscored the challenges BOD faced and mandated greater use of carrots, rather than sticks. It denoted, moreover, the importance of flexibility and better job training instead of increased stringency amongst employees.

Commissioner Hayes—A Moderate Deregulator?

The public face of the FDA from the agency's inception has not been the secretary of HHS, or HEW before that, but the commissioner. The position of commissioner is wrought with troubling pitfalls. A commissioner must maintain fidelity to the agency's mission, to protect America's food and drug supply through accurate, science-based analysis and also approve in a timely fashion innovative products that benefit the general public.

The Reagan administration's choice of FDA commissioner, Dr. Arthur Hull Hayes Jr. was, like Secretary Schweiker, careful and considered. For those interested in the speedier approval of new drugs, Hayes, a wiry, forty-seven-year-old, was hailed as the best possible choice for the commissioner's spot. He was the head of Penn State University's clinical pharmacology division, a member of the United States Pharmacopeia board of trustees, and was well regarded by both the Pharmaceutical Manufacturers Association and the American Medical Association. Hayes was no ideologue, like Secretary of the Interior James Watt or Environmental Protection Agency Chair Anne Burford, but he was no regulatory Pollyanna either. He was camped out on the industry side of medicine, to be sure, having been a regular consultant for many drug companies, at high rates of pay, and he continued to accept financial honoraria as commissioner. *Forbes* magazine classified Hayes as a "moderate deregulator" in 1981.[64] ". . . As I approach the deregulation issue," he remarked to Congress, "I begin from the viewpoint that the public wants and expects the guarantee of protection afforded by FDA."[65] "The public," Hayes added, "has demonstrated its faith in the FDA, and I have tremendous faith in the American public."[66]

Hayes thus echoed Reagan's comments to Elizabeth Drew. He, like the president, accepted the FDA's existence, but he nevertheless felt that the agency had overextended itself and needed reforming. During congressional testimony in 1982, Hayes said he would undertake "critical evaluations of the consequences of the regulatory actions on the American public and the private sector of the economy." He was, he continued, committed to making regulation less burdensome to the regulated industry, to reassessing the need for existing regulations, and to make sure regulation did not stifle innovation or new applications of knowledge. Hayes added, "Rationality, flexibility and economic impact" were essential tools in assessing "whether there are alternative ways to accomplish the same goals."[67]

The commissioner also made clear, as Secretary Schweiker had, that the drug review and approval process was of particular interest to him. He was especially interested in the prospect of—to use a familiar word—streamlining certain processes. ". . . I have been sensitive to, and at times critical of, the time it takes to bring important new drugs from the manufacturers' laboratories to the pharmacy shelves," he asserted.[68] Hayes vowed to speed up the drug approval of totally new drugs, mitigate the drug lag, and "foster a more cooperative spirit" with the pharmaceutical industry through the promotion of "voluntary action." "Drug review can be streamlined," he averred, "existing regulations can be improved," and "we must be sensitive to the impact of our regulatory stance on innovation."[69] To achieve these formidable goals, Hayes's policy agenda included initiatives to study the drug approval process through a twenty-one-member task force, reduce FDA processing time by 15 percent, and continue implementation of the priority review system.[70]

When asked by Representative Elliott Levitas (D-GA), an avid deregulator, whether the FDA's agenda of reform (including proposed revisions to the new drug application) would be harmful to public safety, Hayes adopted a dual approach: he accentuated the importance of both consumer protection and product innovation. On the topic of regulatory reform, Hayes promised there would be no "'loosening up' in the level of public health protection now afforded by the drug approval process." The FDA, he stressed, was "ever mindful not to compromise the safety and effectiveness of new drug products approved for marketing." According to Hayes, however, "weeding out" requirements that were "duplicative" and "unnecessary" was of the utmost importance as well.[71] Taken as a whole, Hayes demonstrated a commitment to the FDA and its mandate as well as unmistakable loyalty to the Reagan administration and its approach to regulation.

As balanced as it seemed, Hayes's regulatory philosophy was not accepted unequivocally within the FDA. Career employees in the agency challenged him to clarify how his approach to drug regulation would affect the Bureau of Drugs and the public at large. The November 1981 issue of *FDA Consumer,* for example, included a lively and candid interchange between long-time Associate FDA Commissioner Wayne Pines and Hayes. In the course of the interview, Pines asked Hayes—his boss—some incendiary and potentially damaging questions about his regulatory beliefs. First, was he opposed to federal regulations? Second, had he received any marching orders from the new administration before he was appointed commissioner? Finally, how much time did he think could be shaved off the drug review process?[72]

Hayes, less than a month into the job, deftly parried the sharp thrust of the questions. On federal regulations Hayes observed: "I believe that this administration [the Reagan government] favors good regulation." He agreed with this regulatory approach, and he added judiciously, "I'm very much in favor of regulation—when it's the best or only way to serve the public good and when the regulations are fair and effective. I'm only against bad and unnecessary regulation, and I hope everyone would be." Hayes also avoided alienating his subordinates, public servants loyal to the FDA identity and the idea of protecting Americans, when he denied that he had received marching orders from the administration. Admitting that he was regularly consulting with HHS Secretary Schweiker and Assistant Secretary Edward Brandt, Hayes insisted, "I haven't had any differences with them and they've let me make the calls at the FDA. I wouldn't want it any other way."[73]

In answering the final question about the acceleration of the drug approval process, Hayes proved adroit at striking a moderate tone. A number of people and institutions shared blame, he said. Culpability for drug lags, and for fixing the delays, rested with the FDA, the public, industry, and the research community and government. If these parties could increase cohesion, communication, and competitiveness, said Hayes, "a year, maybe more," could potentially be eliminated from the drug review process.[74]

Yet the fact that FDA staff members were asking such clarification questions was instructive; it required independence and enterprise on the part of the FDA's career leadership to inquire about the executive's precise intentions. Wayne Pines, the associate commissioner, acted as the agency's emissary and he sought to unpack how the president's appointment felt about drug regulation—in a specific rather than general fashion. Remarkably, he pulled no rhetorical punches in doing so: Was Hayes a lackey and/or a yesman? Would the drug industry gain a greater foothold in the halls of FDA? It required autonomy to ask questions of this kind as well as a degree of faith in the institution itself; such questions were in fact emblematic of the FDA's robust institutional identity, a testimony to the agency's unwillingness to mindlessly assent to the administration's wishes.

Inside the FDA—Being Pushed and Pulled!

As the rather rough treatment of Hayes signified, FDA staff members were not entirely sure what to make of President Reagan, his political appointments, or his regulatory philosophy. Gerald Barkdoll, Associate Commissioner for Planning and Evaluation in 1980–1981, described one tempestuous meeting between long-time career FDA employees. He recalled that his colleagues were curious about their role and the agency's role in society. Had the political and economic landscape shifted? Had a new order been established? Did this mean a more marginal role for the FDA? According to Barkdoll, this stimulating discussion was prompted "by the fact that different people saw the role of the agency differently" and "we were being pushed and pulled by different people."[75]

One useful viewpoint on the FDA came from the director of the FDA's Atlanta District Office during the presidential transition, Ballard Graham. He felt that the early 1980s were acutely difficult times for the FDA, but the agency nevertheless had to be adaptable and receptive to the Reagan administration's regulatory reform policies. "Every four years or every eight years, whatever the case may be," he stated, "you were going to get a new elected official in the position who was going to say, these are my policies and this is how I want to see things ran and done." Graham believed that the FDA's ultimate boss was not the man in the Oval Office, Ronald Reagan, but rather the electorate. The FDA was therefore obligated to deal even-handedly with the new presidential policy:

> I think the American people have spoken. This is the kind of government they want to see. and that's what we have to—like it or not, we make it work the way the American citizenry wishes. [76]

For all the internal debate about being pushed and pulled and the FDA's role in society in 1981, the FDA exhibited a degree of flexibility in dealing with the Reagan administration's conservative economic agenda. The agency reached out to the pharmaceutical industry and business groups in a number of ways; thereafter, the FDA disseminated information to the public about what the Reagan administration's plans for regulatory reform augured for the agency's mandate.

First, the FDA's monthly publication, *FDA Consumer,* explored the Reagan administration's regulatory approach, the traditional relationship between the regulator and the regulated drug industry, and what the future held. [77] In February 1981, editor Roger W. Miller interviewed the president of the Pharmaceutical Manufacturers Association (PMA), Lewis Engman, in a piece titled, "Talking With Industry About Drug Lag, Generics and Breakthroughs." Uncompromising and frank, Miller challenged Engman with a number of tough-minded, incisive questions: "Do you think that one reason for government's growth is that the public has been turning to Government because industry hasn't been responding? How can [PMA] help overcome the drug lag? Are we past the age of real wonder drugs? What is the pharmaceutical industry doing to hold down soaring health costs? Commissioner Goyan maintains that Americans take too many medicines and the health industry relies too much on drugs . . . do you agree with that?" [78] The by-line indicated that the express purpose of the interview was to facilitate to a greater degree a dialogue with industry, as had been the case with the December meetings with executives, "to get industry views on current drug topics." [79]

Four months later in the June 1981 issue, *FDA Consumer* was still devoting pages to understanding the drug industry and the impacts of Reagan's regulatory reform agenda. Reflective and judicious in tone, articles by former FDA chief counsel Richard M. Cooper ("Regulation: Looking to the Future")[80] and Samuel M. Gilston ("Drug Regulation Today: How Much is Appropriate?)[81] posed trenchant questions about how the FDA could redress some of its problems and about its proper role amid the new regulatory climate.

In addition, the FDA increased its communication with agency stakeholders. From the mid-1970s, agency planning and priority setting was assisted through feedback from external stakeholders, mainly consumer groups. Using a questionnaire system, information was gleaned on a number of topics: How should the agency allocate its resources? What were the areas that needed improvement? What industry deserved greater regulatory scrutiny? As the decade came to a close this stakeholder information input program was enlarged and "the nature of the process changed." Following the 1980 election, the Associate Commissioner for Planning, Gerald Barkdoll expanded the agency's communication with stakeholders:

> . . . We ended up with state officials; trade associations; professional health care associations; [business owners]; and others. We had four or five fairly large groups, and we were given literally thousands of ballots [questionnaires] back. Even when we reached the point where we could accurately predict what they were going to say, we continued to do it because of the involvement . . . and . . . they wanted to do it.[82]

Lastly, the FDA signaled harmonization with the new administration's regulatory reform agenda in a final way in the weeks after the election. The *New York Times* reported on November 15 that the FDA announced it was launching a campaign to meet with business owners in New Jersey, Illinois, and California throughout December. The series of meetings were established, according to the article, so that the FDA could hear the "views of small business owners and managers about the regulatory agency and its programs."[83]

In sum, the FDA responded to the new Republican administration—and its attendant regulatory philosophy—with a mixture of resignation and acceptance about the nature of the U.S. electoral system. "It is clear," said John Petricciani, head of the FDA's Bureau of Biologics in 1981, "that the new administration will press for regulatory reform" and the FDA would continue to adopt an "adversary role" toward industry. Nevertheless, he said, "we in the agency have come to realize the commonality of interest that government, industry and academia all share."[84] The agency, in short, was ready for change; however, the FDA also challenged industry to come clean about its own responsibility in mitigating the drug lag. The FDA, as part of the executive branch, indicated that it would harmonize with the new president's political ethos, but like any bureaucracy, it took action to protect itself as well.

The Effectiveness of Executive Order 12291

Once President Reagan took the oath of office he quickly changed the nature of regulation-making at the FDA and within government as a whole with the February 17, 1981, signing of Executive Order 12291. This order required that United States federal agencies prepare cost-benefit analyses for all new major regulations and, in effect, centralized final regulatory authority in David Stockman's Office of Management and Budget.[85] "It came through loud and clear during the election campaign that there is too much regulation," Vice President George Bush commented during the news conference, that "it is acting as a depressant on the economy." "This order," Bush asserted, "provides a mechanism for us to monitor regulatory activity and to coordinate the Administration's program of regulatory relief."[86]

E.O. 12291 was not entirely original, however. Executive Order 12044, issued by President Carter, also required a review of all major regulations. The difference between the two presidential orders lay in the "formality."[87] Carter's E.O. 12044 called for "an informal brand of cost-effectiveness analysis"[88] whereas Reagan's E.O. 12291 called for a "formal" cost-benefit analysis program. Since Reagan's executive order instructed the executive agencies to use the maximum net benefit criterion to choose among regulatory options, primacy was placed on the economic outcome of the regulatory review; this meant Reagan's executive order built and expanded upon Carter's pre-existing framework. Reagan's order, in short, was a more formidable regulatory reform mechanism because it codified cost-benefit analysis and thereby significantly affected the rate at which new regulations at agencies such as the FDA were developed and promulgated.

Not surprisingly, E.O. 12291 was also a divisive policy in that it married to a greater extent economics and health and safety issues in directing agencies to regulate only when the ensuing benefits would outweigh the costs. The *New York Times* reported that this doctrine was problematic because "politics and mathematics are sometimes hard to separate . . . especially when it comes to costly measures to protect consumers."[89] On one side, Representative Al Gore Jr. (D-TN) contended that consumer protection was in danger of "falling into the black hole of Reaganomics."[90] On the other side, the Reagan administration argued that "its actions to reduce the number and cost of Federal regulations would save consumers and businesses over $150 billion in the next decade."[91]

E.O. 12291 soon made an impact on regulation-making at the FDA. Under the old procedure, before President Reagan, a regulation was developed by the FDA, reviewed by the general counsel of FDA, and signed and put into effect by the commissioner. From there it went to the Federal Register, repository of the nation's regulations; but under the new procedure, the complexity of the labyrinth a regulation traveled was intensified, according to FDA's Associate Commissioner for Regulatory Affairs. As Paul Hile observed:

> All of a sudden regulations not only had to go through all of the initial developmental process, developed, drafted in the agency, go through the commissioner's office, be reviewed by the general counsel's office; but then they also had to go to the assistant secretary for Health and Human Services office, where they were reviewed by an office that was established for that sole purpose, and commented on . . . then they went to the department level, where they were reviewed by an office established for that very purpose in the office of the executive secretariat of the department. And you had to be responsive to all the concerns raised by that office. [Finally] they went forward to the OMB, where they were reviewed by an office which was expanded to accommodate the review of all of these questions and concerns that they raised.

E.O. 12291 was a triumph for the Reagan administration. Its impact was immediately felt. It raised havoc inside the FDA and it slowed down regulation-making. Paul Hile described the torturous process:

> You can imagine those drafts going back and forth, being commented on and sent back for reaction to comments, rewritten, redrafted, sent back through to be assured that we were responsive to the concerns and the change agreements we had, and then go to the next level. You don't need to be an expert in administrative process to understand why that was an effective way of delaying and reducing the number of regulations published throughout the federal government and by FDA specifically. [I]t was effective: at every turn, challenge; at every turn, explanation; at every turn, the possibility of rewrite and restructure. For an organization that had for some number of years pretty much had things its own ways, it was really a traumatic change. And that trauma extended down all the way into the agency.[92]

The Constriction of the Budget and Personnel

In 1989, Dr. Samuel Thier, president of the Institute of Medicine, described the FDA as "a demoralized group, being asked to do too much with too few resources." Former chief counsel of the FDA Peter Barton Hutt observed the agency's "problem is resources. There has been a very serious erosion of resources across the board." John Dingell, chair of the Energy and Commerce subcommittee that exposed generic drug violations in 1988–1989, charged "This has been a [period of] slow, persistent strangulation of an agency, and it has led to the damnedest, most unfair and inconsistent regulations." Similarly, Senator Orrin G. Hatch (R- UT) said that the cause of the problems in the agency's generic drug division was "an overburdened and underfunded agency." He added something had to be done soon to help the agency.[93]

The resource cuts at the agency actually began late in President Carter's term, and were magnified and extended when Ronald Reagan took office. Carter, afflicted with a troubled economy, sought to limit government spending, including the FDA. But whereas President Jimmy Carter had attempted to curtail government spending and deregulate certain aspects of the economy with opposition from his own party in the Democratic House and Senate, President Reagan had strong support in the Republican Senate. His support in the Democratic House was lukewarm, yet he was able to persuade a sufficient amount of Democrats to vote for his measures after the March 1981 assassination attempt. This shift, according to economist Mary K. Olson, facilitated more severe budget reductions at the FDA.[94]

Trimming the FDA's budget was not a straightforward task. Reagan's first budget asked for a 5 percent cut in personnel and funding and was met by an overenthusiastic 21 percent cut by the Republican-controlled Senate Labor and Human Resource Committee. The initial Reagan 5 percent request included the loss of nearly 400 FDA jobs, whereas the committee's cutback amounted to the loss of 3,000 jobs. Appalled agency officials immediately began lobbying the Senate Budget Committee. "We feel it's a mistake," one FDA official said anonymously. In the end, Reagan's budget, which required the approval from the Democrat-controlled House of Representatives, sought a relatively modest $17 million cut in the FDA funds requested by the Carter administration for 1982, as well as an immediate $10.5 million cut for 1981.[95]

The Reagan budget also faced opposition besides officials at the FDA. David Stockman, head of the Office of Management and Budget in the early 1980s described how politicians—even Reagan's appointees—often resisted the changes necessary to produce a revolution in Washington. "A good example" of this, according to Stockman, "was the roughly $2 billion in cuts we requested from Dick Schweiker at HHS—the giant Department of Health and Human Services which accounted for a huge share of the domestic budget." Such cuts, Stockman explained, were to be achieved by trimming fat from disease control, mental health, the Food and Drug Administration, and other local health programs; however, Stockman also noted he faced difficulties in implementing these cuts because "what I got back from HHS was a fat protest." Schweiker, for instance, had been on healthcare committees for twenty years in Congress, championing better governance and reform, and he was not willing to "get skinned alive" by his subordinates at the HHS. ". . . He knew exactly where not to cut," and the director of the OMB and secretary of HHS were forced to renegotiate. Stockman wrote that this type of encounter, this resistance to change, "occurred in most of the other departments."[96]

The Reagan administration would eventually succeed in restraining the FDA's budget. When controlled for inflation, the agency's budget in the

1980s in fact remained virtually static. In real dollars, the agency's budget increased just 2 percent over the entire decade, from $320 million in 1980 to $492 million.[97] The FDA's budget increased in the late 1980s but it did not reach its 1978 level until 1989.[98] One area Reagan's budget cutters were careful to leave untouched, though, was the New Drug Evaluation division. During the transition, Reagan officials had promised not to stultify approvals for new and generic drug products. The administration, that is, promised to reform, not retard, the FDA's drug approval process; and according to *Drug Topics*, this part of the Reagan budget reflected "a determination to maintain FDA's present level of activity on product approvals and to make it more efficient."[99]

The agency's overall workforce declined from 8,089 to 7,398 between 1981 and 1989. In President Reagan's first budget, after considerable wrangling, the administration eliminated approximately one-tenth of the FDA's total staff of 7,517. The total number of employees dropped to 7,101 full-time positions in FY 1981, (ninety persons below the ceiling) and then 6,821 in FY 1982 (160 persons below the ceiling).[100] The Bureau of Drugs, responsible for new and generic drug evaluation, lost comparatively fewer employees than the rest of the agency. For example, between FY 1980 and FY 1981, BOD overall staff decreased by forty-eight people. However, it is more difficult to assess 1982 staffing levels precisely. Commissioner Hayes consolidated the Bureau of Drugs (BOD) and Bureau of Biologics (BOB) upon assuming his appointed position, ostensibly for reasons of budget and efficiency.[101]

After a lengthy and fruitless search for a candidate to replace outgoing BOD Director Dr. Richard Crout, Commissioner Hayes opted to amalgamate the bureaus. Dr. Hank Meyer, head of BOB, was awarded the position of director of the newly created National Center for Drugs and Biologics (NCDB). This brand new arm of the FDA did not last long. The National Center for Drugs and Biologics was later renamed the Center for Drugs and Biologics in FY 1983 because, as critics argued, the word "national" was redundant and confusing.

Not everyone thought positively of the initial consolidation. James Larry Tidmore, former director of the Division of Contracts and Grant Management, recalled a colleague describing the bureau merger using a quotation attributed to Petronius Arbitor, in 210 B.C.:

> We trained hard, but it seems that every time that we were beginning to form up into teams we would be reorganized. I was to learn later in life that we tend to meet any new situation by reorganization, and what a wonderful method it can be for creating the illusion of progress while producing confusion, inefficiency, and demoralization.[102]

It is impossible to gauge the prevalence of this pejorative interpretation or whether FDA staffers thought the NCDB amalgamation was a tool used by the Reagan administration to hide how the agency was being starved; but it is accurate to take note of how, once again, agency officials displayed independence. Not everyone at the FDA saw the Reagan administration's changes as wholly negative. Then again, not all FDA staffers viewed the new initiatives as positive either.

The commissioner was himself torn on the agency's budget, yet he put on a brave face for Congress. In September 1981, when Representative Scheuer questioned Hayes about problems inherent in the drug approval process the commissioner was bluntly honest. Fewer resources from the Reagan administration and Congress meant cutting back on redundant personnel:

> Rep. Scheuer: Wait a minute. What are you going to do about that problem?
>
> Commissioner Hayes: I'll do the best I can to have not only enough people but the right sorts of people that, as I suggested earlier in my testimony, understand these sorts of drugs and the pharmacology and the clinical medicine involved. That is not an easy task. I'm not suggesting that it will all be solved by throwing people out, but there's no question when the workload increases, you have to to the extent that your budget and other restrictions will allow you to put not just people there but the right people. [103]

Throughout 1982, Hayes was asked similar questions about the personnel reductions and the budget. "It has been my impression that this Bureau [of Drugs] has a tight staffing situation in relation to its heavy workload, especially for the evaluation of drugs," said Representative L.H. Fountain (D-NC) in early August. "Is this impression a correct one?" Hayes responded that the Bureau of Drugs was hit no harder than any other part of FDA. "The whole Food and Drug Administration is tight on staff," he said, and "I am not sure if it is any different in that particular area of the FDA than others." "By attrition or otherwise, we have lost over 1,000 people in the last three years. So staffing is tight everywhere." [104]

Representative Matthew McHugh (D-NY) asked during FDA budget hearings whether the decrease in both staff members and resources hindered the agency's ability to do its job. "No," Dr. Hayes replied. The impact on FDA was not significant. ". . . We have been asked to do our share in maintaining a lean government [and] we have sustained certain resource reductions in 1981 and 1982, which still leave us with the resources necessary to meet our basic responsibilities." On a more personal level, he added, "I really feel that the agency has been able even with the reduction in personnel and leaner budgets all around to carry out our functions." [105]

Yet the commissioner's staff did not uniformly support such optimistic sentiments. If anything, FDA employees, who were spread all across the country, felt that the Reagan administration and his commissioner had wounded the agency. Bob Hart, a supervisory investigator in Albany, New York, wanted to see that more "adequate resources had been provided so FDA could enforce all the laws we're responsible for." "Unfortunately," he bemoaned, this was not the case and FDA staff members had to "wake up and read about some new recall instead. We keep getting stretched so thin that it gets disillusioning." Rosamelia de la Rocha, a consumer affairs specialist based in Rockville, Maryland, agreed. "I'd like it if the newspaper reported that FDA got additional funds or didn't get a budget cut because FDA had demonstrated it was so important to protect the consumer." She continued, "It would mean no reduction in forces (RIFs) or personnel cuts, which are hurting us now." Juan Tijerina, a consumer affairs officer in San Antonio, Texas, wanted to get "FDA's message to as many consumers as possible in spite of the budget constraints." And Ted Thorsen, a consumer safety officer in Des Plaines, Illinois, commented he wanted to hear the "FDA is going to increase its personnel. Our workload is quite heavy. Recalls have taken a lot of time and we need to get back to our regular course of inspections. I'm sure many districts have had to back off of other areas they want to tackle. We could use a few more new faces, more new people."[106]

Therefore, FDA staff members from across a broad spectrum had dramatically different perspectives than the commissioner. Commissioner Hayes had answered Representative McHugh with a simple rejection; no, he contended, the agency was not significantly affected by budget cuts, nor was it hobbled by the cuts in personnel. According to the agency's career employees, however, this assertion was wide of the mark. The FDA's ability to carry out its regulatory mandate *had* been impacted, indeed impaired, by the reduction in resources and staff.

More Work and Trust: The Tale of a Changing Enforcement Profile

As the budget was essentially frozen and debate ensued over how this affected the FDA, the workload at the agency increased markedly through the 1980s, while the types of drug enforcement actions also changed.[107] These shifts, not surprisingly, are intimately related to the resources allocated to the FDA and the number of personnel hired to carry out the agency's mandate. Some actions, such as inspections, prosecutions, and monitoring, are resource-intensive—problematic when the budget has been cut. Other actions, like collaborative recalls, require few resources, and the number of recalls consequently increased throughout the early part of the decade. The agency was compelled to change its enforcement strategy for lack of resources, but also for ideological reasons: Commissioner Hayes made it clear he was going to fulfill the agency's regulatory mandate through promotion of "voluntary action" and by fostering "a cooperative spirit" with industry.[108]

Starting in the Carter years, the workload at the FDA increased perceptibly and the drug industry steadily increased its demand for certification of its products in these years. From 1976 to 1986, the number of generic drug applications rose from 830 to 5,324 and from 1975 to 1990 the number of new drug applications grew from 325 to 610.[109]

As the workload increased there was a shift in types of drug enforcement actions. Upon assuming office, Hayes emphasized that voluntary industry actions would take precedence over other types of regulatory enforcement actions. FDA drug officials were to cooperate with industry, he declared; they were to act in a collaborative fashion as opposed to a combative one, as consultants rather than cops. By adopting this approach, Hayes believed that FDA personnel could eliminate the traditionally adversarial relationship. "Historically," he told Congress, "the Agency has accepted commitments to voluntary corrective actions when it is reasonable to believe that the commitment is made in good faith." This was such a time and in his estimation, the FDA could maximize its enforcement resources, which had grown scanter, by enlarging the number of times when voluntary actions would be accepted.[110]

The enforcement numbers soon began to reflect the new policy. The Public Citizen Health Research Group, headed by Dr. Sidney Wolfe, reported that the number of enforcement actions declined by 45 percent during Reagan's first year in office. The *New York Times* reported a 50 percent drop. Between 1977 and 1980, the Bureau of Drugs had averaged 1,041 enforcement actions, including seizures, prosecutions, inspections, and recalls. But in 1981 that average amounted to 577 actions.[111] One critic of voluntary compliance was FDA historian Herbert Burkholz, who has described the policy as innately problematic. He has argued, somewhat histrionically, that a closer working relationship between the FDA and industry—voluntary compliance based on trust and a greater faith in business—was tantamount to inviting the lions to lie down with the lambs.

Nevertheless, when Hayes was asked by Congress about the disparity in enforcement actions between 1980 and 1981, he betrayed little reservation about the new policy. Indeed, instead of alarm, Hayes was insouciant. Nothing was wrong with the numbers of enforcement actions; in fact, the data, which illustrated a significant reduction from one year to the next, was, according to Hayes, "not a reliable indicator of enforcement policy." He then

Table 4.1.   New Molecular Entities

	1977	1978	1979	1980	1981	1982	1983
NMEs Approved	22	22	14	12	27	28	14

rationalized the reduction with a plethora of reasons: ". . . Changes are influenced by such factors as shifts in FDA program priorities, changes in budgeted resources, unplanned emergencies either industry-wide or by individual firm and changes in enforcement strategies." The *enforcement actions* data were in fact "relatively meaningless" if not juxtaposed with *enforcement activities* data. As such, Representative Jamie Whitten (D-MS), the chairman of the Appropriations Subcommittee on Agriculture, not the FDA, not Hayes, and not the Reagan administration, was ill-informed about enforcement actions and missing the big picture. In carrying out its drug regulation duties, the FDA's Bureau of Drugs was fulfilling its mandate and acquitting itself admirably. Added Hayes, "I think this is most visibly proven by the number of recalls—rather large in extent—that I think have been handled expeditiously."

But FDA officials, both inside and outside the Bureau of Drugs, were not completely enamored of the commissioner's policy of voluntary compliance. As in the previous case of budget resources, there was little harmony on this issue. Often the policy of "cooperation and collaboration" was regarded as an ineffective regulatory measure, or as a constituent part of a larger, effective drug regulatory policy. Consider the exchange between FDA historian Robert Tucker and Jerome Bressler, director of compliance branch, Chicago district:

> RT: What is your sense of the move in more recent times to a greater reliance on voluntary compliance or industry education? How does that square with your experience?

> JB: . . . I believe in voluntary compliance. There are those, however, who, because of the almighty dollar and greed, are willing to take the chance, because it's costly in many cases to add controls, especially in the manufacture of drugs to make sure that the end product is what it's labeled to be and that it is effective. It costs a lot of money for controls and there are those firms that are waiting to take a chance. And I saw that over the years. All you have to do is look at the history of the various prosecutions and seizures we've made, and

Table 4.2. Human Drug Enforcement Actions

	1980	1981
Citations	4	1
Prosecutions	2	5
Injunctions	6	1
Seizures	234	97
Recalls	219	188
Total Actions	465	292

you wonder why. This involves both small and large firms. I strongly believe in voluntary compliance at those firms that you know are going to comply and make the necessary corrections, based on their established history of compliance.[112]

Or take another example from an interview between Robert Tucker and special assistant to the director in the Office of Compliance, Raymond Newberry:

RT: . . . Would it be correct to infer that you were not entirely enthralled with the move more to voluntary compliance? Did you see that as a weakening of the agency's effectiveness?

RN: Oh, absolutely, yes, yes.[113]

In other cases, voluntary compliance was considered purely a political-driven initiative, and as a usurpation of FDA authority. John Finlayson, director of the plasma derivatives branch in the National Center for Drugs and Biologics, said in 1982, "I would like to read that a regulatory decision was made by the scientists, as opposed to someone in Congress or in the echelons of FDA where people haven't been in a laboratory for years, or anyone down the line above the scientists."[114] Tom Warwick, a Salt Lake City investigator said, "I'd like to see FDA get away from concern with budget cuts and get back to standard practices."[115]

Oraflex and Reye's Syndrome

The story behind non-steroidal anti-inflammatory (NSAID) arthritis drug Oraflex underscores the potential trouble inherent to excessive workloads and the trust component of voluntary compliance. Manufactured by Eli Lilly in the 1970s and granted U.S. approval in April 1982, Oraflex was withdrawn from the market worldwide in August 1982 after it was found responsible for eighty-six cases of jaundice, thirty of which were fatal. Afterward, FDA officials testified before a subcommittee on Intergovernmental Relations that the Bureau of Drugs had overlooked key reports regarding benoxaprofen (Oraflex). John Harter, chief medical officer for NSAIDS, said the FDA had a four-month backlog in reviewing IND data and drug company Eli Lilly had indeed sent the clinical data reports documenting the jaundice; however, this was after the submission of the original new drug application and the jaundice reports were lost at the FDA. Curiously, Commissioner Hayes added during his testimony that even if the agency had been aware of this particular side effect it would not have withdrawn approval of the drug and the drug would have been given the benefit of the doubt. Still, he admitted, "jaundice should have been on the label and the prescribing recommendations given to doctors."[116] Acting director of the Office of New Drugs, Dr. Robert Temple was more critical, calling the agency's mistake "unacceptable and inexcusable."

Eli Lilly's far from blameless conduct during this episode raised questions about the validity of voluntary compliance. Already approved in Britain under the name Opren, the drug had caused twenty-nine deaths that were not reported to the FDA. Eli Lilly's U.S. medical director, William Shedden, knew of the contraindications in the U.K. but failed to disclose this information to the agency. In fact, on May 29, 1982 he lied to the FDA: "No deaths and no jaundice . . . were reported in approximately 2200 carefully followed patients who participated in clinical trials in the U.S." He later admitted this was incorrect and according to sociologist and drug industry scholar John Abraham, "if there is one lesson to be learned from the benoxaprofen case it is surely that regulators should trust, and depend on, pharmaceutical companies far less. . . . Stretching the institutional resources of a regulatory agency can increase significantly regulators' dependence on manufacturers' conduct."[117]

The approach to Reye's syndrome also demonstrated the difficulties and dangers inherent to an influential, anti-regulatory Reagan administration. In June 1982, the Department of Health and Human Services proposed a regulation that aspirin bottles carry a label warning describing that the pain reliever could trigger Reye's syndrome in children suffering from chicken pox or influenza.[118] The proposed regulation was backed by robust findings which supported a link between aspirin and Reye's syndrome. A "consensus of the scientific experts" agreed with this link, including the FDA as well as the federal Centers for Disease Control and Prevention and the American Academy of Pediatrics. The latter issued a report citing a "high probability that the administration of aspirin contributes to the causation of Reye's syndrome."[119]

Despite the presence of strong evidence and an ostensible scientific consensus, the labeling regulation was undermined by figures within the Reagan administration. This occurred in two ways. First, the industry-funded Aspirin Foundation and Committee on the Care of Children moved against the proposed regulation and applied pressure not only on the American Academy of Pediatrics (AAP) but also the Office of Management and Budget. The AAP, for instance, was threatened with massive lawsuits if it published any information casting doubt on the safety of aspirin. Second, Jim J. Tozzi, a deputy administrator of the Office of Information and Regulatory Affairs (OIRA) and a strident, long-standing deregulator who had caught the attention of the Nixon White House in 1970, moved against the regulation.[120] He commissioned an outside scientific assessor to examine the evidence and then told the FDA, "You have not made your case."[121] On November 18, 1982 HHS Secretary Richard Schweiker withdrew the proposal.

This withdrawal proved calamitous for some American families. For example, once the decision was finally taken to label all aspirin bottles in 1986 (after sustained pressure from interest groups), the number of Reye's syndrome cases reported in the United States declined from 555 in 1980 to 36 in 1987; thereafter, the disease all but disappeared.[122] In 1992, researchers at the National Academy of Sciences (NAS) and the School of Public Health at the University of California-Berkeley concluded a study that found that of the hundreds of children who died of Reye's syndrome in the crucial years between 1980 and 1987, 1,470 could have been saved if Schweiker's regulation had been passed and the aspirin bottles had been labeled. "These 1,470 deaths were especially tragic," wrote the report's authors Patricia Buffler and Devra Lee Davis, "because they were, typically, healthy children who never recovered from viral infection or chicken pox."[123] Buffler then noted:

> The Reagan Administration and Bush Administration have been marked by a commitment to deregulation. When it occurs in an area where it has a health impact, the consequences are profound—profoundly averse.[124]

Tylenol

It was not all dark clouds in enforcement and workload in the early years, however. The case of the Tylenol tampering emergency in October 1982 was one silver lining in that it demonstrated just how swiftly and efficiently FDA drug officials could mobilize on a mass, nationwide scale. When a number of individuals died from over-the-counter Tylenol poisoned with potassium cyanide, the FDA wasted little time. The agency asked Bayer, Tylenol's manufacturer, to suspend sales of the drug, responded to over 8,000 calls from a worried public, issued widespread warnings, and its field staff promptly screened over 1.7 million capsules from random sites across the United States. Hundreds of employees sacrificed evenings, weekends, and sleep to secure the safety of a drug that was virtually ubiquitous in American life. In Detroit, for instance, the local FDA office did not have enough money to purchase all the Tylenol for testing. As a result, one employee took out $2,000 dollars from his account; another employee cashed a check and spent it entirely on Tylenol. These employees were compensated to be sure, but their conduct reflects well on the enforcement staff's passionate commitment to protecting Americans.[125]

Thereafter, Commissioner Hayes praised his agents in the field. "I am extremely proud of FDA's handling of the crisis," he told Congress, and this was more than self-reverential, self-aggrandizing rhetoric. Others agreed with his assessment. The University of Maryland awarded its Public Service Excellence Award to the FDA for its outstanding contribution to public safety during the Tylenol Tampering crisis. A Roper Survey found in late 1982 that 81 percent of respondents felt the agency had met its responsibilities well during the scare and 80 percent of those polled understood the agency's mission. The FDA had gained recognition and scored an enforcement victory in the public's eyes. [126]

Spiraling FDA Morale?

The changes in resources, personnel, and enforcement practices at the FDA by their nature produced results. Less measurable and more ephemeral was the impact such changes had on the FDA's spirit, morale, and institutional pride. Associate Commissioner for Regulatory Affairs Joseph Hile described these early years as "very, very difficult times" because neither the Republicans nor Democrats attributed anything of value to the historic federal system or to the career government employee. Yet low morale did not deter agency officials from doing their jobs properly:

> I don't believe . . . that those frustrations or agonies impacted directly or adversely on how employees of the Food and Drug Administration carried out their responsibilities. I really believe that the commitment of the employees to do the very best job they could to protect the interests of the consumer, as good soldiers, and to carry out the policies of the administration in power at the time. . . . I don't think that obligation was compromised in any way. But notwithstanding that, there was a great deal of concern, personal concern, and talk in the halls about how both the Republicans and Democrats had somehow abandoned the career government employee. [127]

This flexible interpretation of these years is crucial to understanding one way in which a significant FDA insider felt about and reacted to the election. If Hile's perception is correct, agency officials set aside their personal frustrations with the rising tide of anti-government, anti-institutional sentiment among the electorate and dutifully carried out their assignments—to protect the nation's drug supply.

Still, other oral records indeed point toward the predominance of pessimism and disenchantment as principal outcomes of Reagan's victory and policy changes. According to Gerald Barkdoll, the Associate Commissioner for Planning and Evaluation, negativism predominated at the top tier of the agency and strategies were developed to ameliorate fear and anxiety:

> When Reagan was elected and there was all the rhetoric about doing away with regulatory agencies, about deregulation, we had a go-away—it was down at NIH. There were people in that room who weren't going to be around in two months or three months, because they were political appointees and the world was changing. We discovered that almost everybody in that room was worried about the agency's future: Was it going to survive? Was it going to get cut in half? What was going to happen? So that go-away turned out to be a catharsis

in that people went back to the roots and the foundations of why FDA existed, and what we were doing, and where our support was. We focused on the agency strengths, why it originally had been established, what was apt to survive through a deregulatory period and a very popular president. We came out saying, 'Sure it's going to be hard times, but we'll survive. We perform an important role, and we'll be here . . .' We came away from that a lot stronger and feeling a lot better. [128]

Other career FDA employees, however, from all across the United States, felt very differently about the Reagan administration than their counterparts having trips and holding therapeutic meetings. Eileen Marshall, computer systems analyst, was exhausted by persistent negativism at the agency. She desired, "Good news, for a change!" Toxicologist Esther Ferri, from Winchester, Massachusetts, wished that "some stability would come for the government employee in FDA and the whole federal family. The way things are now, we don't know whether we will be here or not. Let's go back to doing a job instead of worrying about whether we have one or not." Bruce Williamson, a recall coordinator out of the Los Angeles district said simply, "I hope we're around for 1983." According to Ed Sterner, a regional medical officer in the Denver district, "My first wish would be that I'd like to see morale upgraded." [129]

Unfortunately, there are a number of problems that immediately arise when attempting to measure morale. Ronald Chesemore, who held the position of associate commissioner for Regulatory Affairs, identified the problem of oversimplification in an interview with Robert Tucker. When asked whether he thought that the morale of the agency had improved since the 1980s, Chesemore responded, "I've never been one to generalize about the morale of the agency." Then he added that morale was contingent upon a number of factors: what position a given FDA staffer held, a field inspector or in management at the Rockville headquarters; whether the person received the right opportunities and benefits; what degree of gratification and pride one derived from working at FDA. Overall, Chesemore explained, if certain needs were met, "morale still can be high." [130]

A second problem persists in analyzing morale at FDA: confounding evidence. FDA employee Ken Hansen posits that the early 1980s did not in fact signal a departure from years past. He argued,

The thing that really strikes me, now working for another agency, is that there's a real esprit de corps in FDA. I think the people are united in the sense that they're working for the public health. Even in the really bad times of the Reagan administration and stuff like that, it was always there. There was always that sense. [131]

Kim Stalker, a consumer affairs officer, suggests that FDA morale was already on the decline when Reagan won the presidency because of the Carter administration's budget tightening and deregulation policy. According to Stalker, "When I started with the FDA in 1974, there was a stronger unity throughout the agency . . . because of the budget cuts and everything, some of the spirit has been lost."[132] The perception of morale varies from agency official to official and is thus problematic for the historian of the FDA; in short, depending on the person, agency morale endured in the difficult times that were the Reagan years *and* it had diminished even before Reagan won office.

Results of the Opening Moves

At a reception in the East Room of the White House in September 1981, President Reagan told Congress of how Vice President Bush was successfully spearheading the most vigorous attack on "redtape and overregulation ever conducted." "At the end of our first year," said the President, "the growth in the *Federal Register* will be 50 percent of what it was in 1980." Reagan then quipped he knew Bush's actual goal: "to get it down to pamphlet size." The audience laughed at the deregulation joke.[133]

It is unclear just how ebullient FDA staff members felt in September 1981. The Reagan administration, which had immediately set out to kickstart the U.S. economy and reshape the government, undoubtedly created a stir at the FDA as it targeted the agency for change. Such political appointees as Secretary Schweiker and Commissioner Hayes instilled the Reagan administration's minimalist approach to regulation, promised to trim the fat off bloated, redundant regulations, and thereby shook up the agency. But just how successful was this program and just how successful were the appointments? First of all, the Reagan administration's E.O. 12291 proved to be an effective mechanism that slowed the promulgation and passing of drug regulations. Members of the FDA's top management staff testified that it was successful in disrupting regulation-making. Additionally, the FDA's budget was slashed, albeit moderately, and its personnel levels dipped, even as its workload increased. This was another example of a successful Reagan administration initiative, for this was one of the drivers of a voluntary compliance policy that necessitated more industry/regulator collaboration and trust. However, Representative L.H. Fountain (D-NC) made clear as early as 1982 that this was not positive, as the agency was suffering "significant" and "serious" shortcomings in its policies and procedures, and specifically in the drug approval process.[134]

After the Reagan administration's opening moves in 1981 and 1982, then, things had indeed changed at the FDA. Some pundits, historians, and commentators proclaimed President Reagan set in motion a broad government-wide revolution that remains up for debate; what is not, though, is the fact that he indeed reshaped the FDA, if not in a fundamental or radical manner. Reagan's measures may have recalibrated the balance between the FDA and drug companies and between consumer protection and production innovation, but they did not eviscerate the agency or seek to repeal its enabling legislation. The initial deregulation thrust at the FDA turned out to be moderate and measured, rather than bellicose or dogmatic.

The career employees inside the FDA, for their part, displayed a degree of flexibility and made actionable decisions to work with the new Republican agenda. They met with drug industry representatives throughout the United States immediately after the presidential election. The agency expanded communication with the Bureau of Drugs's stakeholders and it also accepted Secretary Schweiker's initiatives. Yet the FDA did not capitulate entirely to the forces for regulatory reform. In the early 1980s, there was little uniformity of thought and perception. Many FDA career employees disapproved of the ostensible Reagan revolution, the president's philosophy toward government agencies and government employees, and the way he impacted the FDA's ability to carry out its mandate. They feared for the safety of Americans. On a more personal and self-centered level, these particular FDA employees also feared for their jobs. Moreover, career employees sought to obviate, or at least dilute, major changes; a prime example of this occurred when the Bureau of Drugs commissioned its own study of the drug review process, one which undermined, if not wholly contradicted, the results of the Schweiker study. The FDA also asked the newly appointed commissioner to explain his personal views on drug deregulation. In essence, Hayes was challenged to *explain* exactly what he believed and *exactly* what he intended to do in the future; an interview that was then published. Moreover, *FDA Today* made it plain that many career employees were patently unimpressed with the new regime. The long-time personnel, the guardians of the FDA's institutional identity, made clear they were not totally subservient or beholden to the new administration's wishes.

NOTES

1. Phillip J. Cooper, *The War Against Regulation: From Jimmy Carter to George W. Bush* (Lawrence: University of Kansas Press, 2009) 29.

2. Jim Dickinson, "Shackles Loosened, Optimism Returns to FDA," *Medical Marketing and Media* 25, March 1990, 4.

3. Paul D. Erickson, *Reagan Speaks: The Making of An American Myth* (New York: New York University Press, 1985), 97.

4. Judith Stein, *Pivotal Decade: How the United States Traded Factories for Finance in the Seventies* (New Haven, CT: Yale University Press, 2010), 259.

5. Carl Biven, *Jimmy Carter's Economy: Policy in an Age of Limits* (Chapel Hill, N. C.: University of North Carolina Press, 2002), 2–4

6. Ibid.

7. Stein, *Pivotal Decade*, 260.

8. Austin Ranney, "The Carter Administration," in *The American Elections of 1980*, ed. Austin Ranney (Washington, D. C.: American Enterprise Institute, 1982), 1.

9. Elizabeth Drew, *Portrait of an Election: The 1980 Presidential Campaign* (London: Routledge & Kegan Paul Ltd., 1981), 340–342 and William E. Pemberton, *Exit With Honor: The Life and Presidency of Ronald Reagan* (Armonk, NY: M.E. Sharpe, 1997), 90–91.

10. Stein, *Pivotal Decade*, 260.

11. Edmund Morris, *Dutch: A Memoir of Ronald Reagan* (New York: Random House, 1999), 420.

12. Michael Schaller, *Reckoning with Reagan: America and Its President in the 1980s* (New York: Oxford University Press, 1992), 38–39 and Haynes Johnson, *Sleepwalking Through History: America in the Reagan Years rev. ed.* (New York: W.W. Norton and Company, 2003), 88–89.

13. U.N. ambassador Jeanne Kirkpatrick received honorary cabinet status.

14. Michael Schaller, *Right Turn: American Life in the Reagan-Bush Era, 1980-1992* (Oxford: Oxford University Press, 2007), 50–51.

15. Richard E. Neustadt, *Presidential Power and the Modern Presidents* (New York: Free Press, 1990), 270.

16. Alexander M. Haig Jr. *Caveat: Realism, Reagan, and Foreign Policy* (New York: MacMillan Publishing, 1984), 85.

17. Lou Cannon, *President Reagan: The Role of a Lifetime* (New York: Public Affairs, 1991), 142.

18. Martin Anderson, *Revolution* (New York: Harcourt Brace Jovanovich, 1988), 290.

19. Larry Speakes and Robert Pack, *Speaking Out: The Reagan Presidency from Inside the White House* (New York: Charles Scribner's Sons, 1988), 67.

20. Edwin Meese III, *With Reagan: The Inside Story* (Washington, D.C.: Regnery Gateway, 1992), 14.

21. Ibid.

22. Cannon, *President Reagan* 498.

23. Ibid.

24. John Ehrman, *The Eighties: America in the Age of Reagan* (New Haven: Yale University Press, 2005), 91.

25. Cooper, *The War on Regulation*, 29.

26. Ronald Reagan, "Remarks Announcing the Establishment of the Presidential Task Force on Regulatory Relief," *Public Papers of the Presidents—Ronald Reagan, 1981* (Washington: Government Printing Office, 1982), 30–31.

27. Martin Tolchin and Susan J. Tolchin, "The Rush to Deregulate: Government is going to Unravel a Whole Skein of Health and Safety Regulations," *New York Times*, August 21, 1983, SM34.

28. Ibid.

29. Dale Whittington and W. Norton Grubb, "Economic Analysis in Regulatory Decisions: The Implications of Executive Order 12291," *Science, Technology and Human Values* 9 (1) (1984): 64. In historical terms, this order was by no means radical. Every U.S. president since John F. Kennedy has, in Dale Whittington and W. Norton Grubb's words, "attempted to improve management and program evaluation procedures in the federal bureaucracy."

30. Robert M. Collins, *Transforming America: Politics and Culture in the Reagan Years* (New York: Columbia University Press, 2007), 81 and John Ehrman, *The Eighties: America in the Age of Reagan*, 172.

31. Committee on Science and Technology, *FDA Drug Approval—A Lengthy Process that Delays the Availability of Important New Drugs: Report to the Subcommittee on Science, Research, and Technology, House Committee on Science and Technology*, May 28, 1980, 5.

32. James Scheuer, "The F.D.A.: Too Slow," *New York Times*, May 22, 1980, A35.

33. Quoted in Hilts, *Protecting America's Health*, 214. *Mandate for Leadership* proposed a change at FDA to limit the costs on small businesses. MFL states on FDA: "The costs of regulatory compliance frequently work to depress competition and innovation by driving out small business and making private industry less willing to invest in new ideas and new prod-

ucts. The consumer bears the ultimate burden for excessive regulation, in higher prices for the goods he buys and decreased opportunity for choice in the marketplace."

34. Richard D. Lyons, "G.O.P. Group Suggests Health Spending Revisions: No Radical Changes Forseen," *New York Times*, November 16, 1980, 35.

35. Ibid.

36. Quoted in Hilts, *Protecting America's Health*, 214.

37. Jere Goyan, "The Future of the FDA Under a New Administration," *Food Drug Cosmetic Law Journal* 36 (1981) 61–62.

38. David Perlman, "The Debate Over Regulating Drugs," *The San Francisco Chronicle*, February 18, 1981.

39. Hugh D'Andrade Interview, Chemical Heritage Foundation Oral History Collection, 25.

40. Lucas Richert, "Pills, Policymaking and Perceptions," 42–44.

41. Jesse M. Pike, "Letter to President-elect Reagan," *NARD Journal* (1981): 21.

42. James Dickinson, "Washington Report," *Pharmaceutical Technology*, February 1981, 24.

43. Michael Waldholz, "Pfizer Sees 15% Rise in Net and Revenue From New-Drug Sales," *The Wall Street Journal*, March 10, 1981, 20.

44. Phillip H. Wiggins, "Betting the Store on another Tagamet: A Plethora of New Drugs is Making High Flyers of Drug Companies," *New York Times*, May 16, 1982, F14 and Thomas C. Hayes, "The Drug Business Golden Era Ahead," *New York Times* May 17, 1981, F1.

45. Vartanig G. Vartan, "Drug Stocks Finding Favor," *New York Times*, January 21, 1981, D8.

46. Jere Goyan, "The Future of the FDA Under a New Administration," 61.

47. Ibid.

48. Ibid. See also Robert Y. Shapiro and John M. Gilroy, "The Polls-Regulation I," *Public Opinion Quarterly* 48 (2) (1984): 532.

49. Reagan is quoted in speech by Commissioner Jere Goyan, "The Future of the FDA Under a New Administration," 61.

50. Elizabeth Drew, *Portrait of an Election: The 1980 Presidential Campaign*, 111.

51. Ronald Reagan, *The Reagan Diaries*, ed. Douglas Brinkley (New York: HarperCollins 2007), 413.

52. Joseph Paul Hile Interview, FDA Oral History Collection, 88.

53. Gerald Barkdoll Interview, FDA Oral History Collection, 17.

54. Ballard Graham Interview, FDA Oral History Collection, 44–45.

55. Mary Frances Lowe, "Pharmaceutical Regulatory Policy: A Departmental and Administrative Perspective," *Food Drug Cosmetic Law Journal* 39 (1984): 504. Mary Frances Lowe was at the time an executive secretary, Department of U.S. Health and Human Services.

56. Committee on Human Resources, *Testimony of Louis Lasagna, M.D. on Drug Regulation Reform Act of 1978: hearings before the Subcommittee on Health and Scientific Research* (Rochester, New York: The Center for the Study of Drug Development, April 12, 1978), 6.

57. In other words, Reagan officials were worried about "agency capture."

58. Ibid. See also William E. Pemberton, *Exit With Honor: The Life and Presidency of Ronald Reagan*, 95.

59. Committee on Labor and Human Resources, *Drug Regulation Reform Act of 1979: Hearings Before the Subcommittee on Health and Scientific Research*, 96th Congress, 1st Session, May 17 & 10, 1–4. Interestingly, Kennedy called into question the existence of the drug lag saying, "Whether it exists, and if so what its causes are, are hotly debated topics. But whatever each of us concludes about the drug lag and its potential causes, we all agree that new drugs should be marketed as soon as their safety and effectiveness can be demonstrated."

60. "Studies Give Nod to Review Process," *FDA Today*, July 1982, 3.

61. Ibid.

62. Ibid.

63. "Studies Give Nod to Review Process," *FDA Today*, July 3, 1982.

64. Hilts, *Protecting America's Health*, 207–217.

65. Committee on Appropriations, *Arthur Hull Hayes Jr. testimony to Agriculture, Rural Development and Related Agencies Appropriations for 1983*, 97th Congress, 2nd Session, 592–601.

66. Ibid.

67. Ibid.

68. Committee on Science and Technology, *Drug Lag,* 97th Congress, 1st Session, September 16, 1981, 59–60.

69. Committee on Appropriations, *Arthur Hull Hayes Jr. testimony to Agriculture, Rural Development and Related Agencies Appropriations for 1983*, 97th Congress, 2nd Session, 595.

70. Committee on Appropriations, *Justification of Appropriations Estimates for Committee on Appropriations, Fiscal Year 1983—Vol. V*, A Report Presented to the Appropriations Committee, 1983, 70.

71. Committee on Government Operations, *The Regulation of New Drugs By the FDA: The New Drug Review Process,* August 3 &4, 97th Congress, 1984, 293–295.

72. "New Commissioner Finds No Lack of Challenges—Or Satisfaction," *FDA Consumer* 15 (9) (1981): 17–19.

73. Ibid.

74. Ibid.

75. Gerald Barkdoll Interview, FDA Oral History Collection, 17.

76. Ballard Graham Interview, FDA Oral History Collection, 44–45.

77. FDA Consumer is described as "external" because it is designed for the general public, as opposed to FDA Today, which is an "internal" publication for FDA employees.

78. "Talking With Industry About Drug Lag, Generics, and Breakthrough," *FDA Consumer* (1) 14 (1981): 26–28.

79. Ibid.

80. Richard M. Cooper, "Regulation: Looking to the Future," *FDA Consumer* 14 (5) (1981): 64–68. Cooper writes: "I think it's fair to interpret the Presidential and Congressional elections of 1980, together with emergence of an intellectually respectable set of antiregulatory public policy recommendations, as warranting some loosening of regulatory controls on the economy" (64). He adds, however, "In the field of food and drug regulation, major change is unlikely" (66).

81. Samuel M. Gilston, "Drug Regulation Today: How Much is Appropriate?" *FDA Consumer* 14 (5) (1981): 46–50. Gilston asks: "Should there be less drug regulation? Should there be more? How much is enough? Are Federal rules hampering the availability of helpful drug therapies, increasing drug costs, and discouraging industry's investment in research and development? Or are Americans suffering illness and death because of unsafe and ineffective medicines allowed onto the market by overly weak regulation?" (46). He then emphasizes that "FDA staff assigned to NDA review should be enlarged," but because "belt-tightening throughout the government will continue to be part of efforts to control Federal spending and improve the overall economy" the FDA will not receive a greater budget; thus it will be necessary to "reallocate staff and set new priorities to provide resources needed to review NDAs" (50).

82. Ibid.

83. *New York Times.* "F.D.A. Meets with Businessmen" November 16, 1980, 50.

84. David Perlman, "The Debate Over Regulating Drugs," *The San Francisco Chronicle,* February 18, 1981.

85. Dale Whittington and W. Norton Grubb, "Economic Analysis in Regulatory Decisions: 64.

86. Clyde Farnsworth, "Reagan Signs Order to Curb Regulations: Loud and Clear Only Executive Branch Agencies," *New York Times,* February 18, 1981, D13.

87. Whittington and Grubb, "Economic Analysis in Regulatory Decisions," 64.

88. Ibid.

89. Michael DeCourcy Hinds, "Cost Benefit vs. Safety: Politics and Mathematics can be Difficult to Separate When it comes to Regulation," *New York Times,* July 24, 1982, 8.

90. Ibid.

91. Kenneth Noble, "U.S. Expects Deregulation to Save $100 billion Over Next Decade," *New York Times,* August 12, 1983, A8.

92. Joseph Paul Hile Interview, FDA Oral History Collection, 89–97.

93. Quoted in Hilts, "Ailing Agency," *New York Times*, December 4, 1989, A1.

94. Mary K. Olson, "Substitution in Regulatory Agencies: FDA Enforcement Alternatives," *Journal of Law, Economics and Organization* 12 (2) (1996): 389.

95. "Federal drug programs escape cuts," *Drug Topics*, April 3, 1981, 24.

96. David Stockman, *The Triumph of Politics: Why the Reagan Revolution Failed* (London: Bodley Head, 1986), 148.

97. Olson, "Substitution in Regulatory Agencies," 389.

98. Ibid.

99. "Federal drug programs escape cuts," *Drug Topics*, April 3, 1981, 24.

100. See *FDA Quarterly Activities Reports.* 1981, 4th Quarter, Rockville, Maryland: Food and Drug Administration, 21 and *FDA Quarterly Activities Reports.* 1982, 4th Quarter, Rockville, Maryland: Food and Drug Administration, 23. FDA has a staff ceiling and occupied ratio. The ceilings for FY1980, 1981, 1982 are 7745, 7191 and 6981 respectively.

101. Joseph Paul Hile Interview, FDA Oral History Collection, 108.

102. James Larry Tidmore Interview, FDA Oral History Collection, 26.

103. Committee on Science and Technology, *Drug Lag*, 97th Congress, 1st Session, September 16, 1981, 123.

104. Committee on Government Operations, *The Regulation of New Drugs By the FDA: The New Drug Review Process*, August 3 &4, 97th Congress, 1984, 288–289.

105. Committee on Appropriations, *Arthur Hull Hayes Jr. testimony to Agriculture, Rural Development and Related Agencies Appropriations for 1983*, 97th Congress, 2nd Session, 283 and 600.

106. *FDA Today*, January 1982, 4 and *FDA Today*, August, 1982, 2.

107. U.S. Food and Drug Administration, *Milestones in U.S. Food and Drug Law History*, posted at www.fda.gov.opacom/backgrounders/miles.html, consulted November 22,2005 From 1980 to 1989, Congress passed twenty-four laws expanding the FDA's jurisdiction. The 1983 Orphan Drug Act established a new program within the FDA to advance the development of drugs for rare medical conditions, while the 1983 Federal Anti-Tampering Act gave authority to investigate tampering incidents related to products the FDA regulates, including pharmaceuticals. The 1987 Drug Marketing Act required the FDA to restrict the distribution of drug samples, supervise a ban on specific resales of drugs, and police drug wholesalers. Furthermore, the AIDS Amendments of 1988 required it to establish and maintain a registry of new and experimental AIDS drugs. These are a just selection of the laws enacted in the 1980s; altogether, however, the twenty-four new laws would seem to necessitate a commensurate amount of resources to adjudicate these laws rather than opposite.

108. Committee on Appropriations, *Arthur Hull Hayes Jr. testimony to Agriculture, Rural Development and Related Agencies Appropriations for 1983*, 97th Congress, 2nd Session, 592.

109. Mary K. Olson, "Regulatory Agency Discretion Among Competing Industries: Inside the FDA," *Journal of Law, Economics & Organization* 11 (2) (1995): 328. See also Samuel Gilston, "New Drug Pipeline Filling Up," *Medical Advertising News*, November 15, 1983.

110. Committee on Appropriations, *Arthur Hull Hayes Jr. testimony to Agriculture, Rural Development and Related Agencies Appropriations for 1983*, 97th Congress, 2nd Session, 507–508. Unfortunately, Hayes noted, often these types of voluntary enforcement actions were not quantifiable and did not appear in enforcement action data. This was suspiciously convenient to critics of the policy.

111. "Sharp Drop Reported in FDA Enforcement," *New York Times*, January 29, 1982, A12.

112. Jerome Bressler Interview, FDA Oral History Collection, 38–9.

113. Raymond Newberry Interview, FDA Oral History Collection, 25–26.

114. *FDA Today*, August 1982, 2.

115. *FDA Today*, August 1982, 2.

116. Michael DeCourcy Hinds, "F.D.A. Says it Overlooked Drug Data," *New York Times*, August 4, 1982, C1.

117. Quoted in John Abraham, "Distributing the Benefit of the Doubt: Science, Regulators, and Drug Safety," *Science, Technology & Human Values* 19 (1994): 507 and 515–516.

118. Reye's syndrome is an often-fatal illness which attacks the brain, liver, and other organs, and physicians had noticed a link with aspirin consumption in the early 1960s.

119. Quoted in William Kleinknecht, *The Man Who Sold the World: Ronald Reagan and the Betrayal of Main Street America* (New York: Nation Books, 2009), 113.

120. Kleinknecht, *The Man Who Sold the World,* 113.

121. Larry Doyle, "Aspirin-Reye's Chronology: Threat of Suits Delayed Warning Process," *Los Angeles Times,* May 31, 1987, 4.

122. Kleinknecht, *The Man Who Sold thw World,* 113.

123. Quoted in "Delay on Aspirin Warning Label Cost Children's Lives, Study Says," *New York Times*, October 23, 1992, 12.

124. Ibid.

125. *FDA Today*, December 1982, 1.

126. Alan L. Hoeting Interview, FDA Oral History Collection, 46 and Committee on Appropriations. *Agriculture, Rural Development and Related Agencies Appropriations for 1984*, 98th Congress, 1982, 341–345.

127. Joseph Paul Hile Interview, FDA Oral History Collection, 88.

128. Gerald Barkdoll Interview, FDA Oral History Collection, 19 and 27.

129. *FDA Today*, July 1982, 4.

130. Ronald Chesemore Interview, FDA Oral History Collection, 25.

131. Ken Hansen Interview, FDA Oral History Collection, 65.

132. *FDA Today*, August 1982, 2

133. Ronald Reagan, "Remarks on the Program for Economic Recovery at a White House Reception for Members of Congress," *Public Papers of the Presidents of the United States—Ronald Reagan, 1981* (Washington, D.C.: Government Printing Press, 1982), 861–862.

134. Committee on Government Operations, *The Regulation of New Drugs By the FDA: The New Drug Review Process*, August 3 & 4, 97th Congress, 1984, 523–524.

Chapter Five

The Continuing Evolution of the FDA, 1983–1984

"... The executive branch has done what it can." [1]

VP GEORGE BUSH, EXPLAINING THE DECISION TO END THE
TASK FORCE ON REGULATORY REFORM

"After two years, things seem to change. . . . I think there is a different attitude, a different spirit, both in perception and reality, from the beginning of the administration to that later on, when an election is coming." [2]

FDA COMMISSIONER HAYES, RATIONALISING
HIS DECISION TO RESIGN

In 1981, the Reagan administration rolled out a regulatory reform policy that was intended to foster change to the nation's entire regulatory architecture. This policy, which encompassed key political appointments and executive orders at a host of agencies, including FDA, OSHA, EPA, NHTSA, among others, was one constituent part of Reaganomics and aimed to remove an intrusive government from the marketplace. Encompassing the FDA's regulation of drug products, the broader policy of regulatory reform ultimately produced significant but by no means radical changes at the agency in the early 1980s. According to journalist Ed Magnuson, the Reagan administration's efforts to fundamentally alter the FDA "have been foiled by career bureaucrats adhering to the agency's established habits of testing and enforcement." [3]

In 1983, however, the Reagan administration's policy of regulatory reform continued to shift, along with the political and economic circumstances
of the period, and this duly affected the FDA's drug regulation. On the one
hand, Reagan officials, including Vice President Bush, argued that the administration had slashed red tape, reduced the size of the bureaucracy, fulfilled election promises, and respected the wishes of voters. On the other
hand, an array of consumer advocates and public interest groups contended
that any cost savings generated by the broader deregulatory efforts were for
the most part illusory and, worse still, potentially harmful to American consumers. The reality rested somewhere in the space between the two divergent
claims—not only with the FDA, but also the nation's broader regulatory
apparatus.

First of all, the Reagan administration scaled back its deregulatory measures in 1983. According to Vice President Bush, the Reagan administration
had done what it could to alter the government's regulatory architecture—
including the FDA. In 1981–1982, the administration had pushed strenuously
to reduce government interference in the economy; however, in 1983—as the
American economy began to recover—the movement for regulatory reform
stuttered. One White House aide told *Time* magazine: "Deregulation doesn't
have the same priority for us it used to have. The political dividends aren't
very high."[4] Second, the departure of Arthur Hull Hayes, the FDA commissioner, sent ripples throughout the agency. As Hayes left the trappings of
government and returned to academia, he claimed that he had achieved what
he could. The tide had turned against more regulatory reform, he argued, and
public support for deregulation waned. In short, regulatory reform had become something of "a political danger zone."[5] Third, Hatch-Waxman
amendments were passed. Co-sponsored by Senator Orrin Hatch and Representative Henry Waxman, this law benefited consumers and brand-name and
generic companies alike. The booming pharmaceutical industry was given
longer patent times and an ability to submit drug applications without drug
trial data, provided that data was readily available. Hatch-Waxman was a
congressional initiative and, though the president was effusive about the
deregulatory aspects of the law, it demonstrated that non-executive actors
were also effective in implementing change at the FDA.

The years of 1983–1984 thus proved to be complicated times for the
FDA. The agency had undergone a startling, dramatic shock in 1981, to
which the bureaucracy adapted as best it could. Pundits and the press, along
with academics of all political colorations, began to argue whether Reagan
had ushered in a fresh political and economic order. Additionally, such commentators and observers questioned whether the regulatory reform initiatives
had helped or hurt American consumers. In 1983–1984, however, the FDA
now had to confront manifold new challenges: the success and growth of the
pharmaceutical industry, zealous congressional hearings, no commissioner

for a prolonged period of time, and the new pressures of the Hatch-Waxman legislation, which increased the FDA's workload considerably.

The Regulatory State, the FDA, and the Economy in the Mid-1980s

Beginning in 1983, the Reagan administration began to wind down its program of regulatory reform. Such figures as Al Gore, John Dingell, Ted Weiss, Henry Waxman, Sidney Wolfe, and many others, were displeased with the dearth of funding for regulatory agencies, the attendant drop in regulatory actions, and the misplaced faith that American industry was righteous and policed itself adequately.[6] By contrast, Reagan administration officials declared victory and suggested that nothing more could be accomplished. Vice President Bush, who chaired the President's Task Force on Regulatory Reform, declared that $150 billion in savings over ten years—a result of his efforts—would "make an important contribution to the economic recovery now underway . . . ." He added that this would be achieved without jeopardizing "the environment, job or consumer safety, or other regulatory goals."[7]

By contrast, Representative Albert Gore (D-TN), a critic of excessive deregulation, remarked of the Reagan administration that its "No.1 priority is to make certain that no industry is in any way displeased or even slightly disconcerted by any action of Government."[8] According to this perspective, the Reagan administration placed the business of America before the safety of American consumers and thus influenced regulatory activities at multiple agencies. Prior to his election, Reagan had often used the Occupation Health and Safety Administration as a political punch-line and at one point proposed to dismantle the agency. While he backed away from this position, OSHA nevertheless faced tremendous downsizing in 1981–1982. The National Highway Traffic Safety Administration, for its part, lost nearly 30 percent of its staff, sustained a 25 percent budget cut under the Reagan administration, and in the words of one critic, became "a wholly owned subsidiary of Detroit manufacturers."[9]

While one must be cautious of political hyperbole, the size of the U.S. regulatory state certainly diminished after a period of sustained growth. Federal regulatory employment had, in both social and economic terms, increased incrementally (with minor stutters during the Great Depression and World War II) from the Progressive era to the Reagan administration. It was during the 1960s, however, that the growth of the U.S. bureaucracy began its steady, uninterrupted climb until the Reagan era in the 1980s. Historian John Karaagac has called this the "third wave of reform" and he has emphasized that while a new commitment to the environment and product safety was sparked, this wave nevertheless lacked a "broader political symbolism that gave it staying power."[10]

After Reagan's victory in the 1980s, federal regulatory employment as a percentage of civilian employment dropped. The Reagan administration also touted the decline in the bulk of the Federal Register by about a third in two years. The director of the Bush deregulatory task force, Christopher DeMuth, asserted that the flow of new regulatory proposals was down to 15,000 a year from 21,000 in 1980.[11] Moreover, the Reagan administration revoked or revised about 100 burdensome rules and, just as significant, slowed the growth in proposed new regulations by one-third from the last thirty months of the Carter administration. The result, according to the Bush task force report, was that 300 million hours of paperwork had been saved over a two year period.[12]

The Reagan administration's ability to limit the size and scope of U.S. regulatory agencies was not a resounding victory. In fact, the firmament underpinning regulatory reform began to shift at around the time of Hayes's departure; a number of concurrent stories surfaced in the early 1980s that served to undermine the push for deregulation and regulatory reform. Secretary of the Interior James G. Watt, a pugnacious, ardent supporter of deregulation changed his department so much that one official observed ironically, "This is now a captive agency. It is totally a captive of the mining interests."[13] Likewise, negative publicity at the Environmental Protection Agency, headed by Anne Burford, compounded the pejorative perception of deregulators. One political scientist called the lurid tales of scandal at the EPA and Department of the Interior "tragicomedies."[14] Laughable or not, the depressing press reports associated with Watt and Burford were surely detrimental to the Reagan administration and they served to crystallize the impression that something was amiss with the administration's larger plan for the nation's regulatory agencies.

These "tragicomedies" forced the Reagan administration to change its approach. Reagan's pragmatic top advisors counseled a tactical retreat and by mid-1983 the administration gradually gravitated away from regulatory reform.[15] Consequently, the number of federal regulatory employees and regulatory employees as a percentage of federal employees increased after 1984.[16] Another salient example of the shift away from regulatory reform was the termination of the Reagan administration task force on regulation.[17] In 1983, Bush enunciated, somewhat opaquely: ". . . The executive branch has done what it can."[18] According to economist Kip Visuci, regulatory agencies thereafter proposed regulations with greater costs than ever before. The Office of Management and Budget, in his estimation, became less influential in altering the structure of regulation. Regulatory enforcement became even more vigorous than before the onset of the policy of deregulation.[19]

The state of the U.S. economy was also important to the program of deregulation. An economic recession, the worst since the 1930s, began in

1981 and lasted nearly two full years. During this time, unemployment in the United States rose over 10 percent, while business failures, farm foreclosures, and homelessness increased. In December 1981, 59 percent of those asked by pollsters said no when asked if they were better off than last year, and only 36 percent said yes.[20] By November 1982, over 11.5 million Americans had lost jobs. President Reagan's approval ratings hit a low of 35 percent in January 1983, but he nevertheless urged Congress and the American people to "stay the course" and blamed the country's economic woes on the Carter administration.

In 1983, the U.S. economy turned around—as Reagan had predicted. The inflation rate dropped from approximately 14 percent in 1980 to under 2 percent in 1983. Interest rates declined from 21 percent to 11 percent. Moreover, a decrease in the price of oil spurred the economy; and between 1983 and 1989, 18 million new jobs were created.[21] Lawyer and author Peter Wallison wrote "the economy roared back, economic growth continued into the next decade, and the stock markets reached unprecedented levels."[22] As the economy improved and Reagan proclaimed "morning in America" and "America is back," neither the need nor desire for deregulation was as profound.[23] The Reagan administration, for its part, began to shift away from open promotion of a deregulatory agenda.

At the end of Reagan's presidency a general agreement among conservative economists emerged that there were two distinct Reagan regulation agendas—"the deregulation agenda that pertained from 1981 to 1983 and the return to the traditional regulatory agenda from 1984 to 1989."[24] The first period, which covered much of the first Reagan term, was one of deregulation and regulatory reform. It was marked by a rigorous effort to manage the regulatory state. The second period, conversely, saw a marked dip in enthusiasm for regulatory reform and saw a backward slide of influence to the regulatory state. Economist and former Nixon economic advisor Herbert Stein wrote of the shift that "after a few years—say by 1984—public interest in the subject faded and the policy effort languished."[25] Another political scientist, Guthrie Birkhead, argued that widespread regulatory reform was "beyond the reach" of the Reagan administration. He then quoted Murray Weidenbaum, Reagan's chief economic advisor, on the administration's failure: "We will be lucky if, in January 1985, we will be back to where we were in January 1981 in terms of the public's attitude toward statutory reform and social regulation."[26]

When it came to the FDA as part of the regulatory state, two members of Congress compellingly argued that regulatory reform was dangerous. Henry Waxman and Ted Weiss, in particular, each used the power of congressional oversight to investigate and air grievances about the significant shortcomings at the Food and Drug Administration. Henry Waxman (D-CA), considered one of the most liberal members of Congress with an abiding interest in health and the environment, ratcheted up his rhetoric on the FDA and used his position as chairman of the Energy and Commerce Subcommittee on Health and the Environment to investigate the agency. After it was reported in the national press that the number of FDA enforcement actions initiated by the Reagan administration was about half the annual average during the Carter administration, for example, Waxman took aim at the policy of regulatory reform. "I question whether this agency, this administration, and this President are committed to enforcing laws written to protect the public health," Waxman said icily. The Reagan administration, in his estimation, had mistreated the FDA and it was therefore complicit in the declining safety of American drug consumers.[27]

Representative Ted Weiss (D-NY) was another Democrat who perpetuated debate about the FDA's smaller budget and the larger pitfalls of regulatory reform. One of his abiding political interests was the FDA's drug approval process—and how it had been influenced by the Reagan administration. In 1983, Ted Weiss held Government Operations subcommittee hearings on arthritis drug Zomax. A pain reliever in the same vein as Oraflex, Zomax was approved for marketing by the FDA in October 1980; however, McNeil Laboratories, a subsidiary of Johnson & Johnson, neglected to provide the FDA's drug approval division with all the pertinent information, namely, that a number of people taking Zomax in Europe had died. After a number of deaths in the United States, the company opted to independently remove the drug from the market in March of 1983.[28]

The hearings held by Weiss in April 1983 explored the connections between the Zomax-related deaths and the FDA. Just as he had during his hearings on Oraflex, Weiss raised grave questions about what he perceived as an improper relationship between industry, the Reagan administration, and the FDA budget shortfalls. "This situation," he noted, "bears uncanny resemblance to the Oraflex matter . . . An arthritis drug manufacturer did not inform FDA of serious adverse reactions apparently reported to its foreign divisions prior to FDA's approval of the drug."[29] The implication was that drug makers were again taking advantage of the close, cooperative and collaborative relationship with the FDA, whereas the FDA, lacking resources, was far too trusting of the industry it regulated. Weiss touched on the subject of the Bureau of Drugs and its staff levels and he asked "Would it be fair to characterize your resources as being stretched to the breaking point?"[30] Hayes answered cannily that it was inappropriate to discuss resources. "It is not proper for me to discuss, you know, budgets and appropriations and what we would like, could use, or how we would spend it . . ." As an afterthought, he added that "there is no question that budgetary constraints do pose difficulties. One could always do more."[31] Hayes did not address Weiss's larger point, whether or not more resources would have aided the FDA's drug review of Oraflex or Zomax, but he made clear that more funding might ease the lives of FDA regulators.

The Departure of Commissioner Hayes

In August 1983, FDA Commissioner Arthur Hull Hayes announced that he was returning immediately to academia as New York Medical College's dean and provost. Having overseen an increase in drug approvals and decrease in enforcement actions, Hayes maintained it was with "sincere regret" that he left government; nevertheless, he also admitted that his time as commissioner was a draining experience and he had exhausted himself. Other commentators agreed with Hayes's judgment. He was "burned out," "battered," and "spent," and before leaving the FDA in September, Hayes told an interviewer, "after two years, things seem to change."[32]

In the early days of his tenure, Hayes was given a honeymoon, but by 1982 and 1983 his behavior was questioned as national press reports recounted his unwise—some said improper—conduct. Change, as Hayes characterized it, was but one way of describing how stories of his dubious decision-making poisoned his standing as FDA's leader and marred his departure. His dire press coverage, which would hang like a dark cloud over Hayes, began in 1983. A trade publication, *Food Chemical News,* first revealed that Commissioner Hayes had in 1982 accepted $4,300 in honoraria for a number of lectures and speeches. The *Washington Post* soon began an investigation of its own and subsequently discovered that Hayes not only supplemented his FDA salary with an additional $79,662 in honoraria, but also had his travel costs paid for him. In addition, Hayes proved extraordinarily lackadaisical in keeping track of expenses.

Yet Hayes consistently and vehemently denied any wrongdoing, protesting that he was an honest individual and that the national press was exaggerating the extent of his misconduct. The ensuing Justice Department investigation was inconclusive. Adding to the furore, the U.S. Attorney for Maryland declined to prosecute Hayes, and referred the case back to the Department of Health and Human Services. Hayes was ultimately deemed guilty of "insensitivity" to the golden rule of government service, that employees must always avoid the appearance of potential impropriety, and his reputation suffered a minor blow. In his letter of resignation, Hayes made no mention of the mini-scandal and he announced he relished "a challenging opportunity to return to the field of academic medicine."[33]

Hayes explained, during an exit interview, how Washington politics and the political nature of his job had prompted his departure. Somewhat nostalgically, he declared that the beginning of his tenure was marked by enthusiasm and momentum, a drive for reform and change. According to Hayes, however, the FDA hit a quagmire in the fall of 1983 because "everybody is getting ready for the election." "This town," Hayes observed, referring to Washington, "runs almost in a cyclic way. . . ." As such, there was at the FDA "a different attitude, a different spirit, both in perception and in reality."[34] The enthusiasm mutated into political cynicism and, as the elections drew ever nearer, the push for reform faltered.

Hayes was not entirely wrong. One way in which the election cycle impacted the FDA was through oversight hearings. More and more congressional hearings studied the executive branch agencies like the FDA after the creation of new regulatory structures. This trend continued following the Nixon and Ford administrations. In fact, previous FDA commissioners in the 1970s aggressively and lucidly articulated the problem with the politicized nature of certain hearings. It is worth recalling how Commissioner Schmidt decried the misuse of Congress's oversight function in regard to the approval of pharmaceuticals. "By far the greatest pressure that the Bureau of Drugs or the Food and Drug Administration receives with respect to the new drug approval process," he stated in 1974, "is brought to bear through *congressional hearings*." The U.S. Congress needed a greater "perspective" on its use of the "legislative oversight function."[35]

Hayes lamented this fact as well. "We're going to have more hearings because an election is coming," he said. With more than a touch of sourness, Hayes continued:

> Because we have more issues? No. Because we have more problems? No. Because somebody thinks or can document that we've made more mistakes— too much, too little, too fast, too slow? No. Why? We're going to have more hearings because an election is coming, and everybody expects that there will more hearings. People in this agency will spend a lot of valuable time. They will lay other things aside, drop priorities, because there will be hearings.[36]

According to Hayes, then, the political landscape in Washington had altered—as chatter about a dominant conservative order dwindled—and the FDA was affected by this. He did not wish to spend the majority of his time defending the agency's conduct in an overtly partisan atmosphere of congressional hearings. And during his final interviews, he maintained that he had always wanted to be dean of a medical college when he completed his time at the FDA. He simply needed the right offer at the right time and New York Medical College provided Hayes that opportunity.

Measuring Success

Hayes had assumed the office of the commissioner in 1981 with the dual goal of honoring the FDA's institutional identity and promoting regulatory reform. He proclaimed the agency would be "ever mindful not to compromise the safety and effectiveness of new drug products approved for marketing" but "weeding out" requirements that were "duplicative" and "unnecessary" was also of the utmost importance. The FDA's drug review could be "streamlined" and "improved."[37] In view of that, Hayes vowed to advance "a more cooperative spirit" with the pharmaceutical industry through the promotion of "voluntary action" and under his direction the FDA would "be sensitive to the impact of our regulatory stance on innovation."[38] Hayes thus sought to cleave to the FDA's traditional role of consumer protector and implement the Reagan administration's larger ideological goal of regulatory reform. Any barometer of his success or failure, however basic, must measure these two tasks.

The FDA under Hayes's stewardship undoubtedly contributed to the success of the American pharmaceutical industry by approving more drugs. He had promised at the outset of his tenure to support innovation and promote a speedier drug approval process; thereafter, the average time it took to approve a new drug steadily decreased. In 1982, the mean time of approval for 116 NDAs was 22.4 months, compared to the 24.5 months it took for 96 approvals in 1981. This was significantly better than the average in 1979 (33.6 months), 1978 (32.2 months), and 1977 (26.6 months). Hayes also oversaw a higher rate of drug approvals in a more expedient manner.[39]

Moreover, Hayes fulfilled his goal of shifting the agency toward a policy of voluntary compliance and in so doing, he left behind a "healthier agency/ industry environment," according to *Pharmaceutical Technology.* In 1982, the new commissioner promised to foster an accommodating and collaborative atmosphere between the FDA and the pharmaceutical industry. Depending on one's perspective, this was either a positive outcome that facilitated more communication between the regulator and industry or a negative development that necessarily produced drug crises and ultimately harmed consumers.[40]

The American drug industry showed impressive growth during Hayes's time at the FDA. In the aftermath of the 1980 election, this had been predicted in some circles—hoped for in others. Certain economic analysts and pharmaceutical industry insiders had praised Reagan's regulatory reform agenda, while others suggested that a Reagan presidency would translate into pharmaceutical industry profits. "Everyone expects life to be easier for industry under the new Reagan Administration," proclaimed *Pharmaceutical Technology.*[41] Money managers were particularly bullish about drug stocks.[42] Hayes, as leader of the industry regulator, was one architect of the overall growth and in July 1984 one trade publication highlighted how well the pharmaceutical industry had grown and profited as change occurred at the FDA. *Drug Topics* declared: "It was a very good year."[43]

Amid this heady climate, moreover, drug use increased. Approximately 1.5 billion prescriptions were dispensed in 1982, up 5 percent over 1981. New prescriptions increased by 4 percent from 1981 to 1982 and total prescriptions (including new prescriptions and refills) were also on the rise in the early 1980s, after a steady decrease from 1973 though 1979. Drugstore sales increased 8 percent in 1981, 9.7 percent in 1982, and 11.8 percent in 1983, whereas prescription drugs sales were equally impressive, increasing by 21.7 percent to $19.7 billion.[44] Moreover, after little growth in the 1970s, R&D expenditures by U.S. firms grew at a steady rate in the first half of the 1980s (14.3 percent in real terms).[45] Thus, as the FDA's budget was restricted and the policy of regulatory reform was set in motion, precisely the opposite was occurring amongst drug companies—more and more money was being spent on developing new drugs.

Not surprisingly, pharmaceutical companies were profiting during Hayes's time at the FDA. As part of this, according to the U.S. Bureau of Labor Statistics, prescription drug prices increased 38.3 percent between December 1980 and December 1983—far surpassing the overall rate of inflation in the 1980s. Michael Pollard of the Pharmaceutical Manufacturers Association (PMA), in attempting to justify this pricing upswing, declared the trend was just a "temporary departure." The trend was also legitimate, according to PMA, because prescription drugs were the cheapest of all medical therapies and reduced health-care costs by "cutting back on the need for more expensive surgery and hospitalization."[46] Abbott Laboratories, for example, was a mid-sized company based in Abbott Park, Illinois, and it announced that its earnings in the first quarter of 1983 had jumped by 17.9 percent. Johnson & Johnson suffered through a run of bad publicity in 1982–1983, but the company nonetheless raised its quarterly dividend 8 percent in 1983, a move that reflected the company's positive feelings about "the future of our business." In October 1983, Merck & Company completed its acquisition of majority interest in Banyu Pharmaceutical and Torii Pharmaceutical, Japanese drug companies. This type of direct foreign investment in Japan was the first of its kind by an American concern.[47]

The assessments of Hayes and industry growth were not uniformly positive. First, he was unable to curtail the growth of the FDA's drug review backlog. Due to budget restraints, the FDA could not deal with or mitigate all the drugs filing up the approval pipeline, and according to *Medical Advertising News*, the drug industry could expect the FDA's backlog to grow even more.[48]

Second, he was not able to oversee the passage of new administrative rules designed to achieve regulatory reform. The NDA rewrite proposal would have streamlined the new drug application process, for example, by reducing the bulk of NDAs, tightening the enforcement of mandated approval periods, reducing unnecessary supplements, and permitting greater use of foreign data. When Hayes left the FDA, however, the NDA Rewrite rule had not yet wended its way through the Department of Health and Human Services and Office of Management and Budget regulatory channels. The same was true of his proposed investigational new drug (IND) rewrite, a regulation that aimed to advance collaboration between the drug industry and the FDA to further streamline the approval process. Hayes may have instilled a supportive, friendly attitude at the agency, and he may have decreased the length of time to approve a new drug under "current-services resources," but he failed to ameliorate the FDA's backlog or accomplish much in the way of tangible regulatory reform rules.[49]

By the spring of 1984, Hayes's ostensible failure to address the backlog became a significant talking point. "Delay and more delay; the agency's infamous drug lag continues," declared one magazine.[50] Another magazine announced, "the drug industry can expect a lengthening of the time it takes an NDA to travel through the agency gauntlet."[51] In June of 1984, Dr. Richard Lesher, president of the U.S. Chamber of Commerce, professed, "major reform is long overdue for the benefit of the consumer. I hope we get it." According to C. Joseph Stetler, the former president of the PMA and one of the most stentorian critics of drug policy in the mid-1980s, "Many of the drugs that have been held up for long periods of time in the FDA do benefit a segment of society. And believe me, for the people that have that disease or a problem, that drug is important."[52] For all the moderate reform at the FDA in the early 1980s, the drug industry continued to assail the agency.

Stetler, one-time head of the most significant pharmaceutical trade association in Washington, did not reserve his criticism for the FDA alone. In his judgment, the Reagan administration failed to rationalize the drug approval process and provide the FDA with adequate resources to carry out its mandate. Worse still, he stated that Hayes's proposed rules—the NDA and IND rewrites—had been swallowed by the hidebound bureaucracies of Health and Human Services and the Office of Management and Budget. These rules would have facilitated quicker drug approval times, yet the government itself had thwarted this effort. Stetler insisted the Reagan administration was woefully complicit in this inaction: "It is time for the Administration to renew its commitment to FDA regulatory reform," he asserted.[53]

Nevertheless, Stetler also drew attention to significant deficiencies at the FDA. The agency, he averred, required more staff members and better facilities to allay the drug lag and the drug backlog. Without these, it was unlikely that industry could benefit from tangible regulatory reform legislation. "There is a drug lag," he declared while on the business/politics-oriented TV program *It's Your Business.* "To me, that means that drugs come later in the United States than they do in other countries. . . ." The answer to this dilemma, he maintained, was rudimentary: money. It was absolutely essential that the FDA "be given more funding." They also needed more personnel. "I don't think there should be one Bob Temple," referring to his fellow panellist, one of the FDA's foremost drug reviewers, "there should be four Bob

Temples."[54] Stetler hence proffered a complicated position—one that advocated more funds for the FDA but also included new reform measures.

Besides Stetler, the National Academy of Engineering (NAE) criticized Hayes for failing to achieve any lasting regulatory change while commissioner. In September 1983, the same month that Hayes departed, the NAE recommended greater reform measures as well as a revision of the FDA's controls on drugs. As a means of strengthening the competitive position of the American pharmaceutical industry, the NAE offered three suggestions:

1. Extend patent terms for drugs
2. Change FDA regulations to speed up the process for approving new drugs
3. Revise FDA policy to let U.S. companies manufacture for export drugs not approved in the United States

Further to these recommendations, the NAE's report maintained that the U.S. industry's share of the world market was in decline. Profits were inching upward marginally, but between 1968 and 1978 the U.S. global market share fell from 38 percent to 27 percent. Japan's share of world drug production, by contrast, had increased during this same period from 13 percent to 20 percent. West Germany's share had increased from 8.5 percent to 10 percent, while Switzerland's share moved one percentage point from 2 to 3. "A declining U.S. share of a growing industry," the NAE report read, "is as much a concern for U.S. industrial policy as a declining share of an industry undergoing retrenchment."[55]

Donald Rumsfeld, then president and CEO of G.D. Searle, a major pharmaceutical company, endorsed the NAE's findings. He lamented the lack of recognition by American society "that the success of enterprise is of fundamental importance to the success of this country." According to this rationale, streamlining the drug approval process for both new and generic drug applications would foster greater success for American drug industry and, by extension, the United States on the whole.[56] Sidney Wolfe, director of the Public Citizen's Health Research Group strenuously disagreed with the report's recommendations when he said: "they are efforts to remedy a problem that doesn't exist."[57]

The General Accounting Office also contributed to the debate about Hayes's success in instituting regulatory reform at the FDA. In 1983, the GAO released a report evaluating the FDA's conduct from 1981. *Legislative and Administrative Changes Needed to Improve Regulation of the Drug Industry* had its origins in congressional and public interest-group concern about the FDA's diminishing regulatory actions against the American drug industry. The GAO offered multiple suggestions about how the FDA could best take "appropriate and timely" action against those drug makers violating the law while working under the policy of "voluntary compliance." Its most significant recommendation urged the FDA to develop a mechanism measuring the extent to which voluntary corrective actions had resulted in compliance. Irrespective of whether the agency implemented the GAO's suggestions, the release of the report itself signified a growing unease about the state of the FDA in 1983.[58]

Despite such unease and despite the public debate about Hayes's legacy, according to his own stated goals—namely, his vow to protect the agency's institutional identity and promote regulatory reform—the commissioner has to be considered a mixed success. Pharmaceutical industry growth was minimal in the 1970s and, relative to European and Japanese competitors, the American industry had languished, suffering a loss of dominance in its global market share. By contrast, when Hayes left the FDA the American drug industry was in an ascendant position. True, he had fostered a cordial relationship with the American industry and overseen more drugs than previous commissioners. Nevertheless, he had fallen short when it came to the drug backlog and instilling confidence and morale.

Hayes contended that he left the FDA in the midst of an increasingly combative political atmosphere. In his estimation, the clash between regulatory reformers and consumer activists had mutated into a bitter and belligerent struggle, which meant his job was unnecessarily politicized. He also contended that this had stalled reform and curtailed his ability to influence career employees. But was his assessment accurate? The answer must be, in a broader sense, an affirmative. Hayes was correct in thinking that the Reagan administration's program of regulatory reform had decreased as a policy goal.

A Lame-Duck Commissioner?

Few pharmaceutical-oriented observers were shocked when Hayes announced that he was leaving the FDA for academia. In the previous ten years commissioners had averaged approximately two years' tenure in the position and this trend had developed after the job was altered from a career civil servant position to a political appointment. Hayes's departure from the FDA in 1983 was in some measure predictable, but according to the drug industry the destabilized leadership structure at the FDA was not necessarily a cause for celebration. To American Pharmaceutical Association President William Apple, "The constant turnover of FDA commissioners is not in the best interest of the public, the FDA or all those who are being regulated."[59]

With Hayes's resignation in 1983, the hunt was on for a new FDA commissioner. Margaret Heckler, Schweiker's replacement as Secretary of Health and Human Services, commented to Hayes, "You leave a pair of very big shoes which will be hard pressed to fill."[60] Heckler was right on the mark, for this task proved neither quick nor easy; besides the obvious political pitfalls inherent to the job (the negative press, the congressional badgering), potential commissioners knew all too well that the FDA salary was substandard compared to academia and the private sector. In addition, potential candidates for the post probably well understood the position of commissioner offered no stability; until the Reagan administration won another mandate from the American people, the FDA commissioner, whoever he or she was, would be a virtual lame-duck. Not surprisingly, the Reagan administration was turned down by at least six candidates and it took over a year to find a new commissioner.[61]

As the Reagan administration searched for a suitable replacement for Hayes, the FDA's acting commissioner, a career civil servant named Dr. Mark Novitch appointed on September 1, established himself as a first-rate candidate for the job.[62] *Pharmaceutical Technology* reported that Novitch's performance during one Senate hearing "was the most masterful handling of a hostile congressional committee by an FDA chief that this correspondent

Figure 5.1. FROM LEFT TO RIGHT - Margaret Heckler (Secretary of Health and Human Services), Ralph Regula (R-Ohio), Orrin Hatch (R-Utah), James (Jimmy) Quillen (R-Tennessee), Strom Thurmond (R-South Carolina), Henry Waxman (D-California), President Reagan (center) September 24, 1984. President Reagan, Strom Thurmond, Orrin Hatch, and others at the signing ceremony for S 1538 Drug Price Competition and Patent Term Restoration Act of 1984 in the Rose Garden. Courtesy of the Ronald Reagan Presidential Library

has ever seen."[63] Novitch was also regarded highly because he provided much-needed continuity and stability to the commissioner's office.[64] A career FDA employee, Novitch also demonstrated a keen grasp of the nuances, factionalism, and in-fighting that typified the FDA bureaucracy.

Backing Novitch for the post was an incongruous mix of FDA stakeholders, a group notorious for its public wrangling and formidable advocacy. Novitch also found that he had the rare endorsement of industry (in the form of the Pharmaceutical Manufacturers Association) and FDA consumer activists (Public Citizen).[65] This was an unlikely and potent confluence of support and it was indicative of the quality of Novitch's leadership. Despite all this support, however, he was a registered Democrat, and this was a significant obstacle to his appointment. According to FDA historian Philip J. Hilts, Novitch's chance to become commissioner, for this reason, "was soon gone"[66] because the Reagan administration still regarded the agency as a political post—and the commissioner needed to more closely reflect the president's views.

In October 1984, a full year after Hayes's departure, the Reagan administration appointed Dr. Frank Young of Rochester, New York Medical School as FDA commissioner. Holding an M.D. and a Ph.D., Young was a born-again Christian who taught Sunday school. When first asked to serve by the Reagan administration, Young politely declined the post. After a second call, he demurred again; but after a third call Young was, for whatever reason, persuaded to take the job.[67] In spite of his early reluctance to join the FDA, Young articulated that, "The highest calling is really serving the public. That sounds hokey. . . . The problem is, I believe it."[68] He also added, "I like these kinds of challenges" and, although not one of the initial contenders for the job, he stated, "I love to learn."[69]

Young was an appropriate choice for the Reagan administration, though his mandate was not one of change, like his predecessor, but rather one that included getting the agency to run more efficiently.[70] His goal, he stated, was to improve the agency's science capabilities and risk assessment. While dean of Rochester's medical school, Young administered a staff of 6,000 and a budget—at $220 million—reasonably close to that of the FDA. Young was also a world-class pathologist and intimately familiar with the nascent biotechnology industry and the regulation of drug products in general. He not only maintained a strong research record but came equipped with more high-level management experience than any other commissioner in recent years.[71] Compared to Novitch, Young was a neophyte when it came to FDA politics and when Young was queried about his political inclinations he cleverly described himself as apolitical. That was not how entirely how Young was viewed inside the FDA; on the one hand, Young was seen as politically naïve and bullish about building constituencies;[72] on the other hand, according to Joseph Paul Hile, he and other FDA managers "sensed a political dimension to him [Young] that we had not encountered before and, in all candor, it made some of us a little apprehensive, because we didn't know what that might ultimately result in." Hile added, "in my own experience, Frank Young is probably the most politically oriented commissioner that I worked with. . . ."[73]

Yet Young was careful and crafty enough to strike the correct rhetorical chord about the significance of balance between innovation and safety. Like Hayes had been before him, Young was intimately concerned about the drug lag and he underscored his determination to tackle the FDA's long-standing problem. "I've been through the experience of literally having patients dying before my eyes while they're waiting for the medicine to be approved that could save them," he said in one interview. Conversely, he also possessed strong views on regulation and the risk/safety equation, and he noted the most imperative task he faced at the FDA was determining the appropriate risk to which patients should be exposed from new technology. He thus underlined that he would constantly be re-evaluating the balance between safety and risk—that is, what types of new drugs Americans consumers could access and when they could have that access. "We don't live in a risk-free society," he observed. "We take risks all the time. The question is, 'What is the appropriate risk we should take in the area of food and drugs?'"[74]

Frank Young assumed the office of FDA commissioner in the fall of 1984 and immediately sought to shore up an institution he perceived was suffering. The FDA was not a disaster—a "tragicomedy"—like other parts of the U.S. government, but it had been impacted by the Reagan administration's regulatory reform program. Young's long-term goals were to strengthen the agency, promote efficiency, finally overcome the drug lag, and engender a positive relationship with industry. To meet these ends, Young articulated a clear message: a formidable, financially solvent FDA was mutually beneficial for everyone involved—consumers, Congress, the Reagan administration and the drug industry.

Young also indicated to his FDA employees very early on that he was in fact one of them and was concerned about the FDA's institutional identity. In May, after the Reagan administration's announcement of his appointment as commissioner but before he actually held the position Young visited the agency's associate commissioner for Regulatory Affairs—its "top cop." Given a tour of the Chicago district office, Young came away impressed and praised field agents, who were the "first line of defense for the American people." Nonetheless, Young highlighted that the agency's morale was "terrible" because there was no *esprit de corps* due to the frequent "changes at the top." To counter this, Young added that he intended to visit all the regional offices and "shake the hands of 4000 of the 7000 employees" by the end of 1984.[75]

As Young embarked on an extensive public relations campaign with his own staff at the FDA, he also proved attentive to the pharmaceutical industry. He adopted what might be called a centrist approach to product innovation and consumer safety. He deemed a recent consumer study of the agency's declining enforcement actions under the Reagan administration as "meaningless." Moreover, Young met with the leaders of most major drug firms to hear what they, as industry executives, had to say about the FDA's performance in the early 1980s and how its operation might be upgraded. And to assuage any potentially negative reactions and fears about such meetings, HHS Secretary Margaret Heckler announced that they were designed to improve drug regulation, "not to create an opportunity for undue influence."[76]

During his initial meetings with the FDA's pharmaceutical industry stakeholders, Young was unequivocal about the future. Young delivered a candid and aggressive message to the U.S. drug industry and it was summed up this way:

> You know deep down inside [and] you understand deep down inside, that the FDA's not going to go away; regulation of your product is not going to go away; and your industries profit most by having a strong, effective, scientifically and otherwise capable FDA. Except and unless you begin to step forward and talk about that and emphasize that in your contacts with the [FDA] and your contacts with the Congress and your public pronouncements, you're not going to have that [profit].[77]

Young could thus be interpreted as friendly and amenable to change but he *would be* obdurate when it came to protecting American consumers. The FDA, in its various incarnations, had been around for over seventy-five years. Polls consistently demonstrated widespread public support for the agency's work, as well as a high level of popularity relative to other federal regulatory agencies. Young gave the impression that he was acutely aware of this history. Under his guidance, the FDA would be vigilant in carrying out its assigned, statutory duties. The best way the pharmaceutical industry could achieve its goals—i.e., quicker approval times and increased approval rates—was to lend its support to its regulator.[78]

Therefore, Young's approach to industry—one part accommodationist, one part hardliner—informed his forceful and generally successful approach to the FDA's budget process. Early on, Young asserted that the FDA needed more money and more personnel; once HIV/AIDS developed into a nationwide epidemic he grew shriller in his budget requests and increasingly successful in winning more resources. With a larger budget, he told congressional appropriators, the FDA could assist U.S. drug makers in generating profits. In an era of voluntary compliance, of partnership, of bridges rather than barriers, Young asserted it was only natural and necessary to enhance the

Figure 5.2. This ad, which was released in 1984, constituted part of the campaign to bring greater awareness to the costs associated with generic drugs versus brand name drugs. Courtesy of the Food and Drug Administration.

agency's approval process. Accordingly, greater American drug industry profits would be made this way.

Young in fact proved to be a strong, successful advocate for the FDA and he was able to preserve current budget levels and existing services. "When it came to annual budget requests, he was quite aggressive," said Charles Gorton, FDA Director of Planning and Management Communications, Office of Planning and Evaluation.[79] Paul Hile, Associate Commissioner for Regulatory Affairs said ". . . I saw Frank Young as the most effective spokesman for the agency in regards to resources as any commissioner, at least in contemporary time." To Associate Commissioner for Policy and Planning William Hubbard, moreover, Commissioner Young "was indefatigable on the budget side."[80] Indeed, Young won modest funding increases, although he was more successful in arguing for elevated resource levels in the late 1980s, during the tumult over AIDS in America, but the FDA budget did not reach its 1978 level until 1989.[81] While Young may have been aggressive and indefatigable, according to his peers at least, he was effective at winning more funds for the agency only when a public health crisis and attendant fear permitted.

Young was successful in employing that fear as an oratorical weapon. When the HIV/AIDS crisis began to captivate the nation, Young couched his FDA budget requests in evocative and alarming language. He explained that ameliorating the dangers of AIDS was of the utmost importance and required extensive resources. "The enormity of our task is underscored by the diabolic nature of this terrible disease."[82] He also took care to highlight how that task left the FDA exposed to other problems—particularly the drug lag. If Congress did not provide the FDA with more resources, the agency would have to wage the war against AIDS by diverting personnel and shifting workloads; and this shifting of resources would contribute to larger backlogs when, according to Young, "our individuals feel overwhelmed" and "intensity is high."[83] Young emphasized the necessity for a balance between the FDA's longtime adversary, the dreaded drug lag, and efforts to mitigate the HIV/AIDS crisis. It was a balance that required more funding.

Strange Bedfellows: The Hatch-Waxman Legislation

On September 24, 1984, President Reagan signed legislation which restored patent terms for pharmaceutical products and enabled more, cheaper generic drugs to come to the U.S. market. At the same time, the legislation illustrated the evolution of the FDA during the Reagan era. At the signing ceremony Reagan declared that the new law provided "regulatory relief, increased competition, [and] economy in government."[84] The Drug Price Competition and Patent Term Restoration Act of 1984, also known as Hatch-Waxman after its two principal congressional sponsors, represented the first change in U.S. patent terms since 1861. Unabashedly proud of the legislation, Reagan praised the bill. "Best of all," he added, "the American people will save money and yet receive the best medicine that pharmaceutical science can provide."[85]

The Drug Price Competition and Patent Term Restoration Act embodied President Reagan's core goals. The law provided regulatory relief, elevation of unfettered competition, and streamlining of government, but it also conferred other benefits as well. Reagan's remarks cleaved to the concepts of consumer protection and cost-savings and he stressed that the passage of Hatch-Waxman would give Americans increased access to the finest pharmaceutical products available; Americans, moreover, would actually save money when they purchased those drugs. The president's remarks thus cannily framed Hatch-Waxman as a legislative triumph, and one that hewed to the administration's pre-established policy goals.

It is axiomatic, however, that an administration will extol its own achievements, especially when it is a law signed during the September before a presidential election. But what was the veracity of Reagan's interpretation of the Hatch-Waxman legislation? How did it influence the FDA's regulation of drugs? In answering such question, it is crucial to examine the genesis of the statute, appraise the value of the compromise package ingrained in the new law, and once again assess how the FDA was shaped by the legislation. An investigation of Hatch-Waxman adds to the discussion of how the FDA's drug regulation continued to evolve in a parallel fashion with the executive branch's regulatory policy.

The Hatch-Waxman legislation of 1984 had its roots in the late 1970s, as the drug lag issue blossomed in Washington and President Jimmy Carter experimented with a variety of ideas to jumpstart the stalled U.S. economy. In 1978, Carter ordered a domestic policy review of industrial innovation and over 150 representatives from multiple sectors of the American economy were subsequently parcelled into different advisory committees and subcommittees. Two of the subcommittees then proposed increasing the term of a drug patent to compensate for the time lost during the regulatory process.[86] Research demonstrated that the patent life of pharmaceutical products had declined since the 1960s and the passage of the 1962 Kefauver-Harris amendments. From 1966 to 1979, for example, it was estimated that effective patent life had decreased from 13.6 years to 9.6 years. The amendments clearly delayed the introduction of new drugs which had inflated premarket expenditures; politicians and analysts argued that if action was not taken, and taken rapidly, the Japanese pharmaceutical industry, which had evolved markedly from the 1960s, would challenge and perhaps surpass U.S. leadership in pharmaceuticals. Such charges, combined with the fear of an increasingly moribund pharmaceutical industry, emboldened the nation's legislators to tackle patent terms.[87]

Thereafter, a wave of legislative activity addressed the issue of patents. In 1979, Representative Steven Symms (R-ID) proposed a bill that established a fixed seventeen-year patent term (once approval for marketing was granted by the FDA) or, alternatively, a twenty-seven-year patent term from the time the patent itself was awarded. Symms's bill, H.R. 3859, ultimately found little support with either his colleagues or industry; still, his attempt to ameliorate the problem of eroding patent times nevertheless set in motion a series of negotiations and consultations between legislators and the Chemical Manufacturers Association (CMA) and Pharmaceutical Manufacturers Associations (PMA).[88]

In 1980, Senators Birch Bayh (D-IN), Strom Thurmond (R-SC), Charles Mathias (R-MD), and Charles Percy (R-IL) introduced S.2892, while Representative Robert Kastenmeier (D-WI) simultaneously introduced H.R. 7952. Their bill, written with the help of industry, housed the patent framework eventually used by Hatch-Waxman and praised by President Reagan. No action was taken on the bill in 1980, however, for two reasons. First, it was in a queue behind other patent legislation during a busy election year and, second, it came up against intense opposition.[89]

A year later this same piece of legislation was reintroduced and it initially appeared to have a reasonable chance at passing. The Senate passed the bill in a voice vote and the Congressional Office of Technology Assessment concluded that the provisions of the legislation would promote new product innovation. Despite these early signs that the bill would quickly become law in 1982, it was not to be as Representatives Kastenmeier and Sawyer found that there was concentrated opposition to the bill's ultimate goal, to assist companies unduly affected by perceived onerous health and safety regulations. The bill was deemed unsuitably pro-industry and political battle lines were drawn.[90]

Supporting the bill at the time was Commissioner Hayes, who, while testifying before Congress, commented that drug companies required support to remain competitive. In his judgment, drug patent law ought to be extended to reflect the seven years companies lost during reviews by the FDA. Drug companies, Hayes asserted, needed twelve to nineteen years of monopoly sales to earn a reasonable profit on the $54 to $70 million normally involved in the research and development of new drugs. Unfortunately, the overly long drug review process diminished the period of monopoly sales.[91]

The Reagan administration, for its part, stridently supported the bipartisan patent bill and made no effort whatever to pander to consumer activists. Hayes, as already noted, supported aid for drug makers, as did HHS Secretary Schweiker; in fact, the latter proclaimed patent extension legislation would correct an "inequity in the patent laws."[92] Gerald J. Mossinghoff, Reagan's Federal Commissioner of Patents and Trademarks, and who would later become head of the Pharmaceutical Research and Manufacturers Association (PhRMA), also offered his support: "There is no rational reason why a better mousetrap should receive 17 years of patent protection and a life-saving drug should receive only 10."[93]

Opposition to the bill, however, proved strong. Generic drug companies, consumer groups and labor unions, denounced the legislation as a "give-away" to larger, more profitable prescription drug companies. These opponents contended that the bill would prolong the monopoly of brand-name products, delaying the introduction of generic substitutes. According to Representative Gore, large companies "stand to profit enormously" from the proposed changes in the patent law. He charged, moreover, that the legislation would "substantially increase the prescription drug costs to consumers" without any assurance that drug companies would reinvest the extra revenue in research and development.[94]

Henry Waxman (D-CA), chairman of the health subcommittee of the House Committee on Energy and Commerce, was also a resolute opponent of the bill. Like Gore, Waxman fretted over the prices that American consumers were forced to pay by major pharmaceutical companies and he championed the cause of the generic drug industry. In the run-up to the 1982 vote, Waxman rallied his colleagues against a bill that he declaimed to only benefit the brand-name drug industry.[95] In the end, the resistance to patent extension proved overwhelming and it was defeated in the House—meaning the FDA's remit would not be amended. The defeat of the patent bill revealed Waxman to be a commanding figure on health policy, and his concerns about generic drugs would have to be addressed in any future drug legislation.[96]

In 1984, the Drug Price Competition and Patent Term Restoration Act (or Hatch-Waxman amendments) incorporated Waxman's beliefs and much of the earlier, failed patent extension framework. It also included provisions that benefited generic drug companies, which in turn eased American consumers' access to affordable drugs. According to the FDA's own website, Hatch-Waxman expedited "the availability of less costly generic drugs by permitting FDA applications to market generic versions of brand-name drugs without repeating the research done to prove them safe and effective."[97]

Under the new law, brand-name companies could apply for up to five years additional patent protection for the new medicines they developed to make up for the time lost as their products traveled through the FDA's approval process. In short, the expansion of patent rights, or the period of exclusivity, was lengthened by up to five years, with no extension beyond fourteen years. The law also provided for a minimum of five years of protection for all new drugs by not allowing any abbreviated new drug application (ANDAs) during the first five years of market life. At the same time, a generic drug company now only had to submit an ANDA, or a summary of the already approved drug's documentation of safety and effectiveness found in the investigational new drug application (IND) and new drug application (NDA).[98]

The successful enactment of the legislation had much to do with the peculiar but formidable political relationship between Representative Henry Waxman and Senator Orrin Hatch. In 1981, during a House-Senate conference on Orphan Drug legislation, they "discovered that if they worked together, they could do almost anything." Of course the two legislators were vastly different individuals and that only heightened the mystique of the bill. Waxman was short, bald, and moustachioed; moreover, he was a Democrat who possessed a 95 percent voter rating, according to the liberal Americans for Democratic Action (ADA). Hatch, by contrast, was tall, lean, a Mormon bishop, and a Republican whose voting record had a 95 percent rating from the conservative Americans for Constitutional Action (ACA). Their political relationship was so anomalous, so weirdly absurd, that generic drug manufacturers jokingly presented them with nightshirts reading "Politics Makes Strange Bedfellows."[99]

For all their differences, however, Waxman and Hatch held shared beliefs about what they deemed a reasonable drug policy. Both men agreed that their concerns about "health" trumped their deep "political and philosophical differences." According to Hatch, "Henry and I expect to establish a health policy that will satisfy both liberals and conservatives."[100] They were aptly positioned to make headway in this area: as Chairs of the House Energy and Commerce Subcommittee on Health and the Environment and Chairman of the Senate Labor and Human Resources Committee, Waxman and Hatch each wielded a significant amount of clout.

Their law, which immediately changed the FDA drug review processes, was a masterful compromise.[101] It restored part of the patent life lost during the pre-market phase of the FDA's regulatory process, which was good for brand-name drug makers, but the law was advantageous for generic drug makers because they were freed from conducting safety and efficacy studies—they simply had to prove their drugs were equivalent to the original. According to President Reagan, the legislation provided regulatory relief because it "offset the regulatory burdens" placed on drug makers. The law not only aimed to balance the goals of maintaining incentives to invest in developing innovative drugs, it also encouraged generic competition to reduce the prices of older ones.[102] In addition, supporters, including President Reagan, touted the Hatch-Waxman legislation as a consumer-oriented bill that would save Americans money. According to Hatch, "American consumers will save $1 billion in the next 10 years on lower prices for prescription drugs."[103]

Yet passage of this compromise bill was by no means unproblematic. Both Hatch and Waxman were compelled to negotiate with a querulous pharmaceutical industry that was far from monolithic. Precisely because

Hatch-Waxman was a trade-off bill, a compromise between brand-name and generic drug makers, it caused rifts in the traditionally warring factions of the drug industry.[104] A "schism" had emerged. According to James Dickinson, generic and brand-name drug companies had been set against each other for years and the proposed legislation sparked pre-existing rancor.[105] "The long-smoldering fires of change that have been buried deep in both sectors for decades have been released," Dickinson asserted, "and the subsequent reordering of forces that they're now beginning to display have the dynamics of a true revolution." The split, he continued, was wholly unproductive as it had "far more to do with individual product dependence than with long-term philosophy about what was is good overall for the entire industry."[106]

Initially, the Hatch-Waxman law found enough support in Congress and its passage appeared assured.[107] By May and June 1984, however, the fractured consensus was readily apparent. Though a majority of the PMA's thirty-five member board of directors had already voted to support Hatch-Waxman, a coalition of powerful brand-name companies now rebelled and complained openly in the press of how the bill provided insufficient protection against patent infringement—how it essentially favored generic drug companies. This coalition of disgruntled influential firms included Bristol-Myers Co., Merck & Co., Squibb Corp., Hoffman La-Roche Inc., and Johnson & Johnson, who not only ousted PMA President Lewis Engman because he supported Hatch-Waxman, but they also sought to derail the bill. This group of blue-chip companies wielded significant influence, and its representatives were pugnacious during subsequent "eleventh hour" negotiations in August and September. Waxman, undaunted by the setback, commented after meeting representatives of the displeased companies, "I think they don't understand the bill."[108] During testimony to the Senate Labor and Human Resources Committee, a brand-name company representative averred:

> Every recently marketed new drug which has been through the full [FDA] NDA process incurred substantial research and development costs and should be provided with the same reasonable period of exclusivity.

The coalition was ultimately successful in expanding the perimeters of exclusivity and hence their profits for new drugs. The five provisions were included in the Hatch-Waxman legislation during a frenzied period of rewriting in August and early September.[109]

As a direct consequence of Hatch-Waxman, the FDA was inundated with an unprecedented demand for its review and approval of drugs. According to Frank Young, agency budget cuts compounded this dramatic increase in workload.[110] In the wake of Hatch-Waxman, generic drug applications rose from 830 in 1976 to 5,324 in 1986, whereas new brand-name drug applications from 324 in 1975 to 610 in 1990.[111]

For all the changes wrought by the Reagan administration in 1981–1983, the FDA faced a steady number of generic drug applications. In November 1984, the FDA evaluated 270 generic drug industry ANDAs; this was in stark contrast to the forty applications that had been evaluated in the previous month, and generic drug company applications kept pouring in.[112] According to the FDA's own record-keeping, the agency received 1,731 ANDAs in FY 1984. In FY 1985, that number was 2,676. And in F Y1986, that number increased even further, to 5,324. The number of ANDAs *approved* also increased; in FY 1986, 398 generic versions of drug products were approved compared to 117 the previous fiscal year. This was a 340 percent increase over FY1985.[113] These applications, which were facilitated by a piece of legislation touted as a regulatory reform measure, amounted to a remarkable increase in workload and as such, the law, like the earlier opening moves in 1981–1982, had a tremendous impact on the FDA.

In 1984, standing in the White House Rose Garden, President Reagan had promised Hatch-Waxman would provide regulatory relief. The drug approval system, he said, had been modified to assist industry and consumers at large. As the generic drug applications flooded in, the FDA instead found itself swamped with work and the commissioner began to advocate more funding. But was it really the case—as Young averred before Congress—that the FDA was under-funded? In FY 1985, for example, Congress appropriated the FDA an extra $3 million for salaries and seventy-three more employees to implement the Abbreviated New Drug Applications duties provided for in Hatch-Waxman.[114] (To underline the point that the FDA was not starving for resources, it is worth noting that the FDA drug bureau was appropriated an additional $8,350,000 and twenty extra employees to address HIV/AIDS in FY1985).

Furthermore, if the FDA struggled to fulfil its duties under Hatch-Waxman in subsequent years, the agency's budget requests and productivity reports certainly did not reflect such difficulty; the FDA's 1987 budget report to its appropriator, the Committee on Appropriations Subcommittee on Agriculture, stated it was in fact coping with the generic drug applications. "The FDA developed and implemented procedures for processing the large volume of ANDAs submitted when the legislation became effective," the FDA budget report read. It concluded in glowing fashion, "By January 1986, the goal of reviewing ANDAs within 180 days (as required by the Act) was *exceeded*, with average review time reduced to less than 135 days."[115] Commissioner Young stated in 1989 that Hatch-Waxman had placed an enormous burden on FDA staff, but the staff had nevertheless completed their bioequivalence reviews "of almost all submissions" within the maximum allowable period. In short, the generic drug provisions of the Drug Price Competition and Patent Restoration Act did not inflict major damage on the FDA; rather, the FDA demonstrated (or said it demonstrated) it was capable of meeting the requirements of the new legislation and managing the workload.

Conclusions

In 1983–1984, as U.S. pharmaceutical industry prices and profits grew on the domestic front, the FDA was forced to deal with three significant, interconnected events. First, the Reagan administration's enthusiasm for regulatory reform diminished. According to Vice President Bush, the administration had achieved all that it could to alter the nation's regulatory architecture—including the FDA. Second, Arthur Hull Hayes, the FDA commissioner left the institution and returned to the confines of university life. He had grown disgruntled with the interference of Congress and claimed that he had achieved what he could. Third, and most significantly, new legislation was passed, legislation that was emblematic of the times and embodied Reagan's regulatory reform goals. The Hatch-Waxman amendments authorized the FDA to approve drugs without unnecessary duplicative data and lengthened patent terms for new, innovative drugs. The law, though bipartisan in nature, duly affected the FDA—just as the Reagan administration efforts had in the early 1980s.

These events represented further evolution and change at the FDA. The Reagan years had, thus far, been challenging, transitional ones for staff members at the FDA. They were difficult times, which served to confuse and demoralize some employees. Already, the agency had been rocked by scandal and crisis: both Oraflex and the Tylenol poisoning had posed challenges to the FDA. Already, critics had come out and publicly stated that the FDA was not doing its job correctly; moreover, resources had dwindled and it was perceived that morale had shriveled.

Still, the pressure on the FDA to reform—a pressure that emanated from the executive office—was alleviated. If the vice president was correct, the drive to transform the FDA further had abated. It appeared that neither the public nor the Reagan administration possessed the desire to advance the deregulatory experiment any further. The passage of the Hatch-Waxman amendments also demonstrated that multiple actors were effective in implementing change at the FDA. The agency could begin to create a strategy to fulfil its mandate knowing full well that no more dramatic change was coming—knowing the fiduciary restraints with which they had to work.

NOTES

1. "Aid Urged for Drug Industry," *New York Times*, September 5, 1983, 31.
2. James Dickinson, "Washington Report," *Pharmaceutical Technology*, November 1983, 20–23.
3. Ed Magnuson, "Three Steps Forward, Two Back," *Time* 122, August 29, 1983, 16.

4. Ibid.

5. Ibid.

6. Michael DeCourcy Hinds, "Cost Benefits vs. Safety: Politics and Mathematics Can Be Difficult to Separate When it Gets to Regulations," *New York Times*, July 24, 1982, 8.

7. Magnuson, "Three Steps Forward, Two Back," 16.

8. Martin Tolchin and Susan J. Tolchin, "The Rush to Deregulate" *New York Times*, August 21, 1983, SM34.

9. Magnuson, Three Steps Forward, Two Back," 16. See also Phillip J. Cooper, *The War on Regulation*, 33–35.

10. John Karaagac, *Between Promise and Policy: Ronald Reagan and Conservative Reformism* (New York: Lexington Books, 2000), 157.

11. Ronnie Dugger, *On Reagan: The Man & His Presidency* (New York: McGraw-Hill Book Company, 1983), 174.

12. Magnuson, "Three Steps Forward, Two Back," 16–17.

13. Tolchin and Tolchin, "The Rush to Deregulate," SM34.

14. Guthrie S. Birkhead, "Reagan's First Term," *Public Administration Review* 45 (6) (1985): 869–875.

15. Robert M. Collins, *Transforming America: Politics and Culture in the Reagan Years* (New York: Columbia University Press, 2007), 82.

16. Clifford Winston and Robert Crandall, "Explaining Regulatory Policy," *Brookings Papers on Economic Activity, Microeconomics* (1994) 16–17.

17. Tolchin and Tolchin, "The Rush to Deregulate," SM34.

18. "Aid Urged for Drug Industry," 31.

19. Kip Visuci, "The Misspecified Agenda: The 1980s Reforms of Health, Safety and Environmental Regulation," in *American Economic Policy in the 1980s*, ed. by Martin Feldstein (Chicago: University of Chicago Press, 1994), 501.

20. Garry Wills, *Reagan's America: Innocents at Home* (New York: Penguin Books; Company Inc., 1987), 368.

21. Michael Schaller, *Reckoning with Reagan: America and Its President in the 1980s* (New York: Oxford University Press, 1992), 50.

22. Peter J. Wallison, *Ronald Reagan: The Power of Conviction and the Success of His Presidency* (Boulder, CO: Westview Press, 2003), 9.

23. Wills,*Regan's America* 369–370.

24. Ibid.

25. Herbert Stein, *Presidential Economics: The Making of Economic Policy From Roosevelt to Clinton, 3rd ed.* (Washington, D.C.: American Enterprise Institute, 1994), 406.

26. Birkhead, "Reagan's First Term," 872.

27. Michael L. Millenson, "FDA: America's watchdog in distress," *Chicago Tribune*, September 19, 1983, 1.

28. Susan Jenks, "FDA's Inaction on Zomax is probed by House panel," *Washinton Times*, April 28, 1983, no page number—found at FDA Biomedical Library in 1983 Clipping Service.

29. Committee on Government Operations, *FDA's Regulation of Zomax*, 98th Congress, 1st Session, April 26 and 27, 1983, 443.

30. Ibid.

31. Ibid.

32. Ibid. See also James Dickinson, "Washington Report," *Pharmaceutical Technology*, October 1983, 22 and "Search for Hayes' successor will be tough one," *Drug Topics*, September 5, 1983, 10.

33. Robert Pear, "F.D.A. Chief Leaving to Join Westchester Medical School," *New York Times*, July 29, 1983, B8.

34. James Dickinson, "Washington Report," *Pharmaceutical Technology*, November 1983, 20–23.

35. Committee on the Judiciary and Committee on Labor and Public Welfare. *Regulation of New Drug R&D by the Food and Drug Administration*, 93rd Congress, 1974, 207.

36. Ibid.

37. Committee on Government Operations, *The Regulation of New Drugs By the FDA: The New Drug Review Process*, August 3 & 4, 97th Congress, 1984, 293–295.

38. Committee on Appropriations, *Arthur Hull Hayes Jr. testimony to Agriculture, Rural Development and Related Agencies Appropriations for 1983*, 97th Congress, 2nd Session, 595.

39. "Statistical Report, 1987–1988," Offices of Drug Evaluation. Food and Drug Administration (Washington, D.C.: Government Printing Office, 1988) found in the FDA Collection RS.N48 and Samuel Gilston, "New Drug Pipeline is Filling Up," *Medical Advertising News*, November 15, 1983.

40. James Dickinson, "Washington Report," *Pharmaceutical Technology*, November 1983, 20–23.

41. James Dickinson, "Washington Report," *Pharmaceutical Technology*, February 1981, 24.

42. Vartanig G. Vartan, "Drug Stocks Finding Favor," *New York Times*, January 21, 1981, D8.

43. "It was a very good year," *Drug Topics*, July 2, 1984, 22.

44. Ibid.

45. Henry Grabowski, "An Analysis of US International Competitiveness in Pharmaceuticals," *Managerial and Decision Economics* 10 (1989): 27–33.

46. Cristine Russell, "New Studies Find Prescription Drugs 'Least Expensive Form' of Therapy," *Washington Post*, June 20, 1984, A2.

47. "Abbott's Profit Gains by 17.9 percent," *New York Times*, April 8, 1983, D5, "Johnson & Johnson To Raise Payout 8 percent; Sales Gain Reported," *Wall Street Journal*, April 22, 1983, 56, and James C. Abegglen, "Merck Finds a Formula for Success," *New York Times*, October 30, 1983.

48. Gilston, "New Drug Pipeline is Filling Up."

49. Charles Morris, "Interview with Arthur Hayes," *Food Engineering*, October 1983, 18.

50. Shirley Hobbs Scheibla, "Drug on the Market: Examining What's Wrong With the FDA," *Barron's National Business and Financial Weekly*, April 16, 1984, 22–23.

51. Gilston, "New Drug Pipeline is Filling Up."

52. C. Joseph Stetler, "It's Your Business," RADIO TV REPORTS, INC., June 3, 1984. FDA Daily Clipping Service, FDA Biomedical Sciences Library.

53. C. Joseph Stetler, "What Happened to FDA Regulatory Reform?" *Pharmacy Times*, July 1984, 6

54. Stetler, "What Happened to FDA Regulatory Reform?" 6 and C. Joseph Stetler, "It's Your Business," RADIO TV REPORTS, INC.

55. "Aid Urged for Drug Industry," *New York Times*, September, 1983, 31.

56. Ibid.

57. Ibid.

58. *Legislative and Administrative Changes Needed to Improve Regulation of the Drug Industry, Report to the Congress*. U.S. General Accounting Office (Washington, D.C.: Government Printing Office, HRD-83–24 April 5, 1983).

59. "Search for Hayes' successor will be tough one," *Drug Topics*, September 5, 1983, 10.

60. "Hayes Departs for Academia," *FDA Today*, September, 1983, 1.

61. Philip J. Hilts, *Protecting America's Health*, 238

62. "Acting FDA Chief Named," *New York Times*, September 2, 1983, A11.

63. James Dickinson, "Washington Report," *Pharmaceutical Technology*, September 1983, 48.

64. Paul Hile, FDA Oral History Collection, 113–114.

65. James Dickinson, "Washington Report," 48.

66. "Acting FDA Chief Named," *New York Times*, September 2, 1983, A11.

67. Hilts, *Protecting America's Health*, 238.

68. Cristine Russell, "New Chief Casts Widely for New Ideas," *Washington Post*, October 25, 1984, A23.

69. Marjorie Sun, "Young Plans Management Reforms at FDA," *Science* 227, January 18, 1985, 277–278.

70. Samuel Gilston, "FDA's New Commissioner, Frank Young," *Medical Advertising News,* September 30, 1984.

71. Shirley Hobbs Scheibla, "Young Ideas: Meet the New Head of the FDA," *Barron's National Business and Financial Weekly,* June 4, 1984, 13.

72. Sun, "Young Plans Management Reforms at FDA," 277–278.

73. Paul Hile, FDA Oral History Collection, 132

74. Scheilba, "Young Ideas," 13–14.

75. Bill Robinson, "Frank Young takes over 'new challenges' at FDA helm," *Drug Topics,* September 3, 1984, 24–26 and Cristine Russell, "New Chief Casts Widely for New Ideas."

76. Ibid.

77. Paul Hile, FDA Oral History Collection, 132

78. Bill Robinson, "Get on the Bus FDA chief tells health professions," *Drug Topics,* October 15, 1984 and also see Russell, "New Chief Casts Widely for New Ideas," A23.

79. Charles Gorton Interview, FDA Oral History Collection, 18.

80. William Hubbard Interview, FDA Oral History Collection, 32–33. As good as Young was at securing money for the agency, when controlled for inflation the FDA's budget in the 1980s remained virtually static.

81. Committee on Government Operations, *Therapeutic Drugs for AIDS: Development, Testing, and Availability,* 100th Congress, 2nd Session, 1988, 390.

82. Committee on Government Operations, *FDA Proposals to Ease Restrictions on the Use and Sale of Experimental Drugs,* 100th Congress, 1st Session, April 29, 1987, 78.

83. Committee on Government Operations, *Therapeutic Drugs for AIDS: Development, Testing, and Availability,* 100th Congress, 2nd Session, 1988, 389.

84. Ronald Reagan, *Remarks on Signing the Drug Price Competition and Patent Term Restoration Act of 1984,* Sept. 24, 1984, posted at www.reagan.edu/archives/speeches/1984/92484.htm, consulted October 22, 2005

85. Ibid.

86. Alan D. Lourie, "Patent Term Restoration: History, Summary, and Appraisal," *Food, Drug, Cosmetic Law Journal* 40 (1985): 351–362.

87. Henry G. Grabowski, John M Vernon, and L.G. Thomas, "Estimating the Effects of Regulation on Innovation: An International Comparative Analysis of the Pharmaceutical Industry," *Journal of Law & Economics* 31 (1) (1978): 133–163 and Henry Grabowski, "An Analysis of US International Competitiveness in Pharmaceuticals": 27–33.

88. Lourie, "Patent Term Restoration: History, Summary, and Appraisal," 352–353.

89. Ibid.

90. Ibid.

91. "FDA Backs Drug Makers," *New York Times,* February 5, 1982, D8.

92. Robert Pear, "Drug Patent Extension Draws Heavy Lobbying," *New York Times,* July 28, 1982, D1.

93. Ibid. Mossinghoff's full title in the Reagan administration was Assistant Secretary of Commerce, Commissioner of Patents and Trademarks. The position was later changed and called Under Secretary of Commerce for Intellectual Property. Mossinghoff, now one of the most important patent lawyers in the United States, serves as an excellent example of how individual actors in the system of health product regulation might occupy multiple positions and thereby influence the governing structure and agency of the FDA.

94. Ibid.

95. Ibid.

96. Lourie, "Patent Term Restoration: History, Summary, and Appraisal," 351–362.

97. U.S. Food and Drug Administration, *Milestones in U.S. Food and Drug Law History,* posted at www.fda.gov.opacom/backgrounders/miles.html, consulted November 22, 2005

98. Ibid, consulted November 22, 2005. Henry Grabowski and John Vernon, "Longer Patents for Lower Imitation Barriers: The 1984 Drug Act," *American Economic Review* 76 (1986): 197–198.

99. Irvin Molotsky, "This Odd Couple Focuses on Health," *New York Times,* September 14, 1984, A24.

100. Ibid.

101. Doug Bandow, "Demonizing Drugmakers: The Political Assault on the Pharmaceutical Industry," *Policy Analysis* 475 (2003): 19.

102. Ibid.

103. Arlen J. Large, "Drug Patent Bill Clears House on a Voice Vote—Long Debated Measure Gives Extended Patent Rights, Speeds Generic Marketing," *Wall Street Journal,* September 13, 1984, 1.

104. Ibid.

105. "PMA rift healing, exec says" *Advertising Age,* November 12, 1984: no page number available: FDA Biomedical Library Clipping Service.

106. James Dickinson, "Washington Report," *Pharmaceutical Technology,* November 1983: no page number available: FDA Biomedical Library Clipping Service.

107. The PMA, the Generic Pharmaceutical Industry Association, the AFL-CIO, and National Council of Senior Citizens all publicly supported the bill.

108. Irvin Molotsky, "Big Drug Makers Fail to Stall Bill Aiding Generics," *New York Times,* June 8, 1984, D2. The coalition of brand-name drug companies well understood the legislation and its principal objective was to broaden the exclusivity provisions of the pending legislation in five ways. The companies wanted written into the bill (1) protections for drugs which had new indications; (2) new dosage forms; (3) new release mechanisms; (4) new delivery systems and, finally; (5) innovative formulations.

109. Stuart M. Pape, "Market Exclusivity Under the Drug Price Competition and Patent Term Restoration Act of 1984—The Five Clauses," *Food, Drug, Cosmetic Law Journal* 30 (1985): 310–316.

110. Frank Young and James Norris, "Leadership Change and Action Planning: A Case Study," *Public Administration Review* 48 (1988): 564–570.

111. Mary K. Olson, "Regulatory Discretion Among Competing Industries: Inside the FDA," *Journal of Law, Organization & Economics* 11 (1995): 379–405.

112. Janet Ochs Wiener, "FDA Scandal: White Hats, Black Hats, Gray Areas," *Medicine & Health,* December 11, 1989, 12–13.

113. *FDA Quarterly Activities Reports,* Fiscal Year 1986, 4th Quarter, 16.

114. *FDA Quarterly Activities Reports,* Fiscal Year 1985, 1st Quarter, 16.

115. Committee on Appropriations, *Agriculture, Rural Development and Related Agencies Appropriations for 1987,* 1988, 755. Italics are mine.

Chapter Six

Reagan's Leadership, Health Activism, and the HIV/AIDS Crisis

"While there has been much effort to refocus the FDA toward patients the past eight years, there has been relative silence from one man: Ronald Reagan." [1]

WALL STREET JOURNAL, OCTOBER 13, 1988

"Each of those folks [AIDS activists] thought there was a drug that was the next magic bullet that could save lives, if FDA would just put them on the market. And so you had this synergy between these ultraliberal AIDS activists and these almost rightwing conservatives who wanted regulation reduced." [2]

FDA ASSOCIATE COMMISSIONER FOR POLICY AND PLANNING
WILLIAM HUBBARD, JULY 27, 2005

The beginning of the AIDS epidemic in the 1980s placed tremendous strain on the Food and Drug Administration. Much has already been written of it—and this body of literature continues to expand—but careful consideration of this subject matter is of crucial significance to understanding the communication and relationship between regulatory agencies, the executive branch, industry, and the public during the Reagan years. [3]

Periodically, the FDA has undergone phases in which various priorities dominated. At one point or another it has distinguished itself as a regulatory, law enforcement, or science agency, depending on the political party in power, the ideology of the FDA commissioner, and the influence of external stakeholders.[4] The AIDS epidemic, which gave birth to a new and assertive coalition of issue activists, reformers, and libertarians, tested the agency's institutional identity and served as what political scientist Thomas Birkland calls a "focusing event."[5] To other commentators, the FDA's management of the AIDS crisis was a serious blunder.[6] Despite the absence of presidential leadership, the FDA, a bureaucracy with a formidable institutional identity, succeeded in rising to the challenge of the AIDS epidemic in the 1980s by transforming its existing regulatory rules, reaching out to the AIDS movement and the pharmaceutical industry, and maintaining its strong commitment to consumer protection.[7]

The first U.S. cases of what became known as HIV/AIDS occurred in the late 1970s. Homosexual men in San Francisco began showing up at local clinics complaining of swollen glands, and they then began to die of unusual diseases (e.g., Kaposi's sarcoma) and a form of pneumonia not commonly seen in the young, *pneumocystis carinii*. In June 1981, the federal Centers for Disease Control's *Morbidity and Mortality Weekly Report* began alerting doctors nationwide of these new developments and by the end of the year, the number of immune collapse cases in homosexual men rose to 180. In mid-1982, good evidence that the disease was sexually transmitted finally surfaced; at the conclusion of summer, 505 cases had been reported, with 202 dead.[8]

By April 1984, Secretary of Health and Human Services Margaret Heckler announced that scientists had identified the source of AIDS as a retrovirus, soon labeled human immunodeficiency virus (HIV). By the beginning of 1985, AIDS had killed an estimated 5,600 Americans. By January 1989, when Reagan left office, FDA policy changes were well underway and there was still only one AIDS drug on the market even though the Centers for Disease Control had confirmed 82,764 cases and 46,344 deaths.[9]

President Reagan's Lack of Leadership

Amid this growing public health crisis, the FDA was not given a clear policy direction from the White House, Congress, or the HHS. "It was tough," wrote Democratic political operative Bob Shrum, "to get Congress or the administration to act."[10] However, President Reagan's leadership on the HIV/AIDS issue was notably lacking. According to Associate Commissioner for Policy and Planning William Hubbard, it was perceived "within the FDA that the Reagan administration didn't want to talk about AIDS for a long time."[11] Because "Reagan was President," Hubbard added, "AIDS activists concluded that the agency was sitting on lifesaving AIDS drugs and refusing to let patients have them, sort of a ban by the social conservatives."[12] By other accounts, the president was "uncomprehending," "dithering," and "slow to confront the issue."[13] Larry Kramer, a fierce and especially vocal

Figure 6.1.   The AIDS Memorial Quilt was conceived in 1985 and celebrates the lives of those who died of AIDS. It was one effort on the part of activists to generate awareness for the enormity of the AIDS pandemic. From the Library of Congress. Carol M. Highsmith photographer.

militant, went so far as to say "AIDS is our Holocaust and Reagan is our Hitler."[14]

President Reagan's response to HIV/AIDS was indeed questionable. First, he mentioned HIV/AIDS only once publicly before the film actor Rock Hudson (a friend from Hollywood days) died of AIDS in October 1985, at which point the president asked for more information from the White House physician. Reagan did not speak of AIDS again until February 1986 when he instructed his Surgeon General, C. Everett Koop, to make a report on the problem. Second, Reagan elected to ignore the counsel of his wife, who pushed him to endorse the use of condoms. Third, the president allowed his staff to delete mention of Ryan White from a widely awaited address in May 1987 to the American Foundation for AIDS Research. White, a haemophiliac teenager, who had been ostracized in his hometown of Kokomo, Indiana after he had contracted AIDS from a blood-clotting agent, was a pointed example that anyone could contract the disease. Fourth, in June 1987, the Reagan administration established a presidential commission on HIV/AIDS. Its mission was to investigate the disease in its entirety and recommend solutions. After conducting hearings into all aspects of the situation, the presidential commission produced a report in June 1988 which offered a number of measures. According to the House Committee on Government Operations, the president's response to the recommendations was to shelve them until his White House staff had properly studied them. [15]

The FDA's Drug Policy: Balancing Risk and Safety

A risk always exists in ingesting an FDA-approved drug, even though the agency strives to minimize that danger to the greatest extent possible. In short, a sick patient faces a trade-off between possible therapeutic gains and possible adverse reactions. With unapproved, experimental drugs, however, the degree of risk jumps markedly.

Unfortunately, for most dreadfully sick patients the logic of "sound science" means little. When death is imminent, most desperately ill patients will opt to take an experimental drug, with or without the completion of clinical trials and the blessing of the FDA. The predominance of AIDS crystallized this fact in the 1980s. According to author Daniel Harris:

> Much as discrepancies of class cause crime and riots, discrepancies of knowledge also cause social unrest. A case in point is modern medicine: As it becomes more and more inaccessible to the general public, we can see a form of revolt, an uprising in which the masses, starved by ignorance if not by famine, attempt to take back what they have lost to their internists: the control of their health and well-being. [16]

In other words, the HIV/AIDS crisis brought into stark relief the precarious stability between consumer safety and product innovation, the issue of scientific credibility, and the precise role of the drug regulator. Important questions were asked of officials at the FDA. At what point must the regulatory rules be bent or amended? Who has the right to deny someone an unapproved, foreign drug when that person's life hangs in the balance?

Young articulated his recognition of the public's and health community's concerns about regulatory policy. "AIDS has focused attention on the issue of compassionate use of experimental drugs as never before," Young declared in 1987. [17] Young also understood that American laypeople and agency stakeholders demanded a recalibration of safety, innovation, and access. [18] To a gathering at the Institutes of Medicine in 1987, he emphasized that many dying patients will "try anything," even in the face of considerable risk; yet Young also stated that important ethical concerns had to be reconciled with the FDA's "need to study drugs thoroughly and carefully and base our decisions regarding treatment uses on good science." [19] In making these remarks, Young struck a middle ground. He not only defended the agency's opposition to unfettered access to experimental drugs, its reliance on sound science, and fidelity to consumer protection, but as a counterpoint, Young also left the door open for increased compassionate access to certain types of drugs. Moreover, he signaled that the FDA was not unbendingly loyal to the established regulatory protocols; that its institutional identity was mutable rather than fixed, and that its officials were receptive to change rather than rigid.

Young made his rational and balanced rhetoric policy with the August 1987 Action Plan Phase II, a long-term planning document. A year in the making, Action Plan Phase II outlined that the "timely and efficient" review of AIDS therapies was the agency's principal objective. An interrelated goal of Action Plan Phase II was "continued improvement of the drug and device approval process."[20] Quicker approval of AIDS drugs was thus the central goal of Action Plan Phase II.[21]

The FDA's Action Plan Phase II was developed with and underpinned by the understanding that the agency's stakeholders wanted a recalibration of the balance between safety, risk, and innovation. When the FDA's Office of Planning and Management surveyed outsiders, respondents rated new product approval and new drug review as most significant, whereas risk assessment and risk management were regarded as subordinate priorities. The pendulum had seemingly swung away from safety and consumer protection, and the agency's stakeholders wanted a focus on the rapid approval of new drug products. "We must ensure that we act as a bridge between basic and applied research," Young proclaimed in 1988, "not as a barrier."[22]

The development and approval of the first antiviral AIDS drug, brand name Retrovir, acts as an instructive example of the FDA as a bridge. Originally developed in the 1960s as a cancer treatment, the chemical compound azidothymidine, or AZT, had languished in obscurity until Burroughs Wellcome, a major drug company, opened its considerable drug inventory for testing. Duke University and the National Institutes of Health subsequently tested AZT at taxpayer expense. In 1985, Burroughs Wellcome filed the customary new drug application (NDA) for AZT—at which point the FDA's regulatory posture became integral to the swift development of the drug. The FDA approved the first clinical testing of the drug within five days. To determine the safety of the compound, Phase I trials were carried out using approximately twenty-five live test subjects. Thereafter, Phase II trials, using hundreds of patients, commenced. The FDA worked closely with Burroughs Wellcome throughout these clinical trials. When the Phase II trials bore fruit in the form of remarkably positive results the FDA allowed the drug to go on the market without conducting Phase III trials.[23] In the final event, the review and expedited approval of AZT took 107 days, while the clinical trials took twenty-two months.[24]

Both industry and the FDA were pleased with the outcome. FDA official Dr. Ellen Cooper explained: "there has been a strong emphasis within the agency on working to streamline the process by eliminating any gaps in communication."[25] The cooperation with Burroughs Wellcome, Cooper added, was advantageous because it "kept both parties abreast of the other's advances, problems, and needs." This cooperation also had positive results, because it "took less time to review the [drug trial] results than might otherwise have been the case."[26] According to Deputy Director of Biologics Research and Review Dr. James Bilstad, AZT demonstrated "that FDA, industry, and other agencies can work together quickly and effectively to develop, test, and review drugs to combat AIDS."[27] A delighted Dr. David Barry, Burroughs Wellcome's chief researcher, said, "After less than two years, we are at the point we would normally be at after four to five years."[28]

The approval of AZT was the FDA's most visible success against AIDS, and it encapsulated just how much the agency had committed itself to maintaining a balance between consumer protection and regulatory relief, sound science and responsiveness to external group pressures. It also moved on other fronts to further recalibrate the balance between safety and risk.

From 1987 onward, the FDA made three internal bureaucratic changes as a response to the outcry for faster new drugs, and it is worth noting that these were administrative rather than legislative in nature, and thus Congress was not directly involved. First, Deputy Commissioner John Norris contended that the agency had truncated a year from the document-processing time during the drug review process, a major development since it had only recently taken three years for the FDA to study the information that companies submit in conjunction with their drugs. To use bureaucratic argot, this streamlining was called "rationalizing the procedure."[29] Second, in 1987 the agency created a special 1-AA designation for AIDS related drugs. According to Young, the initiative was designed to place greater emphasis on AIDS drugs and it would ensure such drugs received "our highest priority at all stages of the review process."[30] Lastly, in April 1988, the FDA announced the formation of a new division of the Center for Drug Evaluation and Research. The new division, led by Dr. Ellen Cooper, the principal medical officer overseeing the approval of AZT, was charged with reviewing antiviral and anti-infective drugs with direct application for AIDS.[31]

These modifications to existing drug policy signified that the FDA was willing to respond to the AIDS epidemic with rapid reform. Yet these bureaucratic changes were not the only actions taken. The FDA also proposed four formal regulations during the Reagan years that provided greater access to unapproved, experimental drugs and foreign drugs. What follows is an examination of those regulations.

From Informal to Formal Regulatory Change

In response to criticism from a new and vigorous coalition of AIDS activists and regulatory reformers, Commissioner Young implemented a regulatory approach that emphasized safety, but also flexibility and a new consumerist vision.[32] His approach included the promulgation of a number of new regulatory measures to deal with the AIDS epidemic as well as the drug lag. These regulations are outlined below and the key changes were the first and the third of these measures:

1. Treatment use of investigational new drugs (IND)
2. Liberalized interpretation of import regulations
3. Subpart E regulations to speed the approval process
4. Parallel track system to allow drug access early in the testing process

The FDA's first response to the clamor for change in its drug regulations was the treatment IND regulation. It generated a substantial amount of press and faced a commensurate level of opposition; as such, it demonstrates the tensions of the period. The treatment IND was first proposed by FDA in June 1983. Signed off by the Secretary of Health and Human Services and passed onto the Office of Management and Budget (OMB) in July 1985, the regulation held that "treatment INDs are designed primarily for drugs in Phase III, when sufficient evidence of safety and effectiveness has been established to warrant therapeutic use." After a prolonged period of negotiation between the OMB and the FDA, the treatment IND regulation was formalized in June 1987.

All in all, the regulation provided sick consumers greater access to promising new drugs *before* final approval of that drug. Once a drug was given treatment IND status by the FDA, physicians then had the choice to acquire that drug from the pharmaceutical firm. FDA officials also decided that the drug needed to treat a serious or immediately life-threatening illness for which there was no satisfactory alternative treatment and the clinical evidence had to demonstrate that the drug was safe and *may be* effective. In essence, the new regulation formalized access for all patients and physicians to experimental drugs previously available in individual cases or isolated circumstances (but it also benefited manufacturers as well in that it allowed them to recoup costs of research, production, and distribution earlier).[33]

The treatment IND measure was heralded as a major breakthrough and was received with considerable fanfare by activists and the press.[34] *The Economist,* for example, reported that the "FDA's step should be applauded, and then copied elsewhere."[35] Enactment of the regulation was a victory for ill patients and anti-regulatory proponents, but not a substantial one, since it codified established practice; the first antiviral AIDS drug, AZT, had already been tested on 4,000 human subjects prior to the treatment IND regulation, for instance. Still, the new measure was important because it symbolized bureaucratic flexibility, recognition of the magnitude of the current health crisis, and the need to minimize and negotiate negative public feedback. According to the FDA's own polling, newness was what most stakeholders sought, whereas risk management was of less importance. If the agency did not respect the stakeholders and meet the challenge of AIDS by enacting new regulatory policies, respect for the FDA would, in turn, slowly diminish.[36]

The treatment IND regulation was hardly greeted with universal favor. Among its many critics, Senator Edward Kennedy (D-Mass), charged: "The real long term effects of these regulations are likely to be: (1) lengthening of the time needed to develop safe and effective drugs; (2) confusion over the meaning of FDA approval; (3) the inclusion of only poor and low income people in the drug evaluating process and; (4) a marked increase in the number of lay media reports of spectacular therapeutic results. Finally, the possibility of selling experimental drugs is likely to stimulate unscrupulous firms to promote unfounded reports of the new miraculous drugs."[37]

Representative Ted Weiss (D-NY) agreed with Kennedy's broad assessment, but went much further in his condemnation. "Many of the nation's preeminent experts in the public health service have concluded that the new regulations are counterproductive," he declared. "The regulations are a disaster." The provisions of the Treatment IND were, he perceived, unduly dangerous and usurped a degree of the commissioner's traditional authority. In Weiss's assessment, the blame ultimately lay with the Office of Management and Budget for its uneducated heavy-handedness during the development of the regulation. "OMB," he alleged, "under the guise of assisting people with AIDS is, in fact, attempting to dismantle the regulatory complex and OMB justifies this on the grounds that there are many people who are desperately ill who have no hope."[38]

Indeed, the treatment IND regulation also faced opposition inside the confines of the FDA. There was little that resembled a united front. Dr. James Bilstad, a figure so integral in the cooperative approval of AZT, served as an advisor to Ted Weiss's committee and was reported to have told subcommittee staff that he did not know anyone within the Center for Drugs and Biologics who supports the provisions.[39] Another FDA employee, Dr. Robert Temple, took issue with the language of the treatment IND. Notes he provided to the committee read, "Regulations need to say what we mean. Can't regulate through commissioner's speech. No one then knows, inside or out; consistency virtually impossible." He added, "the [regulation's] preamble still seems weak to me and the words of the regulation itself pose many problems."[40]

In 1988, the FDA adopted a second regulation dealing with the illegal importing of drugs for personal use. This regulation allowed a given individual, with the support of a supervising doctor, to import a three-month supply of a given drug. Prior to the enactment of this regulation, patients imported drugs (illegally) through the use of pharmaceutical buying clubs. This import policy, though, was similar to the treatment IND in that it codified a standard FDA practice of noninterference with the buying clubs; the only new provision mandated that the clubs send the drugs directly to individual users. This was a tip of the hat to pharmaceutical firms, so that buyers avoided conflict with regulations prohibiting the import of commercial quantities. [41]

In October 1988, the FDA moved forward on a third regulation, the modification of treatment IND regulations through Subpart E provisions. This important regulation further truncated the drug review process, because the FDA decided to work more closely with drug researchers in industry to design experiments during the first two stages of the human-testing process, thereby eliminating the final phase. Underpinning the Subpart E regulation was the hope that manufacturers (for AIDS and other life-threatening and severely debilitating diseases) would meet with FDA drug officials earlier and more frequently, rather than later and rarely. Such collegiality between FDA officials and drug company scientists was deemed positive, and would naturally result in a streamlined review process. [42]

At the FDA, however, this regulation was not treated lightly nor accepted easily. As in the case of Treatment IND, there was substantial recalcitrance among FDA drug officials, feelings which nearly scuttled the measure. In the fall of 1988, Young faced staunch resistance to the plan. The *Wall Street Journal* reported at the time, "career bureaucrats inside the FDA have dug in their heels to insist on provisions that essentially would eviscerate the initiative's goal of faster approvals of drugs to treat life-threatening diseases." It continued: "Frank Young, though he personally supports the change, is said to have concluded that he can't overcome opposition within his own bureaucracy."[43] Vice President Bush and the Regulatory Task Force had a direct hand in proposing and crafting the regulation; for this reason, activists were likely sceptical of the measure. Right or wrong, these detractors viewed the regulation as subverting the safety of the American public in addition to the FDA's core principles, which rested on sound science and an arms-length distance from industry.

Much of the internal resistance originated in the Office of New Drug Evaluation (ONDE). Its head, Dr. Robert Temple, emphasized that drug approvals should depend on a "meaningful endpoint."[44] Consumer safety, he stated, was compromised when the third phase of clinical trials were abandoned at the behest of the public and politicians. AZT, for instance, had shown a number of contraindications, notably a harmful level of toxicity. It was far from safe and Temple and other ONDE officials feared a loosening of standards in the rush to approve new AIDS drugs. Such figures also feared that the office's regulatory authority was being undermined and the tenuous symmetry between safety and risk was being remodeled. The resistance inside the FDA illustrated that while it was willing to modify its regulatory policy, it was still a multifaceted agency that was loyal to consumer protection.

The showdown at the FDA ended a little over a week after the 700-strong demonstration at FDA Headquarters in Rockville, Maryland. On October 19, 1988, Subpart E provisions were enacted and immediately hailed as a profoundly important recalibration of the balance between risks and benefits. The *Wall Street Journal* was ebullient about the new regulation and it praised both Young and the agency's officials. They "deserve credit," the paper proclaimed, "for committing themselves to such a significant change in long-standing procedures. The nature of a bureaucracy, public or private, is to resist change as an unwarranted challenge to its competence and authority."[45]

The fourth regulatory change made by the FDA was the enactment of parallel track measures. Where the earlier treatment IND status allowed a gravely ill patient access to experimental drugs during clinical trials in Phase II or Phase III testing, parallel track measures allowed patients access to those drugs even sooner. Patients with no available alternatives could now acquire drugs in or after Phase I testing, but only for AIDS or HIV-related illness. The pharmaceutical company provided such drugs. This change was instituted only for AIDS patients with no other available option and for those unable to participate in clinical trials.[46] According to a National Research Council report, "the parallel track was described as an alternative Phase II model" that fit within the FDA's regulatory framework, but "it was in reality an ad hoc concession to public pressure that demanded wide distribution of clinically unproved new drugs."[47]

In a broader sense, the four regulations described above had a profound impact on the way drugs are developed and distributed in the United States. They represented the FDA's capacity to respond to the public's cry for change and how the agency was willing, though not uniformly so, to shift the balance between safety and risk. Though the public and media reaction to the regulations varied, these regulations, in their totality, accelerated the procedures and processes of basic research and clinical investigations.

The FDA and the AIDS Movement

The FDA chose to make bureaucratic policy changes and promulgate new drug regulations during the AIDS crisis for a number of reasons. Chief among those reasons was the pressure from external groups, including the energetic, resourceful, and oftentimes militant AIDS movement.

Both Project Inform and ACT-UP were instrumental in influencing the FDA's response to the HIV/AIDS crisis. San Francisco-based Project Inform, founded in 1985 by Martin Delaney, worked to create awareness of

AIDS and secure speedier approval of drugs. Additionally, Project Inform earmarked funds and solicited scientific assistance from its members in order to conduct its own illegal, underground drug trials. In 1987, Larry Kramer founded another organization, the militant New York-based AIDS Coalition to Unleash Power (ACT-UP), which held the same goals as Project Inform. ACT-UP, however, surpassed its predecessor in generating media attention. In March 1987, ACT-UP successfully blocked off parts of Wall Street in New York. Thereafter, ACT-UP directed its anger at the FDA for perceived complicity during the AIDS crisis and the FDA, to its credit, tackled the AIDS epidemic by reassessing and modifying its regulatory policies but also by extending an olive branch to the AIDS movement.[48]

The AIDS movement was a formidable political force, including grass-roots activists and advocacy organizations, health care providers, journalists, and writers. In the 1970s, there had been a disorganized drive for gay rights, but the gay community needed the awful alarm of AIDS to galvanize itself. The movement, as finally constituted, was uniquely positioned to influence FDA's regulatory policy for several reasons. First, HIV/AIDS was contracted by many citizens in their twenties and thirties, a certain demographic of the population for which there existed, "little social expectation that they will passively await death."[49] Second, this nascent movement consisted of and was dominated by white, middle-class men with fund-raising strengths; that is, people who were themselves doctors, scientists, educators, nurses, professionals, and other intellectuals. These movement characteristics (scientific credibility, economic strength, media savvy) were unique for a group that claimed to be oppressed and they, not surprisingly, increased the likelihood that the group could successfully cooperate with and influence FDA drug officers.[50]

Relations between the FDA and the AIDS movement were far from cordial. The AIDS movement had vehemently impugned the FDA for what it regarded as disastrously antiquated regulatory policies. In one case, ACT-UP founder Larry Kramer hyperbolically likened one FDA official's behavior to that of a "murderer."[51] Predictably, when Young began "the process of reaching out to those folks," it did not go smoothly.[52] Activists advocated open access to all drugs and more drug importation of unapproved drugs. According to Associate Commissioner for Policy and Planning William Hubbard, "there was an effort to try to explain to them why that was a bad idea." That effort, he added, was "initially unsuccessful."[53]

Anxious for regulatory change, activists were not receptive to FDA explanations about the need for clinical evidence and adherence to safety standards. "They didn't see it from our viewpoint," said Hubbard. "They didn't want to hear it. They viewed all of the FDA people as largely political, hating gays, trying to keep them from getting drugs, and overly concerned about process." He added, "The AIDS activists concluded that, because Reagan was President, that the agency was sitting on lifesaving AIDS drugs and refusing to let patients have them, sort of a ban by the social conservatives."[54] Matt Sharp, an AIDS activist summed up the feelings of the AIDS community. The FDA, he said, was "viewed as apathetic in their approach to listening to people who were dying of HIV." He added, more damningly: "They shut the door to us. There was a lot of discrimination. That was the general mindset. It was the same thing that was going on all across the country."[55]

Despite the animus between the FDA and the AIDS movement, one thing is certain: AIDS activists were given a greater voice in finding solutions to vexing regulatory problems. Activists assisted in the development of approval criteria. They were able to gain representation on FDA advisory committees, on institutional boards at local hospitals and research centers, and community advisory boards established by pharmaceutical firms. Credible activists were successful, for example, in shifting FDA policy away from clinical endpoints as markers of effectiveness to surrogate endpoints as conceptual bases for drug approval. At its most basic, this meant that the approval process would be abridged because the scientific foundation for approval had been modified.[56]

According to Alan Hoeting, AIDS activists were able to make such headway because the commissioner was "impressed and persuaded" by those he met. These persons were well organized, they were intelligent, they were articulate."[57] "I believe," Hoeting added, "that his experiences during that period caused the agency to change its attitude somewhat toward the release of investigational new drugs and treatment of persons with AIDS or cancer or other serious condition with these investigational drugs.[58] Dr. Anthony Fauci, director of the National Institute of Allergy and Infectious Diseases, broached one problem inherent to giving AIDS activists a greater voice. Some individuals who were given a seat at the table had "no idea what the hell they're talking about," while others were "brilliant, and even more so than some of the scientists."[59]

In a final show of cooperation, the FDA reached out to the AIDS movement individuals conducting illegal community clinical trials.[60] In 1988, Project Inform had initiated an illegal study of a drug called trichosanthin, an extract of the Chinese cucumber root, which would later be known as Compound Q. The group viewed the government trials as not only slow but totally inadequate. Under the government trials, only a small number of patients would be administered the drug, and only at infinitesimal and possibly subtherapeutic dosages.[61] This was unacceptable to Project Inform. Thus, researchers and physicians in four cities participated in the unsanctioned trials and, despite the risk, more patients were administered more of the extract. An investigational new drug (IND) permit was not filed with the FDA, nor did an institutional review board (IRB) pass judgment on the protocol.[62] Project Inform opted to work outside the confines of standard operating procedure.

The study's clandestine nature and methodology (which lacked a placebo control) drew fire from the mainstream medical establishment, yet FDA officials met with the underground researchers and were presented a summary of the trial's results. Thus, this cooperation offers a further glimpse into how the FDA adapted to the AIDS epidemic. To include previously unheard activists in standard operational protocols like advisory committees was admirable; however, it took more fortitude to break with protocol and embrace underground, unsanctioned drug researchers who shunned the agency and its regulatory mandate altogether.

The FDA's Relationship with Pharmaceutical Companies

The relationship between regulators at the FDA and pharmaceutical companies was dramatically altered by the Reagan administration in the early 1980s, and this relationship took on broader significance as the AIDS crisis grew. Once the AIDS epidemic began to develop, the rapid creation and marketing of AIDS-related drugs became a major priority for the U.S. pharmaceutical industry. That the industry's aim was to minimize negative feedback from Congress and public interest groups—who felt it was dodging the epidemic—and, at the same time, maximize possible earnings should come as no surprise. AIDS had the potential to generate windfall profits if handled correctly. Conversely, if handled badly it could create disastrous public relations problems.

In 1981, before AIDS gained widespread exposure, it was impossible to know with certainty the degree to which President Reagan would affect change at the FDA. Political pundits, economic analysts, and pharmaceutical industry insiders suggested that the future was pregnant with possibility because Reagan as president meant less regulation, which meant more industry growth. The president of the National Association of Retail Druggists (NARD), Jesse M. Pike, for example, was delighted NARD was to see Reagan in the White House.[63] Yet, more generally, the pharmaceutical industry was supremely confident about the future in this new regulatory climate.[64]

The speculation about President Reagan's positive impact on the U.S. pharmaceutical turned out to be correct: the U.S. pharmaceutical industry's earnings grew at a steady pace throughout the 1980s, and this was surely due in part to a stronger working relationship between the FDA and the drug industry. However, if the architect of the robust, friendly relationship between regulator and industry was clearly Reagan, then the builder was Dr. Arthur Hull Hayes. The Reagan administration's first appointment as FDA commissioner, Hayes immediately implemented a program of voluntary compliance. He vowed to speed up the drug approval of totally new drugs, mitigate the drug lag, and "foster a more cooperative spirit" with the pharmaceutical industry through the promotion of "voluntary action." "Drug review can be streamlined," he averred, "existing regulations can be improved," and "we must be sensitive to the impact of our regulatory stance on innovation."[65] In his estimation, the responsibility for drug lags and delays rested with the FDA, the public, industry, and the research community and government. If these parties could increase cohesion, communication, and competitiveness, "a year, maybe more," could potentially be eliminated from the drug review process.[66] Unpalatable and unjustifiable to many consumer activists in the early 1980s, this regulatory philosophy gained greater traction amid a political landscape shaped by AIDS.

In the case of AZT, for instance, the FDA and industry, alongside the university and publicly funded research community, worked swiftly and decisively to bring the first antiviral AIDS drug to market. Significant levels of communication and collaboration between Burroughs Wellcome and FDA drug officials characterized the final stages of the drug approval process. However, according to author and business reporter Merrill Goozner, the tale of AZT has a darker underside. In his view, it was not until the public sector had borne the brunt of the costs, after a testable compound had been isolated that might sell at high volume at a high price, did Burroughs Wellcome involve itself in the development of clinical trials. To Goozner, the AZT saga demonstrated how pharmaceutical companies could shirk responsibility early on and thereafter take advantage of public funding, a close relationship with government regulators, and the relaxation of standards during a health crisis.[67]

Pentamidine, an anti-infective, was, just like AZT, a visible success for the industry, and it highlights not only the competitive climate among drug companies but also the pressure those companies exerted on the FDA to secure exclusivity. Targeted at *pneumocystis carinii* pneumonia (PCP), the largest cause of death in AIDS patients, pentamidine was approved in 1984. In 1988, however, the race to market an aerosolized pentamidine pitted two smaller companies against each other, as Fisons and Lyphomed, firms with "below-average innovative propensity," raced to get approval from the FDA.[68] In June 1989, Lyphomed effectively defeated Fisons, and its drug was granted seven years of market exclusivity.

Though of tremendous benefit to AIDS patients, the approval of Lyphomed's aerosolized pentamidine had, like AZT, a shadowy underside and it is imperative to underline some of the controversies that emerged as a consequence of the FDA approval. First, Fisons protested its drug delivery system was of a higher quality than Lyphomed's—the FDA had, according to the failed competitor, held Lyphomed to a less rigorous standard.[69] Second, even as Lyphomed's aerosolized version of pentamidine was approved, the firm's managers came under heavy scrutiny for trebling the price of its injectable pentamidine. According to Ted Weiss, Lyphomed was "soaking its clientele," sick AIDS victims.[70] Third, in the wake of the approval, questions were asked of Lyphomed's lobbying of the FDA's generic drug division, which was already scandalized by revelations that certain officials had taken bribes.[71] Lyphomed employed persons who had previously pled guilty to giving payoffs to FDA officials, though they were with other generic drug companies when they committed these criminal acts. Thereafter, Dr. John Kapoor, former chief executive of Lyphomed, appeared at congressional hearings in 1991 and declined to testify, citing the Fifth Amendment right against self-incrimination.[72]

In sum, the account of pentamidine encapsulates the complex relationship between the FDA and the drug industry—a relationship incontrovertibly affected by the Reagan administration. To be sure, as fears over AIDS mounted, the FDA faced a vigorous lobby in the AIDS movement led by Martin Delaney and Larry Kramer. Nevertheless, the FDA also faced a robust lobby in the form of the U.S. pharmaceutical industry, an industry that was bent on providing life-saving medicines to sick Americans and ramping up profits and share prices.

The Battle for Resources

As the FDA developed new drug regulations and reached out to the AIDS movement, it also responded to the AIDS epidemic by attempting to shore up its existing programs and acquire more resources. Importantly, the support for increased FDA funding came from the Presidential Commission on the Human HIV Epidemic. Chairman of the commission, Admiral James Watkins, was adamant that the FDA receive more funding. A self-described neophyte in the field of medicine and drugs, Watkins discovered that the FDA was operating "out of a totally inadequate physical plant with crippling manpower restrictions." He was shocked to find, moreover, that while the National Institutes of Health budget had grown by ten thousand percent, "the FDA budget for reviewing new AIDS drugs remained flat." "We need," he said, "to increase the medical review work force, improve the facilities, and upgrade the technological capacity of the FDA."[73]

Commissioner Young was also integral to the FDA's success in securing increased appropriations and staff members. According to Associate Commissioner for Policy and Planning William Hubbard, Commissioner Young "was indefatigable on the budget side." "It was hard to get money in the Reagan administration . . . to support FDA budget increases." He maintained that "only certain programs could get funded, and AIDS did get funded."[74] Director of Planning and Management Communications Charles Gorton added, "When it came to annual budget requests, [Commissioner Young] was quite aggressive."[75]

In 1987, for example, Young employed warfare as a metaphor to frame the FDA's struggle against HIV/AIDS and the necessity for additional funding:

> It is clear that we are now fighting what can only be described as full scale war against AIDS. As in wartime, I believe that FDA is now running a munitions factory, and it is our job to make safe and effective bullets on as timely a basis as possible. . . . An actual bullet must be safe for the person firing the gun and effective at hitting its target and killing the enemy. The same is true of therapeutic bullets. FDA is now entering a wartime phase to produce safe and effective therapeutic bullets against AIDS. [76]

Young explained, furthermore, that combating AIDS left the FDA vulnerable to its long-standing adversary, the drug lag. [77] From the agency's perspective, this was a cleverly constructed and persuasive argument. The drug lag had registered as the FDA's trickiest, most public and political trouble spot, at least since the mid-1970s. A host of new regulatory measures initiatives were taken to meet the AIDS epidemic and applied to other types of drugs, but Young cautioned that if all the agency's resources—limited in his opinion—were diverted to evaluating AIDS-related drugs he could not prevent a backward slide with non-AIDS drugs. An effective war against AIDS and the drug lag, argued Young, required more money.

Only near the end of Reagan's presidency would Young see a marked increase in the agency's AIDS-related budget. Between 1984 and 1986, the entire U.S. Public Health Community, including the NIH, CDC, and FDA, received $93 million. [78] In FY 1986, those appropriations would increase to $145 million. In FY 1987, it was $268 million. A year later they stood at $493 million; however, FDA AIDS-related funding in those budgets were $10 million, $26 million, and $25 million respectively. The year after, Reagan's final budget allotted $65 million to FDA for AIDS-related activities. Frank Young took particular care to draw attention to the disparity between FDA and NIH funding, echoing the findings of Admiral Watkins, chairman of the President's Commission on HIV. [79] This argument, alongside public and congressional arguments, helped increase the agency's budget. In fiscal year 1989, the FDA received 63 percent more funding than in 1988 for AIDS-related activities, which included the review of treatments, vaccines, and diagnostic kits for AIDS. It amounted to $16 million more than the previous year and it meant the FDA could hire eighty-five new full-time employees for AIDS related activities. Reagan's budget request also provided $65 million for the construction of a new FDA AIDS-research facility. [80]

The FDA's Communication with the American Public and Physicians

Beginning in the early 1980s, the FDA regularly apprised Americans of developments in the understanding of and fights against the disease through a number of different publications. The FDA in its publications broached numerous topics. What is AIDS? What are its symptoms? Who gets AIDS? Is it widespread? How contagious is AIDS? And most significantly, what is the federal government doing about AIDS? To this last question, the FDA stressed it was working alongside the entire U.S. health service and taking action on a number of fronts.[81]

When the FDA's publication, *Drug Bulletin,* devoted an entire issue to AIDS in October 1985, the FDA expanded its communication project to include the nation's health professionals. Young wrote that the goal of the initiative was to keep health professionals fully informed.[82] In September 1987, in a second issue devoted exclusively to AIDS, Young wrote "I want to reiterate my pledge that FDA will continue to give the evaluation of products for the treatment and prevention of this disease our highest priority." "We will," he concluded, "keep the medical community apprised of the latest developments in HIV and AIDS."[83]

In October 1987, the FDA devoted another of its publications, *FDA Consumer,* to the AIDS epidemic. It contained such articles as "A Progress Report on AIDS Research," "Fast-tracking the First AIDS Drug," and "Defrauding the Desperate: Quackery and AIDS." It alerted readers to the difficulty the U.S. public health service faced in striking a balance between amassing credible scientific data and determining the correct regulatory posture to take in lieu of such information.[84] Self-aggrandizing, judicious, and shrewd, *FDA Consumer's* AIDS issue offered something for everyone. Dr. Ellen Cooper explained how the FDA worked closely with Burroughs Welcome, Duke University, and the National Institutes of Health to expedite the approval of the first anti-viral AIDS drug. Marian Segal, an author of an article on AIDS, emphasized that medical science was not like Hollywood depicted—too often cures were painfully slow in emerging. "Defrauding the Desperate" explored the pitfalls inherent to relaxing enforcement of existing drug regulation and the article stressed how the sick needed protection from vultures and money-hungry quacks that made over an estimated $1 billion in fraudulent therapies in 1987.[85]

Significantly, the agency addressed AIDS-related quackery again in 1988. At the height of debate about the proper amount and application of regulatory measures, the FDA communicated it was unrelentingly rigid when it came to questionable, unapproved products and the safety of American consumers. In a joint public memo entitled "AIDS: False Hope from Fraudulent Treatment," the Council for Better Business Bureaus and the FDA together reaffirmed that the public would be protected against "charlatans," "con artists," and "quacks." Only one AIDS drug, AZT, had been approved by FDA at this juncture, yet a cornucopia of untested, spurious remedies were available to consumers including vitamin supplements, snake venom concoctions, ice balls, urine injections, hydrogen peroxide injections, Laetrile, garlic pills, processed algae, and booster capsules later found to contain lead and chromium.[86] The FDA/CBBB memo indicated that steps had been taken to make available credible drugs in a speedy fashion, and AIDS drugs would continue to be afforded top priority. It made plain, however, that the regulations regarding the promotion of specious drugs would be adhered to and those individuals touting such bogus medicines would be prosecuted and their products either seized or made to be withdrawn from the market.[87]

Conclusions

It is clear that in a time of contrary pressures and absent a clear policy direction from the Reagan administration the FDA modified its bureaucratic operating procedure through certain document-processing changes and it also created a special 1-AA designation for AIDS related drugs. In addition to these changes, the FDA streamlined the drug review process with (1) treatment use of investigational new drugs (IND); (2) liberalized interpretation of import regulations; (3) subpart E regulations to speed the approval process; (4) parallel track system to allow drug access early in the testing process.

The FDA also reached out to Congress, AIDS activists, the pharmaceutical industry, and the public at large. On the budget side, Commissioner Frank Young was able to secure greater appropriations and hence more staff members. He argued stridently and persuasively that the FDA required more resources to fulfill its mandate. Congress and the Reagan administration eventually agreed. Both *FDA Consumer* and *Drug Bulletin* educated the public about the history, profile, and transmission of AIDS, as well as the actions taken by the FDA to combat the disease. Moreover, the agency was vigilant in protecting Americans against another scourge: quacks and their spurious medicines. Commissioner Young also brought AIDS activists into the fold so that they played a greater role in developing protocols for clinical trials, and he allowed FDA drug officials to confer with the unsanctioned AIDS movement underground.

Undoubtedly, the AIDS crisis, and all the political heat that it generated, profoundly influenced the FDA's regulatory posture. With ardent intensity, a new, dynamic coalition of free market conservatives and liberal AIDS activists demanded modification of what it regarded as a set of deleterious drug policies. HIV/AIDS was imposing tricky, life-affecting decisions on sick Americans, and the FDA had to consider the possibility that it sanction and broaden access to experimental drugs. The FDA responded by taking actionable decisions that recalibrated the standard balance between consumer protection and product safety, revealing, in the final event, that neither the FDA's drug policy subsystem nor the spirit of its employees was rigidly fixed. Amid the AIDS epidemic, the FDA demonstrated a willingness to reassess and transform its institutional identity in a time of widespread disquiet.

NOTES

1. "The FDA for Itself," *Wall Street Journal*, October 13, 1988, A22.
2. William Hubbard Interview, FDA Oral History Collection, 37.
3. See Jonathan Kwitny, *Acceptable Risks* (New York: Simon & Schuster, 1992); Patricia Siplon, "A Brief History of the Political Science of AIDS Activism," *Political Science and Politics* 32 (3) (1999): 578–581; and Kenneth Sherrill, Carolyn M. Somerville, and Robert W. Bailey, "What Political Science is Missing by Not Studying AIDS," *Political Science and Politics* 25 (1992): 688–693.
4. See Stephen J. Ceccoli, *Pill Politics: Drugs and the FDA* (New York: Lynne Rienner Publishers, 2004), 106–108 and Daniel Carpenter, *Reputation and Power: Organizational Image and Pharmaceutical Regulation at the FDA*. Princeton, N.J.: Princeton University Press, 2010). These political scientists, who take a longer view of the FDA, offer significant detail about the different phases in the agency's history.
5. Anthony A. Celeste and Arthur N. Levine, "The Mission and the Institution: Ever Changing Yet Eternally the Same," in *FDA: A Century of Consumer Protection*, ed. Wayne Pines (Washington: Food and Drug Law Institute, 2006), 71–98. According to Thomas Birkland's book, *After Disaster: Agenda Setting, Public Policy, and Focusing Events* (Washington, D.C.: Georgetown University Press, 1997), a specific "focusing event"—calamities as earthquakes, hurricanes, oil spills, and nuclear meltdowns—cause both policymakers and citizens to search for solutions. In the context of the FDA, the AIDS crisis was such an event and helped to reshape the agency's priorities. Another useful book is Thomas Birkland's, *Lessons of Disaster: Policy Change After Catastrophic Event* (Washington, D.C.: Georgetown University Press, 2006).
6. Fran Hawthorne, *Inside the FDA: The Business and Politics Behind the Drugs We Take and the Food We Eat* (Hoboken, N.J.: John Wiley & Sons, 2005), 51.
7. For a similar argument, see Lucas Richert, "Reagan, Regulation, and the FDA: The U.S. Food and Drug Administration's Response to HIV/AIDS, 1980–1990," *Canadian Journal of History* 44 (3) (2009), 467–487.
8. Philip J. Hilts, *Protecting America's Health: The FDA, Business, and One Hundred Years of Regulation* (New York: Alfred A. Knopf, 2003), 237.
9. James Patterson, *Restless Giant: The United States from Watergate to Bush v. Gore*, (Oxford: Oxford University Press, 2006), 179–184 and Robert M. Collins, *Transforming America: Politics and Culture in the Reagan Years* (New York: Columbia University Press, 2007), 133–145.
10. Bob Shrum, *No Excuses: Concessions of a Serial Campaigner* (New York: Simon & Schuster, 2009), 134.
11. William Hubbard Interview, FDA Oral History Collection, 31.
12. Ibid.
13. Collins, *Transforming America* 133–145.
14. Ibid.
15. Committee on Government Operations, *AIDS Drugs: Where Are They?* A report issued by the Committee on Government Operations, October 19, 1988, 18–19.
16. Daniel Harris, "The AIDS Guerillas," *Los Angeles Times*, November 1, 1992. Consult: http://articles.latimes.com/1992-11-01/books/bk-1333_1_jonathan-kwitny.

17. Quoted in Marian Segal, "A Progress Report on AIDS Research," *FDA Consumer* 21 (8) October 1987: 11.

18. Committee on Government Operations, *FDA Proposals to Ease Restrictions on the Use and Sale of Experimental Drugs,* 100th Congress, 1st Session, April 29, 1987, 89–90. "I believe first and foremost," Young said, "there is broad public consensus acceptance and earnest support for the goal of providing promising new drugs to desperately ill patients."

19. Committee on Appropriations, *Supplement to FDA Commissioner Frank Young's testimony to Agriculture, Rural Development and Related Agencies Appropriations for 1988,* 100th Congress, 1st Session, 1987, 532.

20. "Action Plan II Is Here Now," *FDA Today,* August/September, 1987, 1.

21. See *Food and Drug Administration Quarterly Activities Reports,* 1st Quarter, Fiscal Year 1987, 1987, 11. Throughout 1986, the FDA asked external groups for their views on goals for Action Plan II. The agency duly received 502 ballots from consumers, consumer groups, former FDA Policy Board members, state governments, small businesses, and trade associations.

22. Speech by FDA Commissioner Frank E. Young, given 06/14/88, consulted at https://www.fda.gov.bbs/topics/SPEECH/SPE00008.htm.

23. Ceccoli, *Pill Politics: Drugs and the FDA,* (1987): 106–108.

24. *Drug Bulletin,* (Washington, September 1987), 14.

25. "Fast-tracking the First AIDS Drug," *FDA Consumer* 21 (8): 14–15.

26. Ibid.

27. Ibid.

28. Ibid.

29. "Testing Medicines to Death," *Economist,* January 30, 1988, 52.

30. Committee on Appropriations, *Statement by Commissioner Frank Young, Agriculture, Rural Development and Related Agencies Appropriations for 1988,* 100th Congress, 1987, 524–525.

31. "New Division to Review Drugs for AIDS and other Viruses," *FDA Today,* April 1988, 1.

32. "Testing Medicines to Death," *Economist,* January 30, 1988, 52. See also Arthur Daemmrich, *Pharmacopolitics: Drug Regulation in the United States and Germany* (Chapel Hill: University of North Carolina, 2004), 31–33

33. Committee on Government Operations, *AIDS Drugs: Where Are They?* 29.

34. Codified and announced by Commissioner Frank Young the same month that President Reagan established his Commission on HIV/AIDS

35. "AIDS is Different," *Economist,* June 20, 1987, 15.

36. Mary K. Olson, "Substitution in Regulatory Agencies: FDA Enforcement Alternatives," *Journal of Law, Economics and Organization* 12 (1996): 385–390.

37. Committee on Government Operations, Opening Statement of Congressman Ted Weiss, *FDA Proposals to Ease Restrictions on the Use and Sale of Experimental Drugs,* 100th Congress, 1st Session, 2-3.

38. *FDA Proposals to Ease Restrictions on the Use and Sale of Experimental Drugs,* 98–105 and 126.

39. Ibid., 98.

40. Ibid., 103.

41. Joanna E. Siegel and Marc J. Roberts, "Reforming FDA Policy Lessons from the AIDS Experience" *Regulation Magazine* 14 (4) (1991) consulted at www.cato.org/pubs/regulation.

42. Ibid.

43. "The FDA for Itself," *Wall Street Journal,* October 13, 1988, A22. See also "FDA to Shorten Testing Stage For Some Drugs—Plan May Speed Treatment For AIDS and Other Ills Seen as Life Threatening," *Wall Street Journal,* October 20, 1988, B4. The Subpart E regulation was an outgrowth of President Reagan's Task Force on Regulatory Relief, chaired by Vice President Bush. The task force had concluded that when a drug was developed for a disease without an existing therapy, a successful Phase II trial would suffice. It recommended, too, that once a drug proved safe in Phase I clinical trials and showed positive results during Phase II trials that that drug should be sold to desperately ill patients. Surveillance and testing of the

drug would continue after marketing. Vice President Bush played a significant, hands-on role during the development of the regulation. On two separate occasions in 1987 he met with FDA Commissioner Young. According to spokespersons, they discussed the possibilities and pitfalls of treating patients with experimental drugs. They met again in August 1988 to review the progress of the new policy.

44. Ibid.

45. "Finally, the Patients Benefit," *Wall Street Journal,* October 20, 1988, A24. The article concludes: "a drug's real risks should not be allowed to overpower its benefits and prevent approval. In practice, it should allow patients in the most extreme and desperate circumstances to take a long shot. Ask almost any patient facing death or no prospect of gain, and he or she will say that a long shot is all they want."

46. Albert R. Jonsen and Jeff Stryker, *The Social Impact of AIDS in the United States* (Washington: National Academy Press, 1993), 93.

47. Ibid.

48. See Dennis Altman, *AIDS in the Minds of America: The Social, Political, and Psychological Impact of a New Epidemic* (New York: Doubleday, 1986), Larry Kramer, *Reports from the Holocaust* (New York: St. Martin's Press, 1989), and Randy Shilts, *And the Band Played On: Politics, People and the AIDS Epidemic* (New York: St. Martin's Press, 1987).

49. Steven Epstein, "The Construction of Lay Expertise: AIDS Activism and the Forging of Credibility in the Reform of Clinical Trials," *Science, Technology, & Human Values* 20 (1995): 413–414.

50. Ibid.

51. Quoted in Hawthorne, *Inside the FDA*, 52.

52. William Hubbard Interview, FDA Oral History Collection, 31.

53. Quoted in Hawthorne, *Inside the FDA*, 52.

54. William Hubbard Interview, FDA Oral History Collection, 31.

55. Quoted in Hawthorne, *Inside the FDA*, 52.

56. Epstein, "The Construction of Lay Expertise," 422–428.

57. Alan Hoeting Interview, FDA Oral History Collection, 41.

58. Ibid., 41.

59. Quoted in Epstein, "The Construction of Lay Expertise," 419.

60. As early as 1984, the AIDS movement had developed an underground treatment wing. Several chemists, working independently of the FDA, began scouring the European medical literature for possible approaches to thwart HIV and to rebuild the cell-mediated (T-cell) immunity lost in the virus' wake. Key individuals, including Steve Gavin of Baltimore, Rob Springer of Santa Monica, David Mitchell of Pacific Palisades, and Jack Gerhardt of Seattle, found the means to synthesise large quantities of such compounds as DTC (Imuthiol), AL–721, and DNCB, none of which had been approved for human use by the FDA. The chemists then distributed the drugs to patients in the AIDS community while tracking their progress.

61. Paul A. Sergios, "The AIDS Underground, AIDS Activists, and the FDA—A Historical Overview" in *Stop the FDA: Save Your Health Freedom*, eds. John Morgenthaler and Steven William Fowkes, (Menlo Park, CA, 1992), 106–107. Health Freedoms Publications, Preliminary studies indicated the drug destroyed HIV-infected cells—lymphocytes and macrophages—while leaving uninfected cells unharmed.

62. IRB is a committee of physicians, lay people, clergy, and attorneys that approves and periodically reviews experimental protocols to ensure that the rights of human subjects are protected.

63. Jesse M. Pike, "Letter to President-elect Reagan," *NARD Journal*, January 1981, 21.

64. James Dickinson, "Washington Report," *Pharmaceutical Technology*, February 1981, 24. See also Phillip H. Wiggins, "Betting the Store on another Tagamet: A Plethora of New Drugs is Making High Flyers of Drug Companies," *New York Times*, May 16, 1982, F14 and Thomas C. Hayes, "The Drug Business Golden Era Ahead," *New York Times*, May 17, 1981, F1.

65. Committee on Appropriations, *Arthur Hull Hayes Jr. testimony to Agriculture, Rural Development and Related Agencies Appropriations for 1983*, 97th Congress, 2nd Session, 595.

66. "New Commissioner Finds No Lack of Challenges—Or Satisfaction," *FDA Consumer* 15 (9) (1981): 17–19.

67. Merrill Goozner, *The $800 Million Pill: The Truth Behind New Drug Costs* (Berkeley: University of California Press, 2004), 103–105.

68. Peter W. Roberts, "Product Innovation, Product-Market Competition and Persistent Profitability in the U.S. Pharmaceutical Industry," *Strategic Management Journal* 20 (1999): 662.

69. Peter S. Arno, Karen Bonuck, and Michael Davis, "Rare Diseases, Drug Development, and AIDS: The Impact of the Orphan Drug Act," *The Milbank Quarterly* 73 (1995): 239.

70. *AIDS Drugs: Where Are They?* 32.

71. Herbert Burkholz, *The FDA Follies* (New York: Basic Books, 1994), 60–61. Forty-two people and ten companies pleaded guilty to, or were convicted of, fraud or corruption charges. American Therapeutics Inc., My-K Laboratories, and Bolar Pharmaceutical Company were among the generic drug firms that blighted the industry's reputation.

72. Warren E. Leary, "Congressmen Fault FDA On Generics," *New York Times*, March 8, 1991, D3.

73. Committee on Government Operations, *Therapeutic Drugs for AIDS: Development, Testing, and Availability*, 100th Congress, 2nd Session, 1988, 390. 266–268.

74. William Hubbard Interview, FDA Oral History Collection, 32–33.

75. Charles Gorton Interview, FDA Oral History Collection, 18. Even as Young pressed Congress and President Reagan for more funds to fight AIDS, he suffered no illusions. He told an audience at the Institute of Medicine in 1987, "We must always remember that we are facing a future of scarce resources and serious challenges." See also *Agriculture, Rural Development and Related Agencies Appropriations for 1987*, 1988, 530–531.

76. *FDA Proposals to Ease Restrictions on the Use and Sale of Experimental Drugs*, April 1987, 78.

77. *Therapeutic Drugs for AIDS: Development, Testing, and Availability*, 392. According to Young, the FDA had to reduce its efforts in a number of fields because of shortfalls. He proclaimed: "our intensity is high" and "our individuals feel overwhelmed." He noted ". . . when we evaluated AZT in 107 days, it took over 20 people working that 107 days and an expense of $600, 000. There was a slowdown in the approval of new anti-infective drugs during that time, and we still have a backlog because of our diversion there."

78. Marian Segal, "A Progress Report on AIDS Research," *FDA Consumer* 21 (8) (1987): 10–12.

79. "President Asks for More Funds, Added Staff in 1988," *FDA Today*, March 1987, 1.

80. "President Reagan's Budget Request," *FDA Today*, March 1988, 1 and *Congressional Quarterly Almanac*, 100th Congress, 2nd Session, 1988, 517.

81. "What the Experts Know About AIDS," *FDA Consumer* 17 (7) (1983): 16–18.

82. "Letter From the Commissioner," *Drug Bulletin* (Washington: Government Printing Office, October 1985), 1.

83. "Letter from the Commissioner," *Drug Bulletin* (Washington: Government Printing Office, September 1987), 1.

84. *FDA Consumer*, Special Issue 21 (1987): 1–19.

85. Ibid.

86. *AIDS: False Hope From Fraudulent Treatment*, Food and Drug Administration Collection, 1988, 2.

87. Ibid.

Chapter Seven

The Triumph of Conservatism: Scandal and Beyond

"The question of how much money the FDA needs reminds me of the story of what Abe Lincoln said when he was asked how long legs should be. As long is takes to reach the ground."[1]

PETER BARTON HUTT, FORMER FDA CHIEF COUNSEL

"The chronic and pervasive shortcomings that FDA has had to cope with for more than a decade have seriously crippled the Agency."[2]

CHARLES EDWARDS, CHAIRMAN OF
FDA ADVISORY COMMITTEE 1991

In August 1989, America's most widely read newspaper, *USA Today*, reported on its front page that the FDA was "weak." This weakness, according to the paper, had contributed to the recent generic drug scandal that had rocked the FDA's drug review offices and would eventually force Commissioner Young to resign. President Reagan's time in office had just ended, a new Republican president installed, and *USA Today* treated its 6.5 million readers to a disquieting article that hinted Reagan had seriously impaired a federal regulatory agency responsible for protecting American consumer products.[3]

As if the *USA Today* article had sounded a clarion call, a host of expert voices soon started to echo the idea that the FDA was structurally deficient and the public was therefore at risk. Former chief counsel of the FDA, Peter Barton Hutt observed, "The FDA's problem is resources. There has been a very serious erosion of resources across the board." Dr. Samuel Thier, President of the National Institutes of Medicine, described the FDA as "a demoralized group, being asked to do too much with too few resources." Senator Orrin Hatch commented that something had gone wrong at the FDA during the 1980s. From his perspective, the cause of the problem in the generic drug division was "an overburdened and underfunded agency." Ominously, Hatch added that something had to be done, and rather soon, to help the moribund agency.[4]

This help would eventually arrive in the form of the Bush administration. According to *Medical Marketing and the Media*, the new administration's decisions and appointments were not encumbered by "meddlesome ideology."[5] One FDA official suggested that the Bush people were far more practical, "as opposed to the ideological bias in everything the Reagan administration did."[6] Pragmatism, as it were, resulted in the confirmation of acting commissioner James Benson until a permanent candidate could be found, the appointment of Commissioner David Kessler, and, most importantly, budget increases. During the presidential campaign in 1988, George H.W. Bush, who had in 1981–1983 played such a prominent role in the Presidential Task Force on Regulatory Reform, commented on the changes in the FDA's relationship with the drug industry. Bush remarked, "I think we've started to see this philosophical shift, the end of this adversarial relationship." He made no mention of any perceived flaws at the agency, his role in the decline of the agency, and instead focused on the principles of free market enterprise. "Government shouldn't be an adversary," Bush declared. "It should be a partner."[7]

FDA Responsibilities and Pharmaceutical Industry Demands

Opinions about the FDA's vulnerability at the conclusion of the 1980s were indeed accurate, but the question of what needed to be done lingered. Invariably, answers centered on the agency's budget, which operated at a current-services budget level throughout the decade. In 1982, Commissioner Hayes had testified the agency was not unduly affected by the tightening budgets. At the end of the Reagan years, if Hatch and a host of others were to be believed, Hayes was dreadfully mistaken. Both the food and drug industries grew concerned. For instance, John Cady, president of the National Food Processors Association proclaimed, "The problems at the FDA stem directly from the deregulatory process . . . they just do not have the resources to do the job correctly."[8] The National Association of Pharmaceutical Manufacturers also weighed in, stating, "We're concerned about the FDA's ability to function."[9]

Taking a slightly longer view, one that includes President George H.W. Bush, the Food and Drug Administration's yearly budget between 1980 and

1995 ranged from $470,499,000 to $827,877,000. The average budget for these years was $591,000,000, with yearly increases averaging 3.24 percent. Budget changes ranged from cuts of 12 percent to increases of 11 percent yearly.[10] The FDA's budget incontrovertibly affected its enforcement profile and drug review; for example, the FDA's overall workforce declined from 8,089 to 7,398 throughout the 1980s. Only when the HIV/AIDs epidemic gained widespread recognition would the agency see an increase in funding. Moreover, the number of inspections of foods and drugs dropped from 32,778 in 1980 to 19,876 in 1988, whereas the number of seizures, injunctions, and criminal prosecutions dipped from 532 in 1980 to 237 in 1988. To supplement the lack of "boots on the ground" in factories and laboratories, the FDA increased the use of warning letters to promote compliance with its regulatory requirements. The number of FDA-initiated routine criminal prosecutions also substantially decreased, which were in turn replaced by a smaller number of aggressively developed criminal cases against persons engaging in fraud in FDA-regulated areas.[11]

The FDA's drug review process was further impacted by these changes. In 1989, Frank Young told John Dingell of the pressures imposed by the Hatch-Waxman law in 1984. "As we moved from 1981, '82, '83, and into '84, there was a marked surge in the number of applications that came in" and "we were granted only four months to get ready."[12] It is especially important, moreover, to note the remarkable speed of growth in domestic R& D spending by pharmaceutical companies in the 1980s. According to *Pharmaceutical R&D: Costs, Risks, and Rewards*, a technical report prepared by the Office of Technological Assessment in 1992–1993, real domestic R&D spending increased by 3.5 percent between 1975 and 1980. Between 1980 and 1985, however, that spending averaged 11 percent, whereas between 1985 and 1990 it averaged 10.7 percent.[13] In short, the industry's R&D grew from $600 million in 1970 to $8.1 billion in 1990 and it began to demand more from the FDA.

Yet as industry investment skyrocketed at the outset of the Reagan years, the agency's drug review began to suffer. Between 1980 and 1989, the agency's staff declined by 10 percent. More startling, however, the FDA's research staff devoted to drugs actually declined 28 percent. Even more striking was the total number of new product applications increasing 82 percent between 1980 and 1989, with the average approval time culminating in a shockingly high 32.5 months. It was certainly the case that the FDA received increased funding in the wake of the HIV/AIDS epidemic; however, according to Angela Ritzert, the effect of more FDA funding was actually slower approval times.[14]

The stagnancy of FDA funding would have perhaps been more manageable if Congress had not simultaneously expanded the FDA's statutory duties.[15] Instead, the FDA was deprived of a commensurate amount of resources to deal with a set of new laws. From 1980 to 1989, Congress passed twenty-four laws expanding FDA jurisdiction and while not all of the laws directly impacted the Bureau of Drugs (later the Center for Drug Evaluation and Resources) the enactment of animal drug laws or food laws created a knock-on effect, because resources needed to be reshuffled and diverted. The 1983 Orphan Drug Act established a new program within the FDA to advance the development of drugs for rare medical conditions, while the 1983 Federal Anti-Tampering Act gave the FDA authority to investigate tampering incidents related to such products as pharmaceuticals. Hatch-Waxman amendments sparked a substantial increase in abbreviated new drug applications, whereas the 1987 Drug Marketing Act required the FDA to restrict the distribution of drug samples, supervise a ban on specific resales of drugs, and police drug wholesalers. Furthermore, the AIDS Amendments of 1988 required the FDA to establish and maintain a registry of new and experimental AIDS drugs.[16] The laws named above, though a small selection of the legislation passed in the 1980s, created an environment in which the FDA found it difficult to sustain its mandate and protect American consumers.

Meanwhile, another gloomy episode demonstrated that something had gone awry at the FDA during the Reagan years. In the late 1980s, the agency was marred by the improper and illegal conduct of certain generic drug officials. A distressing scandal, the episode culminated with the conviction of FDA drug officials for taking bribes from drug companies. The event not only neatly paralleled and informed the perception of the FDA as weak and vulnerable, but it also raised questions about the Reagan administration's ethical and regulatory effects on the FDA during the 1980s.

The Generic Drug Scandal and the Departure of Commissioner Young

In the summer of 1988, as the nation prepared for a presidential election, an unforgettably dark chapter in the FDA's history began to unfold. In 1986, Michigan Democratic representative John Dingell, chairman of the Subcommittee on Oversight and Investigations and the longest-serving member of the House of Representatives, initiated a sweeping congressional analysis of the safety of the nation's generic drug supply and at the same time got to the bottom of the FDA's reputed troubles. Dingell's investigation, which lasted a total of three years, engulfed the agency in controversy and unprecedented scrutiny.[17]

Since as early as 1986, the Generic Drugs division has been overshadowed by rumors of ethical problems, if not outright corruption. The discussion of improprieties had begun when Roy McKnight of Mylan Laboratories, a mid-sized generics manufacturer, went to the FDA and asserted that his competitors were bribing FDA officials. Initially, McKnight and Mylan Laboratories were thwarted because they did not possess hard evidence of du-plicity; the FDA bureaucracy, for its part, initially rallied around its own and action was not immediately taken. At the center of the controversy was Dr. Charles Chang, head of the generic drug division, but his superiors were suspicious of the drug industry's accusations against him. Perhaps it was an elaborate ruse to garner favored treatment for Mylan's pending applications? Perhaps it was a clever way to circumnavigate the queue? Mylan Laborato-ries also undermined its own cause—and justice—when their director of regulatory affairs and chief FDA liaison, Dr. Cheryl Blume, used racial epi-thets to describe Chang. The focus shifted, therefore, from the original claims of corruption within the FDA to claims of insensitivity and racism. [18]

Yet the generic drugs industry was unwilling to allow the matter to rest. Mylan Laboratories, along with Barr Laboratories and Barre-National, again came forward and made accusations about the duplicity of officials in the Division of Generic Drugs. The principal claim, that other drug companies were buying preferential treatment at the FDA through gifts and meals, was taken more seriously in light of a second important claim. According to the aggrieved companies, Dr. Marvin Seife, the director of the Division of Ge-neric Drugs (and Chang's immediate superior) was himself possibly under-handed. If nothing else, Seife had demonstrated unresponsiveness to the original claim of corruption. [19]

By June of 1988, however, the FDA determined there was no clear "im-proper handling" of generic drug applications. A number of generic drug applications had been reassigned by Chang to different generic officials and this had inevitably slowed the review process. These reassignments were, the FDA concluded, far from irrefutable proof of crooked behavior. Rather, Chang had gone forward with the reassignments because certain FDA gener-ic drug reviewers left the agency.

John Dingell had by this point involved himself, and he not only regarded the generic industry accusations as grave, but he disagreed with the FDA's contention that the generic approval process was fundamentally sound. Al-ready, Dingell, using his Subcommittee on Oversight and Investigations, had humiliated and undermined such Reagan administration figures as Michael Deaver, Environmental Protection Administrator Ann Gorsuch Burford, and Interior Secretary James Watt. Adamantly opposed to excessive deregulation and corruption, he now turned his attention to the FDA. The "Food and Drug administration has a long and proud tradition of protecting the American people," proclaimed Dingell. "It is a distinguished Agency." Nevertheless, "troubling information regarding possible criminal misconduct" had prompted him to investigate the agency. [20]

From the outset, the relationship between FDA officials and Dingell's subcommittee was fraught with acrimony. Dingell, a tenacious investigator and ferocious interlocutor, surely contributed to the tension when he observed, "a few public hangings will be of immense value."[21] This type of belligerent, wild-west rhetoric surely did not sit well with FDA officials, who were all too aware of the negative feedback caused by such investigations and were concerned about the inherent danger of sensationalizing the hearings. The combative Dingell was soon at loggerheads with the FDA's gruff chief counsel, Tom Scarlett, a man highly regarded within the agency. A key flashpoint between the two men was the FDA's ostensible lack of transparency and uncooperativeness in the face of a congressional investigation. On one occasion, Dingell's subcommittee aides, who had unsuccessfully demanded access to FDA documents, entered the FDA building without notice and started rifling through and seizing files. According to the Associate Commissioner for Policy and Planning William Hubbard, at that point, Tom Scarlett basically stopped them at the elevator and said, "You're not taking anything out of here." Unfortunately, that put Scarlett "in a position of opposing John Dingell and other investigators and probably was the beginning of his leaving, essentially being pushed out."[22] In July 1989, after a series of moves by Dingell and the top officials in the Department of Health and Human Services, Scarlett was dismissed as chief counsel, which sent shockwaves through the FDA. According to one report, the chairman demanded Scarlett be "excluded from all further contacts with Dingell's subcommittee and its staffers."[23]

Dingell's subcommittee hearings ultimately revealed several instances of corruption, not only in the FDA's Division of Generic Drugs, but in the wider generic drugs industry as well. Chang, who had been accused of crimes in 1986, was found guilty of accepting globetrotting holidays and expensive furniture worth $24,300. He pled guilty to racketeering and bribery, and in late 1989, to reduce his sentence he cooperated with the Maryland law enforcement authorities to bring down other criminals.[24] Marvin Seife, Chang's former superior, was also found guilty of perjury and an all-too-close and inappropriate relationship with the drug industry. Overall, over forty people and ten separate companies were found or pled guilty to either corruption and fraud. American Therapeutics Inc., My-K Laboratories, and Bolar Pharmaceutical Company were among the generic drug firms that blighted the generic drug industry's reputation. Bolar's former president faced the sternest sentence, five years in prison and a $1.25 million fine, as U.S. authorities sought to send a message to other companies.[25] Christine Gorman, writing in *Time*, emphasized how the entire industry was likely to suffer.[26]

In the wake of the acrimonious investigation and hearings, it became clear that the Reagan administration had played a role in the scandal, albeit minor. The policy of voluntary compliance, which called for increased cooperation and communication between industry and regulator, for instance, came under fire for establishing the conditions, if not motivations, for malfeasant behavior. One FDA employee was quoted saying "Maybe we went to extremes [to help drug companies], but it would have been alright if a few hadn't acted dishonestly."[27]

As important as voluntary compliance was, however, the generic drug crisis had its origins in the 1984 Hatch-Waxman amendments. It was here, moreover, that the Reagan administration and the U.S. Congress played a second, overlapping role in the generic drug debacle, namely by depriving the FDA of necessary funds—the weakness described earlier. As has been shown, the enactment of the Hatch-Waxman legislation encouraged a tremendous influx in abbreviated new drug applications (ANDAs); these demonstrated that a given generic drug was equivalent to an original brand-name drug about to lose its patent. According to Young, this increased the aggressiveness in an already competitive generic drug industry. Generic drug companies soon pushed, harassed, and pressured FDA generic drug officials to expedite their application as opposed to another company's. (Of course John Dingell's hearings revealed just how unscrupulous certain drug companies were willing to be.) Young, during congressional testimony, explained the economic motivations for possible malfeasance on the part of generic drug makers:

> Companies were anxious to receive first approval to market a new generic product so they could enjoy a period during which they were the exclusive marketer of the generic drug before other companies received FDA approval to market the same product. There was also a perception within the industry that the first firm to penetrate the market would have a long-term competitive advantage in terms of market share and revenue over later entrants into the marketplace.[28]

The enactment of Hatch-Waxman, according to this perspective, ramped up the competitiveness between generic drug makers and raised the stakes in securing an approval.

Yet amid this hyper-competitive, overworked climate, the FDA was not appropriated sufficient resources or staff "to do the job efficiently" or ameliorate the potential for drug firms to coerce FDA officials. As previously demonstrated, the FDA had been made vulnerable. *Medicine & Health* noted how the FDA faced an "onslaught" of ANDAs that were "stacked by the ream around the agency." "A small staff—30 workers, including 8 to 12 chemists—had to track ANDAs by the thousands, read millions of pages, storing them on shelves, chairs, desks, and tables."[29] It was a near impossible task to perform efficiently.

As the House investigation proceeded apace, Frank Young was forced to resign. He was vilified for a failure of leadership—for adopting and following the Reagan administration's philosophy of "relaxed regulation."[30] To such critics, Young's tenure at the FDA was marked by a friendly posture toward the pharmaceutical industry when it ought to have been scrutinizing it more thoroughly. By this reasoning, Young was therefore partly culpable for the debacle. According to Sidney Wolfe, a high-profile consumer activist, Young pandered to industry; the cost was "hundreds of lives and injuries to many more." Ralph Nader, a colleague of Wolfe's at the Public Citizen Health Research Group, ratcheted up the criticism even further when he described Young as "by far the worst FDA Commissioner in 18 years." Young's departure from the FDA, in Nader's judgment, would "improve the health of the American people."[31]

Young was not entirely abandoned in the political wilderness. He found mild approbation from an unlikely source. AIDS activists praised his deregulatory measures that quickened the approval of AIDS drugs. John Dingell, the architect of Young's downfall, came out in support of the commissioner when he said Young's intentions were honorable, "but he was handicapped by the budgets and attitudes of an Administration that let the agency [FDA] go to seed."[32] Dingell added: "Frank Young had the misfortune to preside at the FDA during a time when it was virtually guaranteed that rogues and knaves would prosper and honest people would face great difficulty."[33] Senator Orrin Hatch, for his part, indirectly supported Young. "If anyone is to blame," he said of the FDA's weakness and the generic drug scandal, "it is Congress, because the people at the FDA are worked to death."[34]

Young left the agency on December 18, 1989 and took up a new post at the Department of Health and Human Services. He was obviously reluctant to leave the FDA, having described his position as "the best job in the world."[35] An unnamed source commented on how Young was forced out by Bush administration officials; they wanted him gone because "it's just been one thing after another at the FDA, and people were unhappy."[36] According to investigative reporters Jack Anderson and Dale Van Atta, Young's association with President Reagan and his policy of regulatory reform served as his political undoing:

> He [Young] was a good soldier for the Reagan regime, serving as head of the FDA for six years. But a good soldier in Ronald Reagan's army had to be an advocate of deregulation and hands-off government, even in the agency that is supposed to protect consumers from dangerous foods and drugs. The hands-off approach didn't work for the FDA much better than it worked for the savings and loan industry, the Defense Department or the Housing and Urban Development Department. Now, with Reagan enjoying retirement, people like Frank Young are paying for what they did to please the big guy.[37]

In Anderson and Van Atta's estimation, Young's firing was inextricably linked to the failure of Reagan's economic policies at the FDA.

Forced to resign from a besieged, scandal-plagued agency, Young demonstrated both resentment and disillusionment. He claimed to love his "rough-and-tumble" years on the job but begrudged how his position had become overly politicized. "Every day," Young told one reporter bitterly, "a new grenade comes through the window."[38] During a separate farewell speech, Young adopted an even more combative tone as he reprimanded Washington lawmakers and returned to his theme of FDA politicization. In his judgment, the FDA was not receiving the support that was needed and this had contributed to the numerous problems that occurred under his watch. "We've had enough—too much—of politicians who view civil servants as part of the problem," he stated flatly. "To fully get through this [scandal and crisis], the FDA needs a little breathing room to reassess its priorities and to develop a strategy for the next decade." Young subsequently added, as others already had, "the agency deserves the guarantee of no new responsibilities without concomitant resources."[39] In a final, rancorous parting shot, Young accused Congress, and specifically John Dingell, of distorting the truth—to the detriment of the FDA:

> While the FDA is most willing to accept constructive criticism from the Congress, such criticism should be factually based and consistent with a reasonable assessment of agency priorities. . . . The agency should respectfully ask members of Congress to resist the temptation to grandstand of FDA issues.[40]

Similar to former Commissioner Schmidt's earlier claim in 1974, Young asserted that Congress had to improve its oversight of the FDA through greater diligence and less politicking. Only with this adjustment could the FDA move past the profligate and illegal behavior of a small number of bad apples. Only with this adjustment, moreover, would the FDA be able to carry out its mandate of consumer protection and product innovation in the near future.

As the news of Young's resignation echoed throughout the halls of the FDA, his former co-workers lamented the circumstances surrounding his departure. The word "sacrifice" began to be used to describe the event. "Young was kicked out because there were too many accusations against the agency," claimed one newspaper source. "There had to be a sacrifice. He was it."[41] Burton Love, who worked closely with Young, recognized the damning nature of the generic drugs scandal and, indeed, that Young was responsible as agency head, but he was unable to accept that Young was entirely accountable:

> . . . one of the most devastating things to have happened, of course, on Young's watch with the generic scandal. I mean, we took such a bath over the poor behavior of such a few that that was really hard to stomach. Very, very difficult. And, of course, it was not Dr. Young's fault. He didn't have a clue. He was simply the scapegoat, of the sacrificial lamb, or whatever you want to call it.[42]

However much or little FDA staff members believed that Young served as a sacrificial lamb did not matter. Young was responsible for the agency and he was gone, shunted off to a newly created position in the Department of Health and Human Services. A career FDA employee named James Benson replaced him.

The FDA, meanwhile, continued to negotiate the aftermath of the scandal in his absence. It was critical to stave off further bad press—that is, negative feedback—and get to grips with the underlying causes, the antecedents, of corruption and weakness at the FDA. Reassessment was necessary. Thus, in December 1989, Louis Sullivan, the secretary of HHS, announced the formation of a blue-ribbon panel to "to examine the mission, responsibilities and structure of the Food and Drug Administration" so that the FDA could be "strengthened to benefit the public health."[43]

Assessing the FDA: The Edwards Report

In March 1990, Sullivan appointed Dr. Charles Edwards to head a blue-ribbon FDA advisory committee. Edwards, a Nixon-era FDA commissioner, was intimately familiar with the policy subsystems, organizational framework, and decision-making structure at the FDA. As such, he was charged with re-evaluating the FDA's *raison d'être* at the end of the Reagan years. According to Stephen Ceccoli, author of *Pill Politics*, Edwards was "generally known to be sympathetic toward industry views."[44] Nevertheless, Sullivan, upon naming Edwards, observed that he was "uniquely qualified" to carry out the review of the FDA. Edwards and his fifteen-person committee (consisting of academics, industry representatives, patient groups, and physicians) were told to examine how the drug industry had itself changed during the 1980s, how equipped the FDA was to perform its duties, and whether the agency was sufficiently balanced to ensure speedy review of new drugs while still protecting the American public.[45]

As the Edwards committee began its investigation of the FDA, the politicization and rule-making autonomy of the agency surfaced as significant points of discussion. The Reagan administration, according to the committee, had transformed the FDA in two fundamental ways. First, certain Reagan administration officials, namely HHS Secretary Richard Schweiker, had stripped the FDA of its authority by adding extra layers to the regulation-making process back in 1981. Whereas once the FDA could develop and pass its own regulations, Schweiker had engineered it so regulations had to pass through the HHS bureaucracy. Second, President Reagan's Executive Order 12291 had stripped the FDA of a degree of autonomy. The Office of Management and Budget, as stipulated by E.O. 12291, was charged with reviewing FDA regulations using a cost/benefit scale, leaving the agency in an even deeper bureaucratic morass. Clearly, then, the Reagan administration had modified the FDA's ability to craft and formalize its own rules, independent of some politically oriented third party.[46]

Thereupon the questions of political control and political influence gained greater traction and generated increased debate. Who, the committee asked, ought to control the FDA? What political arrangement would best serve the FDA's staff and, more importantly, the American consumer? The Department of Health and Human Services? The Office of Management and Budget? Congress? One thing was certain—the status quo was no longer feasible. Some sort of adjustment was desperately needed. "If you've been to the FDA, you got to know what an awful mess it is," noted Terry Lierman, a lobbyist in favor of more FDA resources.[47]

The Edwards committee subsequently considered a number of proposals, radical and otherwise, that sought to enhance the FDA's stature and authority. Two of the more drastic ideas saw the FDA completely reorganized within the American government, with the purported goal to limit presidential control over the agency and thus change the immediate political control over the FDA. One option was to refashion the FDA in the mold of the Environmental Protection Agency, an independent body within the executive branch. A second option was to place the FDA under the control of Congress, much like the Federal Trade Commission, so that the FDA was completely free of the executive branch and presidential influence. This meant, ultimately, that the FDA's rule-making would no longer be beholden to the Office of Management and Budget.[48]

A less severe option, however, was to leave the FDA in its position in the government and simply have Health and Human Services Secretary Louis Sullivan rescind Richard Schweiker's ten-year-old order about HHS approval of regulations. In short, this would return regulation-making control to the FDA. Sherwin Gardner, the former head of the Bureau of Drugs and a member of the Edwards committee, encapsulated the debate when he observed, "you can achieve independence inside or outside the agency in a number of different ways." This independence, he noted, was lost in the very early Reagan years and reestablishing that power "would clearly enable the agency to function in a more vigorous way than it is now functioning."[49] Edwards agreed and he explained this to the Senate Committee on Labor and Human Resources. The "FDA," he declared, "must be separated from the Public Health Service" and the commissioner must have total authority to "run the Agency's operations including regulations, facilities, equipment, and personnel."[50]

The Final Report of the Advisory Committee on the Food and Drug Administration was ultimately released in May 1991. After a thorough examination and discussion of the FDA's leadership, management systems, resources, and the effectiveness and authority of the FDA, the report concluded, alarmingly, that something had indeed gone astray at the FDA. According to author Herbert Burkholz, the report was "damning both in general and in detail."[51] It contended there were deficiencies in the FDA's administration and management and, in a broader sense, the FDA was "overextended, underfunded, and shackled by bureaucratic constraints." In addition, it argued that even though "the FDA has routinely lived with controversy, the magnitude of current pressures is unprecedented in nature and scope."[52] (Those pressures, of course, came from all sides—the U.S. Congress, AIDS activists, consumer advocates, drug company officials, and the media.) However, the authors of the report added essential caveats to this larger, menacing finding—namely, their assertions were not to be taken as an attack on the FDA itself or its employees, both Congress and the Executive Branch bore responsibilities for the FDA's moribund state, and, thankfully, the public health had not been significantly threatened.

The report found, moreover, that no single FDA official or department, such as Arthur Hull Hayes or Frank Young or the Division of Generic Drugs, was culpable for the deterioration of the FDA during the 1980s. Instead, the problems facing the FDA were broad and dynamic. Leadership was also an issue. Not only was the FDA weak in a funding sense, not only was morale low, and not only was the FDA having problems with management systems, but the agency could not lure strong leaders to its ranks. This dearth in leadership trickled down to the foundational levels.[53]

In describing the significance and necessity of the report, the committee found that an energetic FDA was essential to Americans. It also underlined the importance of the FDA in the future:

> The impact of a strong and effective FDA goes beyond protecting and enhancing the public health; the Agency's actions can have a profound economic impact as well. A robust FDA will enable American companies to obtain the regulatory approvals they need to move products quickly from laboratories into the hands of patients and consumers.[54]

Ripple Effects

In 1989, at the end of the Reagan years, the *cause célèbre* that was the generic drug scandal cast a pall on the generic drug industry and on the FDA itself. As the sensational details of bribery and a rigged approval process emerged, staff members at the highest levels of the FDA turned on Congress and each other. Commissioner Young, trapped in the "cheerless halls" of the FDA, blasted John Dingell and the House Energy and Commerce Committee for politicizing the issue.[55] Yet Young himself was criticized for the abandonment of FDA Chief Counsel Tom Scarlett, a man well-liked at the agency who was nevertheless dismissed by the Health and Human Services during the investigation. To make matters worse, Young, after he was made to resign, bitterly observed that he had been undone by excessive politicking, a paucity of resources, and by his own staff.

Such troubles at the FDA had profound ripple effects in the early 1990s. First, there was an important change of leadership. Dr. David Kessler, a hard-driving and political individual who subsequently strove to reinvigorate the agency's enforcement profile and public standing, replaced the interim commissioner James Benson. Kessler was an author of the Edwards report and his colleagues on the committee applauded his appointment—indeed, they indicated clearly that Kessler, even at thirty-nine, was a fitting choice to institute the report's recommendations and fully supported him. One of the most-qualified commissioners in the agency's history, Kessler possessed an M.D. from Harvard and law degree from the University of Chicago. Thereafter, while completing his residency at Johns Hopkins University, he also consulted for Orrin Hatch's Committee on Labor and Human Resources. According to Kessler, "I caught up on sleep on the train" between Washington and Baltimore; and because he worked so tirelessly, he was able to obtain an insider's view of the political process.[56] A moderate Republican, Kessler believed in a curious mix of regulation, reform, and enforcement.

By any measure, the FDA was an ailing agency when Kessler assumed the office of the commissioner. Explaining this, in his 2001 autobiography, *A Question of Intent*, he contended that the FDA had been "weakened by years of ideological intervention, especially during the Reagan era, from 1981 through 1988 . . ."[57] Thus, upon taking the job he quickly identified various treatments for the sick agency. First, in the wake of the generic drug scandal he aimed to restore the agency's credibility. Second, he sought to clear the backlog of drugs and products that were months, if not years, behind schedule for their final approval. Third, and perhaps most difficult: improve management. Finally, Kessler made it clear that he needed to seek staff funds and regulatory authority to improve morale and build a stronger agency. These priorities, though driven by different imperatives and circumstances, were reminiscent of the Hayes and Young tenures. The rhetoric emanating from the commissioner, however, shifted rather dramatically under Kessler's leadership. "The honor system is out the window," stated a tougher-talking, more enforcement-driven commissioner. "The FDA is a policeman" and "we're going to take up enforcement a notch in the agency."[58] The softer, industry-friendly language of commissioner Hayes, for example, became a distant memory.

Relatedly, a second significant ripple effect of the 1980s was landmark legislation. In 1992, the U.S. Congress designed and passed the FDA Revitalization Act and the Prescription Drug User Fee Act. This legislation authorized prescription drug and medical device user fee programs—i.e., a system in which drug companies paid the FDA to review their applications; however, the legislation also authorized provisions to improve drug safety, track clinical trials, publicize clinical trial results, and increase data on the safety and efficacy of drugs and medical devices used by children.[59]

The Revitalization Act contained four separate pieces of prescription drug and medical device legislations: the Prescription Drug User Fee Act (discussed below), the Medical Device User Fee and Modernization Act, the Best Pharmaceuticals for Children Act, and the Pediatric Research Equity Act.[60] These provisions aimed to correct flaws in the FDA review process and in its enforcement profile, and they were emblematic of widespread recognition—by the media, by Congress, by the bureaucracy—of a variety of problems hindering the agency. The Prescription Drug User Fee Act (PDU-FA), though just one part of the FDA Revitalization Act, deserves special attention, for the implementation of user fees was nothing less than a fundamental modification of the status quo at the FDA. In the wake of the Edwards report, PDUFA was designed to inject the FDA with extra resources and thereby quicken the drug approval process. With the legislation's passage in 1992, the FDA immediately began to charge drug companies fees to review their drug applications: companies were charged an annual fee of $50,000, as well as $6,000 for each product already on the market and $100,000 for each new application. In addition to this payment system, the Act established deadlines for the FDA's drug reviewers to reach their decisions about products.[61]

The passage of the Prescription Drug User Fee Act underlined how much the FDA had changed during the Reagan years. During the early 1980s, both drug companies and Republicans and Democrats opposed the implementation of user fees. According to congressional Republicans, user fees were no less than hidden taxes on drug companies. For Democrats, the fees posed a clear threat to FDA appropriations levels because they might allow their conservative counterparts the leverage to trim the current FDA budget. Yet, recent circumstances—the drug scandal, dwindling regard for the FDA (exacerbated by enfeebled enforcement and budget numbers), and the Edwards report—established the conditions that enabled the passage of the Prescription Drug User Fees Act.[62] In 1991, Commissioner Kessler felt the conditions were right to advance and implement user fees to increase the agency's resources. Once Kessler won the support of Gerald Mossinghoff, the influential president of the Pharmaceutical Manufacturers Association, it became more likely that a congressional bill would find support. Indeed, familiar figures, Henry Waxman and John Dingell, sponsored a bill in the House of Representatives, while Orrin Hatch and Ted Kennedy proposed a version in the Senate. President George H.W. Bush later signed the bill and it surely reflected his feeling that there ought to be less of an adversarial relationship between the drug industry and the FDA.

The passage of this legislation definitely aided the FDA's drug review process tremendously as the number of reviewers and funding increased and review times fell. By 2004, user fees funded about half of all new drug costs. The implementation of user fees enlarged the new drug review staff two-fold between 1992 and 2004—from 1,277 full-time staff to 2,503. The median approval time for priority new drug applications dropped from 13.2 months in 1993 to 6.4 months in 2003. Between 1992 and 1995, the time needed to act on a drug decreased from thirty to seventeen months. Since the passage of PDUFA, moreover, the FDA approved over 1,000 new drugs.[63] With the addition of industry payments to the FDA and greater collaboration between companies and FDA officials, the approval process was enhanced and more drugs subsequently came to the U.S. market.

Gingrich and Conservatism

By 1994, in a startling reversal, the FDA had once again become a "lightning rod for antigovernment sentiments," forcing commissioner Kessler to comment, "It's not fashionable to be a regulator these days."[64] Having been reappointed as head of the FDA following the Clinton victory in 1992, Kessler was determined to further speed up the drug review process, particularly in the inchoate bio-tech industry. He had been on the job for four years and had already made some progress, but the FDA nevertheless remained the focus of considerable criticism. "I just don't get it," declared Kessler, "I think we've delivered."[65] While that may have been partly true, by most accounts the FDA still needed to enhance its relationship with industry during the IND phase of drug development. Besides this, Kessler had proven irascible— some said antagonistic—during his time in office. Instead of building constituencies and courting allies, he had garnered enemies.[66]

At the same time, there was a broader shift in American politics itself. A "conservative paradigm" continued to govern the period and the "Republican revolution" of 1994 was an important element of the increased pressure on the FDA. More specifically, during the 1994 midterm elections a fiercely antigovernment brand of Republicans led by Representative Newt Gingrich of Georgia won majorities in both the House and Senate. His "Contract with America" demonized President Clinton, promised to end the "scandal and disgrace" of the Democratic Congress, and explicitly outlined small government and antiregulatory principles. According to David Halberstam, the very conservative right wing that had birthed this contract were "the "children of the Reagan revolution now coming of age, driven by their own passions and, like many true believers before them, accustomed to talking only with people who agreed with them."[67] "They were deeply distrustful," moreover, "of the very government that they, like it or not, were now an important part of . . ."[68]

The FDA's pharmaceutical policies, which constituted part of what the new breed of conservatives deemed an intrusive and overbearing government, were especially singled out. Speaker Gingrich called the FDA the nation's "number one job-killer" and underlined a desperate need for FDA reform.[69] And by 1995 a full-scale anti-FDA campaign was underway, with conservative pundit James Brosvard encapsulating the struggle: "One of the clearest tests of whether a Republican Congress can begin to rein in big government will be the . . . battle over the future of the FDA."[70] Yet, both patient-consumer groups and the pharmaceutical industry demonstrated a degree of division and reluctance about wholesale change of drug policies at the agency. For example, the Patient Coalition, a collection of patient groups, articulated strident support of the FDA, whereas the Public Citizen's Dr. Sidney Wolfe, who had made a career out of critiquing the agency, warned of the dangers in weakening the agency—in abandoning its high standards. Representing another patient-consumer opinion, however, were "phony grassroots groups" and other patients and families, who had been flown into Washington specifically for the FDA reform debate. Their message, according to Philip J. Hilts, aligned with the "hard right" Republican view: Americans were dying of red tape and the FDA ought to be dismantled.[71]

The pharmaceutical industry, for its part, struck an uneasy balance between support for the FDA and attempts at reform. The Pharmaceuticals and Research and Manufacturers of American (PhRMA), which represented all drug makers in the United States, was placed in peculiar position where it advocated "quantum changes" in FDA operations, but also sought to prevent significant and irreparable damage to the agency.[72] "Drug companies were doing well—business was good and getting better, profits were high, the FDA was moving faster than ever—but the companies had no desire to alienate the new Republican leadership."[73] It thus allied with such groups as the Cato Institute, Citizens for a Sound Economy, Progress and Freedom Foundation, and Washington Legal Foundation, which had competed with each other in 1995–1996 to produce and promote radical FDA reform measures. At the same time, the pharmaceutical industry did not entirely accept "conservative mythology" and often publicly employed softer terms like modernization and bipartisanship when discussing possible changes at the FDA.[74] PhRMA President Alan Holmer announced publicly the industry wanted, "consensus or noncontroversial FDA modernization items as amendments to PDUFA."[75] Privately, however, certain industry insiders worried that Congress was overreaching and could potentially derail the FDA's all-important drug reviews, thereby hurting the business in the long term.

Efforts for FDA reform reached their zenith in 1996. Representative Ron Wyden (D-OR) had introduced an omnibus bill in 1995 that would have expedited the drug approval process and strengthened the role of outside advisory panels, though this failed to gain traction. The following year, Senator Nancy Kassebaum (R-KS) proposed a bill that aimed to accomplish the same outcome: she incorporated a six-month deadline for FDA action on

NDAs, a 120 day deadline for approval of drugs to treat life-threatening illnesses or those for which no other treatment existed, and a provision that allowed U.K.- or E.U.-approved products on the American market. In the House of Representatives, however, Thomas Bliley (R-VA) proposed an alternative vision of FDA reform. Earlier in the year, the Progress & Freedom Foundation (PFF), which had strong ties to Gingrich's office, unveiled a new plan for FDA reform that included privatizing and eliminating the agency's gatekeeping powers through "third party" reviewers.[76] These outside reviewers, designated as Drug and Device Certification Bodies (DCBs), would essentially serve as independent bodies advising manufacturers on the design and conduct of trials and FDA rules.[77] Representative Bliley, for his part, was very much in support of this type of solution to what he perceived as the FDA's problems. Thus, the legislative efforts in 1996 sought to streamline the FDA drug approval process, either through rigid time limits on FDA action or outsourcing some of the decision-making.

During committee hearings in 1996, the anti-FDA sentiments were front and center and the debate over consumer choice and sound FDA regulation created considerable publicity. In particular, Bliley's House Commerce Committee began hearings on May 1, 1996. Commissioner Kessler, for his part, regarded the Bliley bill and the hearings themselves as parochial and potentially dangerous for Americans. "This is as serious as it gets," he told one reporter the day of his testimony.[78] From the critical opening statement, made by Representative James Greenwood (R-PA), who would later become the head of one of the leading U.S. biotechnology industry trade groups, the Biotechnology Industry Organization (BIO), the FDA found itself on the defensive. Vilified for its slow approval times and denying sick Americans life-saving drugs, the FDA was portrayed in the broadest stroke possible but also as solely culpable for delays. The nuances inherent to an incredibly difficult task like drug approval—be it the "experience" of a company in preparing an acceptable application or how the FDA fared relative to other regulatory bodies—were noticeably absent. In the face of such criticism, Kessler was unrepentant, if not fully pugnacious, as he explained that the FDA rested at the interface of business and industry, physicians and academic researchers, patient-consumer groups, and politicians. Over several hours of testimony he carefully defended the agency, stressed its role in protecting the public health, and highlighted the unmistakable radicalism of the "reform" bills.

Although he avoided outright truculence, Kessler nevertheless declared strongly that the agency's long-standing bugbear—the drug lag—was mainly solved yet it still seemed an obsession for members of Congress. "Those who fail to recognize the [FDA's] performance and achievements," he pronounced, "threaten to undermine the real progress the Agency has made."[79] Thereafter, Kessler addressed what he viewed as the extremist elements of the proposed legislation. First, one of the provisions about which he raised concerns was the provision to modify the agency's mission statement. Instead of simply protecting the public's health and safety, the statement was now to reflect a business agenda. At its most basic, this encapsulated the ideology that drove FDA reform and symbolized the triumph of conservatism in Washington policy-making. Second, proposed restraints on the FDA's power to fully review and approve products were, in Kessler's estimation, pernicious. Hard deadlines and restrictions on comparing the effectiveness of two commercial drugs, just two provisions that Kessler pointed toward, not only limited the agency's ability to ask the proper questions and receive answers from the drug industry.

According to Philip J. Hilts, the authors of the reform legislation, while not aware of FDA history, certainly understood what was irritating to drug manufacturers:

> The conservatives were proposing that the hard-won gains of the previous century to establish testing and the standards of science be erased in a few paragraphs. America would enthrone the judgment of doctors and companies again, and opinion rather than science would rule. The system they proposed to replace the FDA was a fragmented, information-light system that might well be slower that what it replaced, and could certainly lead to medical catastrophes. [80]

The Kassebaum bill, which emerged from the Senate Labor and Human Resources Committee and aimed to significantly reform the FDA, failed to generate sufficient support. Senator Edward Kennedy (D-MA), still involved in the functioning of the FDA, made a speech denouncing Kassebaum's approach, which arguably reflected the moderation of the Senate—the notion of altering the FDA's fundamental approval authority and making the agency more of a supervisory body was far too radical for most legislators. In Kennedy's view, Kassebaum's bill went in the "wrong direction" and the "lessons of the past have been turned on their heads." [81] But the bill demonstrated, as in the earliest days of the Reagan presidency, how FDA reform initiatives were guided by conservative think tanks, in this case the Progress and Freedom Foundation (PFF). Moreover, the policies contained within the bill signaled not only the triumph of conservatism but also showcased how the contours of conservatism had changed under Gingrich's leadership. While Reagan's more moderately conservative approach to FDA reform had been supplanted by notions of privatization and mandated time-lines, his imprint was markedly apparent. Nevertheless, Alicia Ault Barnett, writing in *The Lancet*, speculated that the PFF plan would not likely form part of the finalized FDA reform. [82]

By the early fall of 1996, as the presidential election race gained momentum, Barnett proved to be correct. While Kassebaum's bill made it out of her committee, Bliley's bill did not. Common ground among Democrats and Republicans was scarce and during committee staff meetings it became clear that, unlike with Hatch-Waxman, there was no so-called "radical" deal to be had. Concurrently, the belligerent talk about FDA reform began to moderate, leading eventually to a more balanced approach to FDA legislation. In December 1996, Kessler, who had led the agency for over six years, announced he would be leaving the FDA in the near future. Not surprisingly, the retrospective accounts of his tenure were particularly divided. On the one hand, he was lauded for re-establishing the FDA's reputation and power, and often his approaches to Big Tobacco, silicone breast implants, and restrictions on "off-label" use of drugs are used to make this case; on the other, Kessler was severely criticized for his willingness to limit consumer choice. According to the Institute for Policy Innovation, a conservative think tank, "Kessler believed that the FDA exists (in part) to relieve people of the burden of choosing their risks, and to prevent them from making their own positions."[83]

In 1997, an FDA reform law was finally passed, although it was recast as "FDA modernization." Wide-ranging at 202 pages long, the Food and Drug Administration Modernization Act (FDAMA) ultimately reflected the Republican efforts to modify the agency, particularly the alteration of its mission statement and the tightening NDA deadlines through prescription drug user fee re-authorization. But it failed to achieve conservative goals in other ways. The outsourcing of drug approval, for example, which was referred to as third party review, was not legalized. From the FDA's perspective, FDAMA represented continuity and, while it had strongly objected to various provisions, including statutory deadlines, the agency was forced to "make concessions in light of the inevitable passage of this bill."[84] The National Consumer League, in addressing the passage of FDAMA, suggested it was a manifestation of "antigovernment sentiment" and might "diminish the agency's regulatory capacities." Even so, other provisions, including off-label prescriptions, were clearly intended to help consumers.[85] Richard Wolgemuth, a representative of Glaxo Wellcome, was generally positive about FDAMA and was hopeful that the promise of the Act would be achieve—i.e., genuine streamlining of the regulatory process. However, he insisted that more effort was needed: "the FDA, academia, other regulatory agencies, and the health care industry must truly work together to promote public health—not just protect it."[86]

NOTES

1. Quoted in Malcom Gladwell, "Burdened with New Duties, FDA is Seen Handicapped by Reagan-Era Cuts," *Washington Post*, September 6, 1989, 21.

2. "Proposed Remarks of Dr. Charles Edwards," Before the Senate Committee on Labor and Human Resources, May 15, 1991: Consulted online at http://tobaccodocuments.org/pm/2046936986-6992.html.

3. James Dickinson, "Realignment at FDA," *Pharmaceutical Technology*, November, 1989, 16–19 and Tim Friend, "Weak FDA Caused Drug Scandal," *USA Today*, August 25, 1989, A1.

4. Ibid.

5. Jim Dickinson, "Shackles Loosened, Optimism Returns to FDA," *Medical Marketing and Media* 25, March 1990, 4.

6. Ibid.

7. Quoted in Philip J. Hilts, "Ailing Agency—The FDA and Safety; A Guardian of U.S. Health is Under Stress," *New York Times*, December 4, 1989. A1.

8. Quoted in Dick Thompson, "What's the Cure for Burnout? Budget Cuts Leave FDA Sickly and Corporations Concerned," *Time* 134, December 25, 1989, 68.

9. Janet Ochs Wiener, "FDA Scandal: White Hats, Black Hats, Gray Areas," *Medicine & Health*, December 11, 1989, 12–13.

10. Angela Beth Ritzert, *Essays on the Development and FDA Approval of Pharmaceutical Drugs*, Unpublished PhD Dissertation (University of Kentucky, 1999), 121 (in 1992 dollars).

11. Anthony A. Celeste and Arthur N. Levine "The Mission and the Institution: Ever Changing Yet Eternally the Same" in *FDA: A Century of Consumer Protection*, ed. Wayne Pines (Washington: Food and Drug Law Institute, 2006), 76–77.

12. Janet Ochs Wiener, "FDA Scandal: White Hats, Black Hats, Gray Areas," 12–13.

13. A Report from the Office of Technology Assessment, *Pharmaceutical R&D: Costs, Risks, and Rewards*, February 1993, 40–42.

14. Ritzert, *Essays on the Development and FDA Approval of Pharmaceutical Drugs*, 135.

15. Dickinson, "Realignment at FDA," 16

16. U.S. Food and Drug Administration, *Milestones in U.S. Food and Drug Law History*, posted at www.fda.gov.opacom/backgrounders/miles.html, consulted November 22, 2005

17. James Benson and Robert C. Ecclestone, "Generic Drugs: A Crisis in Confidence" in *FDA: A Century of Consumer Protection*, ed. Wayne Pines (Washington: Food and Drug Law Institute, 2006), 180–181.

18. Committee on Energy and Commerce, *Generic Drug Hearings Part II*, 101st Congress, May–June 1989, 397–400.

19. Christine Gorman, "A Prescription for Scandal," *Time*, August 28, 1989. Consulted online at http://www.time.com/time/magazine/article/0,9171,958423,00.html.

20. Committee on Energy and Commerce, *Generic Drug Hearings Part I*, 101st Congress, May–June 1989, 1–3.

21. Committee on Energy and Commerce, *Generic Drug Hearings Part II*, 101st Congress May–June 1989, 397–400.

22. William Hubbard Interview, FDA Oral History Collection, 28–29.

23. Dickinson, "Realignment at FDA," 16.

24. "New Regs Proposed, Ex-FDAers Sentenced," *FDA Today*, November 1989, 1.

25. Herbert Burkholz, *The FDA Follies* (New York: Basic Books), 60–61.

26. Christine Gorman, "A Prescription for Scandal," consult at http://www.time.com/time/magazine/article/0,9171,958423,00.html.

27. Janet Ochs Wiener, "FDA Scandal: White Hats, Black Hats, Gray Areas," 12–13.

28. Committee on Energy and Commerce, *Generic Drug Hearings Part I*, 101st Congress, May–June 1989, 70–71.

29. Janet Ochs Wiener, "FDA Scandal: White Hats, Black Hats, and Gray Areas," 12–13.

30. Laurie Jones, "Dr. Young Leaves the FDA," *American Medical News*, November 24, 1989, 3. Young was also criticized for his (mis)handling of improperly labeled foods and contaminated batches of Chilean grapes.

31. Lois Ember, "FDA's Young Leaving for New Post," *Chemical and Engineering News*, November 27, 1989, 45–46.

32. Ibid.

33. Laurie Jones, "Dr. Young Leaves the FDA," 3.

34. Janet Ochs Wiener, "FDA Scandal: White Hats, Black Hats, and Gray Areas," 12–13.

35. Marlene Cimons, "FDA Chief Gets New Post but is Seen as Scapegoat," *Los Angeles Times*, November 14, 1989, A26

36. Ibid.

37. Jack Anderson and Dale Van Atta, "Young's Tumble From FDA," *Washington Post*, December 14, 1989, C20.

38. Tom Paulson, "Outgoing FDA Chief Rebuts Critics," *Seattle Post-Intelligencer*, December 8, 1989, D7.

39. Kevin Davis, "Sullivan to Name Panel to Study Troubled FDA," *Los Angeles Times*, December 13, 1989, A5.

40. Ibid.

41. Enrique Gonzales, "A Rudderless FDA Drifts, Awaits Congressional Action," *Washington Times*, December 8, 1989, B6.

42. Burton Love FDA Oral History Collection, ACC 98–16, 51.

43. "Sullivan Naming Panel on F.D.A. Problems," *New York Times,* December 14, 1989, B14.

44. Stephen J. Ceccolli, *Pill Politics: Drugs and the FDA* (New York: Lynne Rienner Publishers, 2004), 104.

45. Larry Thomas, "HHS Secretary Sullivan Announces FDA Review," *Washington Post*, December 12, 1989, B5 and "Former FDA Commissioner to Chair 'Blue-Ribbon' Panel," *FDA Today*, April 1990, 1.

46. Excluding the politically-appointed FDA commissioner.

47. Enrique Gonzales, "A Rudderless FDA Drifts, Awaits Congressional Action," B6.

48. For a more theoretical discussion about this see Daniel Drezner, "Ideas, Bureaucratic Politics, and the Crafting of Foreign Policy," *American Journal of Political Science* 46 (4) 2000: 733–749. The two options about the FDA's potential position in the government are directly related to Drezner's conception of "embedded" and "insulated" government agencies. Drezner contends on page 733: "agencies that are insulated from other bureaucracies have a better chance of surviving, but are unlikely to influence the broad contours of policy. The reverse is also true; embedded agencies have a much lower chance of keeping their ideational mission intact, but if they do survive, their odds of thriving are greater."

49. Malcolm Gladwell, "Breaking Bureaucratic Grip on FDA: Is Independence the Answer?" *Washington Post*, July 17, 1990, A17.

50. "Proposed Remarks of Dr. Charles Edwards," Before the Senate Committee on Labor and Human Resources, May 15, 1991. Consulted online at http://tobaccodocuments.org/pm/2046936986-6992.html.

51. Burkholz, *The FDA Follies*, 4.

52. Ann Gibbons, "A Fix for the FDA," *Science* 252, April 19, 1991, 370.

53. *Final Report of the Review Panel on New Drug Regulation*, Department of Health, Education, and Welfare (Washington, D.C.: May 1977), 5–6.

54. Ibid.

55. Jim Dickinson, "Shackles Loosened, Optimism Returns to FDA," *Medical Marketing and Media* 25, March 1990, 4.

56. Ann Gibbons, "Can David Kessler Revive the FDA?" *Science* 252, April 12, 1991, 200–203.

57. For insight about David Kessler's background and personal characteristics see his book, *A Question of Intent: A Great American Battle with a Deadly Industry* (New York: Public Affairs, 2001), 7. In describing the atmosphere when he first took office, Kessler suggested: "virtually no one was happy with the FDA."

58. Ibid.

59. "S.1082—The Food and Drug Administration Revitalization Act," Democratic Policy Committee (April 30, 2007) consulted at www.democrats.senate.gov.

60. "Legislative Notice: S.1082—The FDA Revitalization Act," Senate Republican Policy Committee (April 30, 2007) consulted at http://rpc.senate.gov.

61. Nicole Ciewhon Quon, *Decisions at Scientific Agencies: How do the NIH and FDA Balance Expert Opinions, Changing Agendas, and Political Pressure?* Unpublished PhD Dissertation (Yale University, 2007), 10–15.

62. Stephen Ceccoli, *Pill Politics*, 110.

63. "Legislative Notice: S.1082—The FDA Revitalization Act," Senate Republican Policy Committee 13 (2007) consulted at http://rpc.senate.gov. Also see Richard Stone, "Kessler's Legacy: Unfinished Reform," *Science* 274, December 6, 1996, 1603–1604.

64. Andrew Lawler and Richard Stone, "FDA: Congress Mixes Harsh Medicine," *Science* 269, August 25, 1995, 1038–1041.

65. Ibid.

66. See Kessler, *A Question of Intent*, 2001.

67. David Halberstam, *War in a Time of Peace: Bush, Clinton, and the Generals* (New York: Scribner, 2001), 298.

68. Ibid.

69. Quoted in Greg Anrig, "Who Strangled the FDA?" *The American Prospect*, December 12, 2007: Web Version Only. Consulted online at http://www.prospect.org//cs/articles;jsessionid=aS2rKBbxapH53-DB0h?article=who_strangled_the_fda

70. Quoted in Philip J. Hilts, *Protecting America's Health: The FDA, Business, and One Hundred Years of Regulation* (New York: Alfred A. Knopf, 2003), 313.

71. Ibid.

72. "FDA in 1996: Twice as NCE," *Medical Marketing and Media* 32, February 27, 1996, 6.

73. Hilts, *Protecting America's Health*, 311.

74. Robert Dreyfuss, "Popping Contributions: The New Battle for the FDA," *The American Prospect* 33, July/August 1997, 58.

75. Ibid.

76. James G. Dickinson, "Gingrich plan for the FDA leaves questions," *Medical Marketing and Media* 31, March 1995, 10.

77. Under this law, FDA personnel would be empowered to certify the DCBs and maintain postmarketing surveillance.

78. Hilts, *Protecting America's Health*, 313.

79. Testimony of David Kessler, U.S. House of Representatives, Committee on Commerce, Subcommittee on Health and the Environment, FDA Reform, May 1, 1996 (Washington, D.C.: Government Printing Office).

80. Hilts, *Protecting America's Health*, 317.

81. Ibid., 330.

82. Alicia Ault Barnett, "Conflict continues over plans for FDA reform," *The Lancet* 347, February 17, 1996, 464. See also Henry I. Miller, "Failed FDA Reform," *Regulation* 21, (1998): 24.

83. For example, see "Preserve David Kessler's Legacy," *New York Times* November 27, 1996, A24; "Building on Kessler's Legacy," *Los Angeles Times*, June 25, 1998, B8; Richard Stone, Kessler's Legacy: Unfinished Reform *Science* 274 December 6, 1996, 1603–1604; Robert Goldberg, "David Kessler's Legacy at the FDA," A Policy Report Summary by the Institute of Policy Innovation, 1997: consulted at www.ipi.org/docLib/QS143FDA.pdf-OpenElement.pdf. His leadership at the agency was unmistakable and he achieved a great deal. Moreover, as an MD and a trained lawyer who served both Democratic and Republican administrations, he established a new template for future commissioners. On the other hand, highly critical scholars and commentators, such as Goldberg, argue that Kessler essentially created a brand new FDA in his own image at the expense of individual choice, the public's health, and the public's well-being. According to Goldberg, for example, ". . . under Kessler the FDA became the only legitimate arbiter of what is regarded as a threat to the public health." He continues: "Kessler's particular justification of FDA's power demanded that the agency be accountable to no one and that neither he nor the agency accept responsibility for the consequences of its decisions and behavior."

84. Peter H. Rheinstein, "Overview of the US Food and Drug Administration's Reform Legislation," *Clinical Therapeutics* 20 (1998), C6-C7.

85. Linda Golodner, "The US Food and Drug Administration Modernization Act of 1997: The Impact on Consumers," *Clinical Therapeutics* 20 (1998), C20–C23. Golodner specifically addresses these provisions: off-label promotion, drug companies' ability to provide economic information, fast tracking of drugs (expedited drug review), codifying clinical trials, establishing a new clinical trials database, and the reauthorization of the PDUFA.

86. Richard Wolgemuth, "Realizing the Promise of the US Food and Drug Administration Modernization Act," *Clinical Therapeutics* 20 (1998), C2930.

Chapter Eight

Conclusion

"We all must realize that by the very act of living in a society we must give up some individual rights. We can never have complete freedom of choice on all matters."[1]

FDA COMMISIONER GOYAN, 1980

"It's simplistic to think that a President or an Administration can turn around an agency when you're dealing with one with a history and tradition like FDA. You can't change that easily, which is both a great weakness and a great strength."[2]

PETER BARTON HUTT, 1983

Ronald Reagan was elected president at a crucial moment in history. "The 1970s were a time of testing for Americans," according to historian Robert M. Collins, and "many came to fear that the nation had lost its ability to master its problems." "Serious observers began to talk of an American climacteric, of a sclerotic society irreversibly succumbing to the ravages of age."[3] Reagan, writes historian David Halberstam, was the answer. "In that period, Reagan ever self-assured—no American had a jauntier walk—was the welcome antidote" to the nation's troubles. "He believed in America, and America, of course, believed in him."[4]

First and foremost on the new president's agenda was the reversal in fortune of the domestic economy. Reagan subordinated all priorities to the economy and he emphasized that a combination of high tax rates and bureaucratic regulations acted as barriers to growth.[5] Unfettered market forces when combined with low tax rates were best equipped to create and distribute wealth, he believed. The unleashing of American industry was a natural good.

Once implemented, his policies helped engineer an economic recovery that would, besides a brief recession in 1990–1991, last for nearly two decades.[6] This was achieved in two ways. First, his "fiscal, deregulatory, and antitrust policies all played a role in facilitating the emergence of a new entrepreneurial economy."[7] Second and more crucial was Reagan's willingness to stay the course to fight inflation with a strict monetary policy executed by the Federal Reserve. Biographer Lou Cannon called this "the most notable economic accomplishment of the Reagan years. . . ."[8] It was brave because the administration was forced to weather the politically damaging recession. Republicans lost ground in the 1982 elections and Reagan's personal popularity dipped; nevertheless, his resolve in struggling through the recession was pivotal in the revitalization of the long-term health of the U.S. economy.

The Reagan administration also touted the unshackling of private enterprise as a key component of its economic agenda and the nation's economic recovery. However, the repeated reference to the virtue and successes of deregulation obscures the plain truth that it was largely a phenomenon of the 1970s. By the time Reagan assumed office in 1981, the deregulation of the airline, trucking, and railroad industries had been essentially completed. Besides that, the deregulation of the electric power, natural gas, and financial services had all been initiated. In addition, the push for that deregulation in the 1970s was bipartisan in nature—not a left or right, Democratic or Republican, issue—and it emerged from a diverse group of economists, legislators, regulators, as well as presidents of both parties.[9] Neither Reagan himself nor officials in his administration could accurately claim credit for instigating meaningful long-term deregulation of government in the 1980s, because its history was far too extensive and complex.

When the Reagan administration turned to the social regulatory regime, to matters of the environment, health, and safety, it discovered that such agencies as the Occupational Safety and Health Administration, Environmental Protection Agency, and Food and Drug Administration were not only well-regarded by the public but also had powerful special-interest lobbies to protect them. In 1987, a Roper survey found that 75 percent of respondents rated the FDA and EPA among the top three government agencies.[10] Reforming health and safety regulatory agencies was troublesome in the first place and this difficulty was compounded by the fact that Americans accepted the existence and practices of such agencies; according to political scientist R. Shep Melnick, "the public now expects the federal government to protect it from a wide variety of hazards."[11]

Consequently, the Reagan administration sought reform at the FDA, not wholesale deregulation, and it did so with tempered rhetoric and a balanced approach. The reform agenda, which Commissioner David Kessler called "ideological intervention,"[12] was advanced at the FDA in increments. And an administrative approach was used, rather than a legislative one. Reagan's Executive Order 12291 restructured the FDA's ability to propose and pass regulations, while Richard Schweiker and Arthur Hull Hayes instilled and oversaw the policy. Moreover, the FDA changed its informal practices and protocols at the behest of the executive branch, but it also modified its relationship with the drug industry. The agency's budget was trimmed and its personnel levels dipped, even though the agency's workload increased. This in turn enabled the FDA to move forward with a policy of voluntary compliance, which necessitated a stronger working relationship between the drug industry and the agency.

Still, having delivered on its promise of promoting regulatory reform at the FDA, the Reagan administration would be unable to claim total victory, since the thrusts and initiatives of that effort were relatively moderate. The agency's enforcement profile was reconfigured, though this was not achieved in radical ways, and no significant attempt was made by Congress to repeal the 1962 Kefauver amendments, which provided for effectiveness.[13] Even more telling, by the mid-1980s, the Reagan administration scaled back its regulatory reform initiatives at the FDA to the chagrin of many deregulators in the Republican Party and industry.[14] In Phillip Cooper's view, this forced antiregulation warriors to leave the administration unhappily.[15] According to historian John Ehrman, Reagan "never risked his political support by pushing for a fundamental restructuring of the role of government, nor did he try to impose drastic changes on existing social arrangements."[16] And as Wilentz contends in *The Age of Reagan,* subsequent Republican leaders, including Speaker Gingrich and George W. Bush, practiced a more ideologically charged verson of conservative politics. The FDA was a prime example of this political behavior in action.

Still, the policy of regulatory reform was nonetheless embedded at the FDA (and government more broadly), and it lingered. In the late 1980s, for instance, Reagan's leadership during the HIV/AIDS epidemic was noticeably absent. Yet the FDA initiated four regulations truncating the drug approval process and liberalizing access to unapproved, sometimes toxic drugs. Besides that, after Congress grappled with the agency over improper conduct in the Generic Drugs Division user fees were proposed by the FDA, and these further reformed the drug approval process.

A broader claim, which holds that Reagan succeeded in shifting the policy discourse about the size and scope of federal government programs, also applies to the FDA. According to political scientist Dan Carpenter, ". . . the rise of libertarian models and conservative politics in the United States" helped weaken the authority and force of the agency's capacities and actions.[17] Reagan was an important element in this, for he succeeded in shifting the policy discourse about the size and scope of federal government programs and he moved the discussion about which government program to launch or expand into how much of a program's or agency's budget *ought to be cut*. First principles, in short, were modified as Reagan instilled a reformist imprint on policy makers in the government and in traditional liberals who had once fought resolutely against Reaganomics (i.e., Ted Kennedy).[18] There was no considerable enlargement in the size of federal social programs during the George H.W. Bush administration, for instance, and this included the FDA. Also, Bill Clinton was unable to influence a Democratic Congress to pass his health care plan. The rise of a "Republican revolution" in 1994, moreover, placed new political exigencies on an already centrist Democratic president in Bill Clinton. In fact, one of Clinton's signature victories, welfare reform in 1996, was an effort to "triangulate," or undermine conservative Republicans' ability to attack him from the right.[19] His was a plan aimed at reducing the role of government in Americans' lives, and it owes much to the influence of Reaganism. During his presidency, moreover, centrist Democrats joined Republicans in a broader reform effort. It was not until the passage of Medicare reform of 2003 that government was significantly expanded and George W. Bush committed American taxpayers to an expensive social program on par with Medicaid and Social Security.[20] Bush, for his part, received withering criticism from members of the conservative establishment who believed he was radical and ultimately betraying the Reagan legacy of limited government.[21]

From the FDA's perspective, the measures and goals advanced by the Reagan administration represented continuity. Policy makers and politicians had attempted to rationalize, streamline, and reform the agency's drug regulation in the 1970s. A political backlash developed against the effectiveness requirement by the early 1970s and Congress began to place significantly more pressure on the FDA. Commissioner Schmidt, for his part, defended the agency and criticized the manner in which its practices were being politicized.[22] Besides this, the agency also contested the proponents of Laetrile, a set of libertarians who argued that the government was protecting people to death. At the end of the 1970s, the FDA had accrued some useful practice in the deliberate obstruction and open negotiation with advocates of regulatory reform.

During the Reagan years, however, the FDA compiled a record that challenges analysis. That record mixed disappointment and success, and it saw the emphasis shift back and forth from consumer protection to product innovation. The FDA sadly failed on a number of fronts. For instance, the agency approved dangerous products, as in the case of Oraflex, and was then quickly made to backtrack. When it came to Reye's syndrome the agency did not rigorously carry out its mandate. In fact, the FDA's enforcement profile changed so much so that commentators accused the nation's drug regulator of under-enforcement. Finally, and most egregiously, certain officials in the FDA engaged in bribery and corruption. According to William Hubbard, these breakdowns at the agency, while dramatic and dangerous, actually assisted the FDA in the long term: "If you look at FDA's history, it's through the tragedies and the problems, that's when you get help—you know, Silent Spring, thalidomide, sulfanilamide, generic drugs, you name it. Those are the things that have gotten FDA boosts in money and resources."[23] In spite of everything, it was not all ill tidings at the FDA and there were also accomplishments to the agency's credit. In lieu of sufficient resources, it won praise and awards for its handling of the Tylenol poisonings in 1982, the agency accelerated the drug review process, and it rose to the formidable challenge of the AIDS crisis—one of the nation's worst public health epidemics—and developed innovative policies.

The outcomes of regulatory reform initiatives at the agency were thus varied. In fact, the Reagan administration's key achievement was not deregulation of the FDA but rather a restrained transformation combined with the prevention of further regulation-making. In a broader sense, this epitomized the administration's approach to the regulatory state on the whole. The approach, while moderate compared to later policies, nonetheless demonstrated the potential for significant unintended consequences as the balance between innovation and consumer protection was recalibrated. The FDA during the Reagan years embodied all the tensions and dynamics inherent to a political and economic order in transition.

An authoritative assessment of the FDA during the Clinton and George W. Bush administrations remains to be written and there is certainly scope for expansion in the future. Avenues of research might include the FDA's regulation of Chinese pharmaceuticals and the approval of sophisticated new security technologies to safeguard the U.S. drug supply and identify counterfeits. These technologies include radio frequency identification, micro-barcode tags, organic tags, optically variable devices, laser perforations, and digital watermarks.[24]

President George W. Bush left office in 2009 and, similar to twenty years earlier in 1989, the strength of the FDA was contemplated and examined. The public discussion began in earnest in September 2006, as a blue-ribbon panel of experts concluded that the federal system for approving and regulating drugs was in serious disrepair. A host of dramatic changes were needed to fix the problem, proclaimed the fifteen-member panel. The report, released on September 22, 2006, represented a watershed moment after nearly two years of high profile controversy over the safety and side effects of such widely used drugs as pain relievers and antidepressants. It was recommended that the FDA implement a number of initiatives, ranging from restrictions on consumer advertising, to increasing the authority of the FDA, to eliminating squabbling within the agency.[25] By 2009, the negative news reports had not abated. The *Washington Post, New York Times,* and *Boston Globe* ran articles in which the FDA featured as a weakened arm of a government that was unable to meet the demands of the twenty-first century bio-pharmaceutical industry. The public health was at risk because the FDA lacked the tools to sufficiently regulate industry, but industry growth was similarly at risk since a drug lag was a natural corollary of budget and personnel deficiencies. Thus, while President Obama assumed control of an agency that was "struggling" and "beleaguered," the challenge for the FDA remained the same as it had during the Reagan years.[26] The agency still had to balance the public's insistence on personal access and choice with the public's expectation that the products from which they have to choose are safe and effective.

The pitfalls inherent in the FDA's thorny regulatory job were demonstrated chillingly during the final years of the George W. Bush administration. In February 2008, it was found that the FDA was utterly shambolic. The agency was, in the words of former FDA chief counsel, Peter Barton Hutt, "barely hanging on by its fingertips."[27] Not only did the FDA lack scientists who understood wondrous and rapidly emerging genomic- and nano-technologies, it was hobbled by an antiquated information technology system. That meant a dangerous informational asymmetry characterized the relationship between the regulator and regulatee. Just as dangerous, the FDA was found bedeviled by a weak organizational structure, a high rate of turnover, and a dwindling inspection force.[28] Joseph E. Stiglitz and Linda J. Bilmes chronicled in March 2008 how the escalating cost of the war in Iraq "crowded out spending on virtually all other discretionary federal programs," including the FDA.[29] In November 2008, the *Washington Post* reported that the Obama administration would "inherit an FDA widely seen as struggling to protect Americans from unsafe medication, contaminated food and a flood of questionable imports from China and other countries." The new administration was slated to take control of an agency that was "one of the many federal agencies where Bush administration critics say ideology has trumped science."[30] It seemed the FDA was again suffering under the leadership of a Republican president, just as it had at the end of the Reagan years.

Of course, the FDA's fragility in 2008 was not entirely the Bush administration's fault. Though the administration displayed little appetite for a major increase in funding between 2000 and 2008, much of the blame for the critical condition of the FDA must fall on the U.S. Congress. The legislature heaped new responsibilities on the agency—passing a hundred statutes between 1988 and 2008—but did not appropriate additional funding for this expanded mission. Rather, over a fourteen year period, between 1994 and 2008, the FDA's funding dipped by $400 million inflation-adjusted dollars.[31] Consequently, the conclusion of the Bush years bore a striking resemblance to the end of the Reagan years: the FDA was low in morale in 1988 and 2008, and federal reports in both years indicated the FDA needed an infusion of monies. In 1988, it was feared that the agency needed more money to prevent further corruption on the part of FDA bureaucrats and, once and for all, quash the drug lag. In 2008, the fear of a destabilized FDA centered more on the globalized nature of the U.S. economy and, specifically, the potential for unregulated foreign (especially Chinese) foods and drugs to enter the U.S. market.[32] As the Obama administration took office, the parallel between 1988 and 2008 was clearly evident, as once again the clarion calls rang in Washington and in the national press about the danger of a weakened FDA after eight years of Republican presidential leadership.

NOTES

1. Jere Goyan, "The Future of the FDA Under a New Administration," *Food Drug Cosmetic Law Journal* 36 (1981): 61–62.
2. Ed Magnuson, "Three Steps Forward, Two Back," *Time* 122, August 29, 1983, 16.
3. Robert M. Collins, *Transforming America: Politics and Culture in the Reagan Years* (New York: Columbia University Press, 2007), 7.
4. David Halberstam, *War in a Time of Peace: Bush, Clinton, and the Generals* (New York: Scribner, 2001), 146.
5. Ronald Reagan, *An American Life* (New York: Pocket Books, 1990), 224.
6. Michael Schaller and George Rising, *The Republican Ascendancy: American Politics, 1968–2001*, (Wheeling, Illinois: Harlan Davidson, 2002), 93 and Robert Dallek, *Ronald Reagan: Politics of Symbolism*, (Cambridge, MA: Harvard University Press, 1984), 5. Dallek also argues that the Reagan era ushered in greed, avarice, self-interest, inequality, conspicuous consumption, and corruption.
7. Collins, *Transforming America*, 236.
8. Lou Cannon, *President Reagan: The Role of A Lifetime* (New York: Public Affairs, 2000), 237.
9. Richard H.K. Vietor, "Government Regulation of Business," *The Cambridge Economic History of the United States, vol. 3, The Twentieth Century*, eds. Stanley L. Engerman and Robert E. Gallman (New York: Cambridge University Press, 2000), 1000-1009. See also Collins, 82–83.
10. "FDA Rates in Top Three Among Federal Agencies," *FDA Today*, February/March, 1987, 1.
11. R. Shep Melnick, "Risky Business: Government and the Environment after Earth Day," in *Taking Stock: American Government in the Twentieth Century*, eds. Morton Keller and R. Shep Melnick (New York: Cambridge University Press, 1999), 158.
12. David Kessler, *A Question of Intent: A Great American Battle with a Deadly Industry* (New York: Public Affairs, 2001), 7.
13. Collins, *Transforming America*, 82.
14. C. Joseph Stetler, "What Happened to FDA Regulatory Reform?" *Pharmacy Times*, July 1984, 6
15. Cooper, *The War on Regulation*, 29.
16. John Ehrman, *The Eighties: America in the Age of Reagan* (New Haven, CT: Yale University Press, 2005), 206.
17. Daniel Carpenter, *Reputation and Power: Organizational Image and Pharmaceutical Regulation at the FDA* (Princeton, NJ: Princeton University Press, 2010), 730–731.
18. John Sloan, *The Reagan Effect: Economics and Presidential Leadership* (Lawrence: University Press of Kansas, 1999), 7–8 and Charles W. Dunn and David J. Woodard, *The*

Conservative Tradition in America rev. ed. (Lanham, MD: Rowman and Littlefield, 2003), 13–14.

19. Nigel Hamilton, *Bill Clinton: Mastering the Presidency* (New York: Public Affairs, 2007), 414–415 and Bob Woodward, *The Choice: How Clinton Won* (New York: Simon & Schuster, 1997), 25.

20. Arnold Relman, *A Second Opinion: Rescuing America's Healthcare* (New York: Public Affairs, 2007), 83–85.

21. Michael Tanner, *Leviathan on the Right: How Big Government Brought Down the Republican Revolution* (Washington, D.C.: Cato Institute, 2007) and Bruce Bartlett, *Imposter: How George W. Bush Bankrupted America and Betrayed the Reagan Legacy* (New York: Doubleday Books, 2006). See also Lucas Richert, "Radical in the White House?" *AmeriQuests Journal* 7 (1) 2010.

22. The FDA's annual appropriation is still a part of the agricultural appropriations process, and this allocation is reviewed by the Agricultural Subcommittees of the House and Senate Appropriations Committees. Also, the FDA's authorizing committees are the Senate Committee on Labor and Human Resources and the House of Representative's Committee on Energy and Commerce. These Committees, as well as the Committee on Government Operations, have taken a strong interest in the FDA's activities and thereby influenced the agency through political pressure, investigations, and hearings.

23. William Hubbard Interview, FDA Oral History Collection, 28.

24. Food and Drug Administration. *FDA Counterfeit Drug Task Force Interim Report*, October 2003, consulted on www.fda.gov.

25. Shankar Vedantam, "FDA Told U.S. Drug System is Broken," *Washington Post*, September 23, 2006, A01.

26. Rob Stein, "Ailing FDA May Need a Major Overhaul, Officials and Groups Say," *Washington Post*, November 26, 2008, A02 and "The FDA in Crisis: It Needs More Money and Talent," *New York Times*, February 3, 2008: found online at http://www.strengthenfda.org.

27. "The FDA in Crisis: It Needs More Money and Talent," *New York Times*, February 3, 2008: found online at http://www.strengthenfda.org.

28. "Condition Critical at the FDA," *The Boston Globe*, February 3, 2008: found online at http://www.strengthenfda.org. In 2007, for example, the FDA inspected just thirty of several thousand foreign drug-manufacturing plants in China and Brazil and elsewhere and 100 of 190,000 food plants.

29. Linda J. Bilmes and Joseph E. Stiglitz, "The Iraq War Will Cost Us $3 Trillion, and Much More," *Washington Post*, March 9, 2008, B01.

30. Rob Stein, "Ailing FDA May Need a Major Overhaul, Officials and Groups Say," *Washington Post*, November 26, 2008, A02: consulted online at http://www.washingtonpost.com/wp-dyn/content/article/2008/11/25/AR2008112502219.html.

31. "Condition Critical at the FDA," www.strengthenfda.org.

32. Stein, A02. See also "FDA Crackdown on Illegal Products," *FDA Consumer* 38 (2004): 36–37.

Bibliography

PRIMARY SOURCES

Interviews

Gerald Barkdoll Interview (1998) FDA Oral History Collection. National Library of Medicine, Accession Number: 1998–018.

Jerome Bressler Interview (1999) FDA Oral History Collection National Library of Medicine, Accession Number: 1999–049.

Ronald Chesemore Interview (1998–1999) FDA Oral History Collection. National Library of Medicine, Accession Number: 2004-045.

Richard J. Crout Interview (1997) FDA Oral History Collection. National Library of Medicine, Accession Number: 2001–051.

Hugh D'Andrade Interview (6 November 1998) Chemical Heritage Foundation Oral History Collection. Chemical Heritage Foundation. Interview Number: 0172.

Charles Gorton Interview (3 December 1997) FDA Oral History Collection. National Library of Medicine, Accession Number: 1998–020.

Ballard Graham Interview (17 June 2003) FDA Oral History Collection. National Library of Medicine, Accession Number: 2004–021.

Ken Hansen Interview (13 June 1990) FDA Oral History Collection. National Library of Medicine, Key Information: 4th Series, 1982–1990 Box 1. (no accession number available).

Alan L. Hoeting Interview (21 April 1999) FDA Oral History Collection. National Library of Medicine, Accession Number: 1999–053

Joseph Paul Hile Interview (4 August 1988) FDA Oral History Collection. National Library of Medicine: Accession Number: 0756.

William Hubbard Interview (27 July 2005) FDA Oral History Collection. National Library of Medicine, Accession Number: 2006–044.

Fred Lofsvold Interview (25 August 1991) FDA Oral History Collection. National Library of Medicine. (no accession number available).

Burton Love Interview (1996) FDA Oral History Collection. National Library of Medicine, Accession Number: Accession Number 1998–016.

Robert P. Luciano Interview (25 June 1999) Chemical Heritage Foundation Oral History Collection. Chemical Heritage Foundation. Interview Number: 0183.

Raymond Newberry Interview (2004) FDA Oral History Collection. National Library of Medicine, Accession Number: 2004–054.

James Larry Tidmore Interview (2004) FDA Oral History Collection. National Library of Medicine, Accession Number: 2004–021.

Public Papers and Government Documents

Benson, James S. *State of the Food and Drug Administration*, delivered May 18, 1990. Posted at www.fda.gov/bbs/topics/SPEECH/SPE00004.htm, consulted November 3, 2005.

Congressional Quarterly Almanac, 99th Congress, 1st Session, 1986, 397–398.

Congressional Quarterly Almanac, 100th Congress, 2nd Session, 1988, 517.

Diamond v. Chakrabarty (United States Supreme Court) 447 U.S. 303, 206 USPQ 193: consulted online at http://digital-law-online.info/cases/206PQ193.htm.

Department of Health, Education and Welfare. *Drug Regulation Reform Act of 1978: The Administration Proposal, Section-by-Section Analysis.* Washington, D.C.: Government Printing Office, 1978.

Goldberg, Robert. "David Kessler's Legacy at the FDA," A Policy Report Summary by the Institute of Policy Innovation, 1997: consulted at http://www.ipi.org/docLib/QS143FDA.pdf-OpenElement.pdf.

"Laetrile/Amygdalin." National Cancer Institute, August 10, 2012. Consulted at http://www.cancer.gov/cancertopics/pdq/cam/laetrile/HealthProfessional/page1/AllPages/Print.

Offices of Drug Evaluation. Food and Drug Administration. "Statistical Report, 1987–1988," Washington, D.C.: Government Printing Office, 1988: found in the FDA Collection RS.N48.

Reagan, Ronald. *Public Papers of the Presidents of the United States: Ronald Reagan, 1981–1989.* Washington, D.C.: Government Printing Office.

———. *Remarks on Signing the Drug Price Competition and Patent Term Restoration Act of 1984,* Sept. 24, 1984, posted at www.reagan.edu/archives/speeches/1984/92484.htm, consulted October 22, 2005.

"S.1082—The Food and Drug Administration Revitalization Act," Democratic Policy Committee (April 30, 2007) consulted at www.democrats.senate.gov.

Schmidt, A.M. U.S. Food and Drug Administration. *The Commissioner's Report of Investigation of Charges From Joint Hearing.* Washington, D.C.: US Government Publications Office, 1975.

Testimony of David Kessler, U.S. House of Representatives, Committee on Commerce, Subcommittee on Health and the Environment, *FDA Reform,* May 1, 1996. Washington, D.C.: Government Printing Office, 1997.

U.S. Congress. House. Committee on Government Operations. *AIDS Drugs: Where Are They?* Washington, D.C.: U.S. Government Printing Office, 1988.

U.S. Congress. House. Subcommittee on Appropriations. *Agriculture, Rural Development and Related Agencies Appropriations for 1983.* 97th Congress, 2nd Session. Washington, D.C.: Government Publishing Office, 1983.

———. Subcommittee on Appropriations. *Agriculture, Rural Development and Related Agencies Appropriations for 1984.* 98th Congress. Washington, D.C.: Government Printing Office, 1984.

———. Subcommittee on Appropriations. *Agriculture, Rural Development and Related Agencies Appropriations for 1987.* Washington, D.C.: Government Publishing Office, 1988.

U.S. Congress. House. Committee on Science and Technology. Subcommittee on Natural Resources Agricultural Research, and Environment. *Drug Lag.* 97th Congress, 1st Session. Washington, D.C.: Government Printing Office, September 16, 1981.

U.S. Congress. House. Committee on Interstate and Foreign Commerce. Subcommittee on Health and the Environment. *Drug Regulation Reform—Oversight, New Drug Approval Process.* 96th Congress, June 25, 1980. Washington, D.C.: Government Printing Office, Washington, 1980.

U.S. Congress. House. Committee on Science and Technology. *FDA Drug Approval—A Lengthy Process that Delays the Availability of Important New Drugs: Report to the Subcommittee on Science, Research, and Technology, House Committee on Science and Technology,* May 28, 1980. Washington, D.C.: Comptroller General, 1980.

U.S. Congress. House. Committee on Government Operations. Subcommittee on Intergovernmental Relations. *FDA Proposals to Ease Restrictions on the Use and Sale of Experimental Drugs.* 100th Congress, 21st Session, April 29. Washington, D.C.: Government Printing Office, 1987.

U.S. Congress. House. Committee on Government Operations. *FDA's Regulation of Zomax.* 98th Congress, 1st Session, April 26 and 27. Washington, D.C.: Government Printing Office, 1983.

U.S. Congress. House. Committee on Energy and Commerce. Subcommittee on Oversight and Investigations. *Generic Drug Hearings Part I.* 101st Congress, May–June. Washington, D.C.: Government Printing Office, 1989.

———. Committee on Energy and Commerce. Subcommittee on Oversight and Investigations. *Generic Drug Hearings Part II.* 101st Congress, May–June. Washington, D.C.: Government Printing Office, 1989.

U.S. Congress. House. Committee on Government Operations. Intergovernmental and Human Resources Subcommittee. *Oversight of the New Drug Review Process and FDA's Regulation of Merital.* 99th Congress, May 22. Washington, D.C.: Government Printing Office, 1986.

U.S. Congress. House. Committee on Labor and Public Welfare and the Committee on the Judiciary. *Regulation of New Drug R&D by the Food and Drug Administration, 1974.* 93rd Congress, 2nd Session. Washington, D.C.: Government Printing Office, 1974.

U.S. Congress. House. Committee on Government Operations. *Therapeutic Drugs for AIDS: Development, Testing, and Availability.* 100th Congress, 2nd Session. Washington, D.C.: Government Printing Office, 1988.

U.S. Congress. House. Subcommittee on Health and Scientific Research and Committee on Human Resources. Testimony of Louis Lasagna, M.D. on Drug Regulation Reform Act of 1978. Rochester, New York: The Center for the Study of Drug Development, April 12, 1978.

U.S. Congress. House. Committee on Government Operations. *The Regulation of New Drugs By the FDA: The New Drug Review Process.* August 3 & 4, 97th Congress. Washington, D.C.: Government Printing Office, 1984.

U.S. Congress. Senate. Subcommittee on Health and Scientific Research of the Committee on Labor and Human Resources *Drug Regulation Reform Act of 1979.* 96th Congress, 1st Session, May 17 & 19. Washington, D.C.: U.S. Government Printing Office, 1979.

U.S. Congress. Senate. Committee on Labor and Public Welfare. Subcommittee on Health and Administrative Practice and Procedure. *Examination of the Pharmaceutical Industry (Part 7)*, 93rd Congress, August 5 and 16, 1974. Washington, D.C.: Government Printing Office, 1974.

U.S. Congress. Senate. Senate Republican Policy Committee. *Legislative Notice: S.1082—The FDA Revitalization Act.* Number 13, April 30, 2007. Consulted at http://rpc.senate.gov.

U.S. Congress. Senate. Committee on Labor and Human Resources. *Proposed Remarks of Dr. Charles Edwards.* May 15, 1991: Document consulted at http://tobaccodocuments.org/pm/2046936986-6992.html.

U.S. Congress. Senate, *Regulation of New Drug R&D by the Food and Drug Administration.* Hearings before the Committee on Labor and Public Welfare and the Committee on the Judiciary. 93rd Congress, 2nd Session. Washington, D.C.: Government Printing Office, 1974.

U.S. Food and Drug Administration. *A Brief History of the Center for Drug Evaluation and Research,* FDA History Office, posted at www.fda.gov/cder/about/history/Page44, consulted June 13, 2006.

U.S. Food and Drug Administration. *AIDS: False Hope From Fraudulent Treatment.* Rockville: Food and Drug Administration, 1988. Found at FDA collection at A26.A3568.

U.S. Food and Drug Administration. *Drug Bulletin.* September 1987. Washington, D.C.: U.S. Government Printing Office.

U.S. Food and Drug Administration. *FDA and the 96th Congress.* Washington, D.C.: Food and Drug Administration, 1980.

U.S. Food and Drug Administration. *Food and Drug Administration Quarterly Activities Reports*, 1970–1994. Washington, D.C: Government Printing Office.

U.S. Food and Drug Administration. *Justification of Appropriations Estimates for Committee on Appropriations, Fiscal Year 1983—Vol. V*. Rockville: Food and Drug Administration, 1983.

U.S. Food and Drug Administration. *Milestones in U.S. Food and Drug Law History*, posted at www.fda.gov.opacom/backgrounders/miles.html, consulted November 22, 2005.

U.S. General Accountability Office. *FDA Drug Approval—A Lengthy Process that Delays the Availability of Important New Drugs*. Comptroller General's Report to the Subcommittee on Science, Research, and Technology House Committee on Science and Technology. Washington, D.C.: Comptroller General of the United States, May 28, 1980.

U.S. General Accountability Office. *Legislative and Administrative Changes Needed to Improve Regulation of the Drug Industry*. Washington, D.C.: Government Printing Office, HRD-83–24, April 1983.

Young, Frank E. *Remarks to the Association of Food and Drug Officials*. June 14, 1988. Posted at www.fda.gov/bbs/topics/SPEECH/SPE00008.htm, consulted on November 22, 2005.

Unpublished PhD Theses

Doshi, Ami K. *Biopharmaceutical Strategic Alliances: Interorganizational Dynamics and Factors Influencing FDA Regulatory Outcomes*. University of Southern California, 2000.

Gieringer, Dale. *Consumer Choice and FDA Drug Regulation*. Stanford University, 1984.

Quon, Nicole Ciewhon. *Decisions at Scientific Agencies: How do the NIH and FDA Balance Expert Opinions, Changing Agendas, and Political Pressure?* Yale University, 2007.

Resnick-Troetel, Barbara. *Three Part Disharmony: The Transformation of the Food and Drug Administration in the 1970s*. City University of New York, 1996.

Ritzert, Angela Beth. *Essays on the Development and FDA Approval of Pharmaceutical Drugs.* University of Kentucky, 1999.

Seoane-Vazquez, Enrique C. *Analysis of the Patent Life of New Molecular Entities Approved by the FDA Between 1980 and 2001*. University of Minnesota, 2002.

New York Times

Abegglen, James C. "Merck Finds a Formula for Success." *New York Times,* October 30, 1983.

Carey, Ted. "At What Price?" *New York Times,* December 19, 1982, F22.

Cowan, Edward. "The Push is On for Legislation." *New York Times,* October 10, 1982, F27.

"Court Ruling on Laetrile Seen by F.D.A. as Curb." *New York Times*, February 27, 1980, A19.

deCourcy Hinds, Michael. "Cost Benefit vs. Safety: Politics and Mathematics Can Be Difficult to Separate When it comes to Regulation." *New York Times,* July 24, 1982, 8.

deCourcy Hinds, Michael. "F.D.A. Says it Overlooked Drug Data." *New York Times,* August 4, 1982, C1.

deCourcy Hinds, Michael. "Speeding F.D.A. Drug Review." *New York Times,* September 22, 1982, C1.

Dougherty, Philip H. "Advertising: Doctors are the Targets." *New York Times,* October 26, 1983, D21.

Farnsworth, Clyde. "Reagan Signs Order to Curb Regulations: Loud and Clear Only Executive Branch Agencies." *New York Times*, February 18, 1981, D13.

Fowlkes, Frank V. "Fair and Vital Legislation on Drug Patents." *New York Times,* August 11, 1982, A22.

Hayes, Thomas C. "The Drug Business Golden Era Ahead." *New York Times,* May 17, 1981, F1.

Hilts, Philip J. "Ailing Agency—The FDA and Safety: A Guardian of U.S. Health is Under Stress." *New York Times,* December 4, 1989, A1.

Leary, Warren E. "Congressmen Fault FDA On Generics." *New York Times*, March 8, 1991, D3.

Lyons, Richard D. "G.O.P. Group Suggests Health Spending Revisions: No Radical Changes Forseen." *New York Times*, November 16, 1980, 35

MacAvoy, Paul W. "Deregulation: A Letter to George Bush." *New York Times*, August 30, 1981, 126.

Molotsky, Irvin. "Big Drug Makers Fail to Stall Bill Aiding Generics." *New York Times*, June 8, 1984, D2.

———. "Critics Say FDA in Reagan Years is Unsafe." *New York Times*, January 4, 1987, A2.

———. "This Odd Couple Focuses on Health." *New York Times*, September 14, 1984, A24.

New York Times. "Abbott's Profit Gains by 17.9%." April 8, 1983, D5.

———. "Acting F.D.A Chief Named." September 2, 1983, A11.

———. "Aid Urged for Drug Industry: Study Urges Aid for Drug Industry." September 5, 1983, 31.

———. "Delay on Aspirin Warning Label Cost Children's Lives, Study Says." October 23, 1992, 12.

———. "Drug Agency Fills Post." March 18, 1983, B13.

———. "The Drug Business Sees a Golden Era Ahead." May 17, 1981, F1.

———. "FDA Backs Drug Makers." February 5, 1982, D8.

———. "F.D.A. Drug Agency Fills Post." February 5, 1982, D8.

———. "The FDA in Crisis: It Needs More Money and Talent." February 2008: found online at http://www.strengthenfda.org.

———. "F.D.A. Meets with Businessmen." November 16, 1980, 50.

———. "Preserve David Kessler's Legacy." November 27, 1996, A24.

———. "Sharp Drop Reported in FDA Enforcement." January 29, 1982, A12.

———. "Sullivan Naming Panel on F.D.A. Problems." December 14, 1989, B14.

———. White House Sought F.D.A. Data to Help In-Law of President." November 20, 1981, A29.

Noble, Kenneth. "Fulfilling a Promise on Deregulation." *New York Times*, August 19, 1983, A16.

———. "U.S. Expects Deregulation to Save Over $100 Billion." *New York Times*, August 12, 1983, A8.

Pear, Robert. "Drug Patent Extension Draws Heavy Lobbying." *New York Times*, July 28, 1983, D1.

———. "F.D.A. Chief Leaving to Join Westchester Medical School." *New York Times*, July 29, 1983, B8.

Reinhold, Robert. "Pills and the Process of Government." *New York Times*, November 9, 1980, SM24.

Scheuer, James H. "The F.D.A. Too Slow." *New York Times*, May 22, 1980, A35.

Tolchin, Martin and Susan J. Tolchin. "The Rush to Deregulate: Government is going to Unravel a Whole Skein of Health and Safety Regulations." *New York Times*, August 21, 1983, SM34.

Vartan, Vartanig G. "Drug Stocks Finding Favor." *New York Times*, January 21, 1981, D8.

Wiggins, Phillip H. "Betting the Store on another Tagamet: A Plethora of New Drugs is Making High Flyers of Drug Companies." *New York Times*, May 16, 1982, F14.

Wall Street Journal

Crossen, Cynthia. "Shock Troops: AIDS Activist Group Harasses and Provokes to Make its Point." *Wall Street Journal* (Eastern edition) December 7, 1989, 1.

Davidson, Joe. "ICN May Have Pushed Virazole to Fight AIDS—House Panel Data Suggest Firm Tried to Sell Drug Without FDA Approval." *Wall Street Journal* (Eastern edition) May 29, 1987, 8.

Davidson, Joe and Carolyn Phillips. "Eli Lilly Admits it Failed to Inform U.S. of Deaths, Illnesses to Tied to Oraflex Drug." *Wall Street Journal* (Eastern edition) August 22, 1985, 2.

Gieringer, Dale H. "The FDA Continues to Commit Regulatory Malpractice." *Wall Street Journal* (Eastern edition) March 27, 1985, 34.

Ingersoll, Bruce. "Chief of FDA to Step Aside After 5 Years—Frank Young, Often Mired in Controversies, Takes New Federal Post." *Wall Street Journal* (Eastern edition) November 14, 1989, A3.

Large, Arlen J. "Drug Patent Bill Clears Congress on a Voice Vote—Long-Debated Measure Gives Extended Patent Rights, Speeds Generic Marketing." *Wall Street Journal* (Eastern edition) September 13, 1984, 12.

———. "House Votes to Extend New Drug Patents and Allow Earlier Marketing of Generics." *Wall Street Journal* (Eastern edition) September 7, 1984, 8.

McQueen, Michael and Gerald F. Seib. "FDA Clears Use of Experimental Drugs; Reagan is Likely in Favor of AIDS Testing." *Wall Street Journal* (Eastern edition) May 22, 1987, 22.

Schorr, Bert. "Bill to Speed Marketing of Generic Drugs and Change Patent Rules Clears Senate." *Wall Street Journal* (Eastern Edition) August 13, 1984, 8.

———. "FDA Allowed Sale of Thousands of Drugs Without Safety Testing, House Panel Says." *Wall Street Journal* (Eastern edition) November 15, 1984, 4.

Swartz, Lucinda Low and Sam Kazman. "FDA Comes Looking for a Revenue Dose." *Wall Street Journal* (Eastern edition) December 23, 1985, 14.

Waldholz, Michael. "Drug Firms Hope FDA Broadens Plan to Speed Approval of Some Medicines." *Wall Street Journal*, October 21, 1988, B3.

———. "Pfizer Sees 15% Rise in Net and Revenue From New-Drug Sales." *The Wall Street Journal*, March 10, 1981, 20.

———. "Plan to Speed Approval of Test Drugs Pits Small Companies Against Big Ones." *Wall Street Journal*, April 3, 1987, 33.

———. "Prescription-Drug Maker's Ad Stirs Debate Over Marketing to Public." *Wall Street Journal*, September 22, 1987, 35.

Wall Street Journal. "Centennial Journal: 100 Years in Business—America Awakens to the AIDS Crisis, 1985." December 18, 1989, B1.

———. "FDA to Shorten Testing for Some Drugs—Plan May Speed Treatment for AIDS and Ills Seen as Life Threatening." October 20, 1988, B4.

———. "FDA Rules Changes on Breakthrough Drugs." October 29, 1987, 33.

———. "FDA Under Siege." October 12, 1988, A18.

———. "Finally, the Patient Benefits." October 20, 1988, A24.

———. "Ill Treatment." August 7, 1985, 16.

———. "Letters to the Editor: Evaluating Drugs." November 7, 1985, 31.

———. "Johnson & Johnson To Raise Payout 8%; Sales Gain Reported." April 22, 1983, 56.

———. "Review & Outlook: The FDA for Itself." October 13, 1988, A22.

Winslow, Ron. "There's Psychology in Drug Company Gift-Giving—Freebies Create Relationship, Reciprocity is Expected, Authors of Study Contend." *Wall Street Journal* (Eastern edition) December 22, 1989, 1.

Assorted Newspaper Sources

Anderson, Jack and Dale Van Atta, "Young's Tumble From FDA." *Washington Post*, December 14, 1989, C20.

Bilmes Linda J. and Joseph E. Stiglitz. "The Iraq War Will Cost Us $3 Trillion, and Much More." *Washington Post*, 9 March 2008, B01.

Brinkley, Douglas. "The Long Shadow." *New York Times Sunday Book Review*, May 18, 2008, http://www.nytimes.com/2008/05/18/books/review/Brinkley-t.html.

"Building on Kessler's Legacy." *Los Angeles Times*, June 25, 1998, B8.

Cimons, Marlene. "FDA Chief Gets New Post but is Seen as Scapegoat." *Los Angeles Times*, November 14, 1989, A26.

Collins, Dave. "Lawyer challenging reported Pfizer settlement." *Washington Post*, May 26, 2009.

"Condition Critical at the FDA." *The Boston Globe*, February 3, 2008: found online at http://www.strengthenfda.org on August 12, 2008.

Davis, Kevin. "Sullivan to Name Panel to Study Troubled FDA." *Los Angeles Times*, December 13, 1989, A5.

Doyle, Larry. "Aspirin-Reye's Chronology: Threat of Suits Delayed Warning Process." *Los Angeles Times*, May 31, 1987, 4.

Edsall, Thomas B. "Business Coalitions Form to Win Congressional Clout." *Baltimore Sun*, February 27, 1980, A6.

Gladwell, Malcolm. "Breaking Bureaucratic Grip on FDA: Is Independence the Answer?" *Washington Post*, July 17, 1990, A17.

———. "Burdened with New Duties, FDA is Seen Handicapped by Reagan-Era Cuts." *Washington Post*, September 6, 1989, 21.

Gonzales, Enrique. "A Rudderless FDA Drifts, Awaits Congressional Action." *Washington Times*, December 8, 1989, B6.

Harris, Daniel. "The AIDS Guerillas." *Los Angeles Times*, November 1, 1992.

Jenks, Susan. "FDA's Inaction on Zomax is probed by House panel." *Washington Times*, April 28, 1983.

Millenson, Michael L. "FDA: America's watchdog in distress." *Chicago Tribune*, September 19, 1983, 1.

"New Chief Casts Widely for New Ideas." *Washington Post*, October 25, 1984.

Paulson, Tom. "Outgoing FDA Chief Rebuts Critics." *Seattle Post-Intelligencer*, December 8, 1989, D7.

Perlman, David. "The Debate Over Regulating Drugs." *The San Francisco Chronicle*, February 18, 1981.

Russell, Cristine. "New Chief Casts Widely for New Ideas." *Washington Post*, October 25, 1984, A23.

———. "New Studies Find Prescription Drugs 'Least Expensive Form' of Therapy." *Washington Post*, June 20, 1984, A2.

Sanders, Bernard. "Let's Demand Lower Drug Prices." *Rutland Daily Herald*, July 25, 2001, A11.

Stein, Rob. "Ailing FDA May Need a Major Overhaul, Officials and Groups Say." *Washington Post*, November 26, 2008, A02.

Thomas, Larry. "HHS Secretary Sullivan Announces FDA Review." *Washington Post*, December 12, 1989, B5.

Vedantam, Shankar. "FDA Told U.S. Drug System is Broken." *Washington Post*, September 23, 2006, A01.

Assorted Magazine Sources

Anrig, Greg. "Who Strangled the FDA?" *The American Prospect*. December 12, 2007: Web Only. Consulted online at http://www.prospect.org//cs/articles;jsessionid=aS2rKBbxapH53-DB0h?article=who_strangled_the_fda.

"AIDS is Different." *Economist*, June 20, 1987, 15.

Barnett, Alicia Ault. "Conflict continues over plans for FDA reform." *The Lancet* 347, February 17, 1996, 464.

"Challenging the Apricot-Pit Gang." *Time*, July 25, 1977, 64.

Chi, Judy. "New FDA Will Stress Scientific Approach." *Drug Topics*, June 1984, 41.

Colvin, Geoffrey. "We Hate Big Pharma, But We Sure Love Drugs." *Fortune*, December 2004, 56.

"Deregulation: A Fast Start for the Reagan Strategy." *Business Week*, March 9, 1981, 62–67.

Dickinson, James. "Realignment at FDA." *Pharmaceutical Technology*, November 1989, 16–19.

Dickinson, James G. "Gingrich plan for the FDA leaves questions." *Medical Marketing and Media* 31, March 1995, 10.

Dickinson, James G. "Goodbye, Goyan! Some parting shots and pleasant memories." *Drug Topics*, March 1981, 84–86.

Dickinson, James. "Washington Report." *Pharmaceutical Technology*, February 1981, 24–26.

Dickinson, James. "Washington Report." *Pharmaceutical Technology*, November 1983, 20–23.

Dickinson, James. "Washington Report." *Pharmaceutical Technology*, October 1983, 22.

Dickinson, Jim. "Shackles Loosened, Optimism Returns to FDA." *Medical Marketing and Media* 25, March 1990, 4.

Dreyfuss, Robert. "Popping Contributions: The New Battle for the FDA." *The American Prospect* 33, July/August 1997, 58.

Ember, Lois. "FDA's Young Leaving for New Post." *Chemical and Engineering News*, November 1989, 45–46.

"FDA in 1996: Twice as NCE." *Medical Marketing and Media* 32, February 27, 1996, 6.

"Federal drug programs escape cuts." *Drug Topics*, April 3, 1981, 24.

Friend, Tim. "Weak FDA Caused Drug Scandal." *USA Today*, August 25, 1989, A1.

Gibbons, Ann. "Can David Kessler Revive the FDA?" *Science* 252, April 12, 1991, 200–203.

Gilston, Samuel. "FDA's New Commissioner, Frank Young." *Medical Advertising News*, September 30, 1984.

Gilston, Sam. "New Drug Pipeline Filling Up." *Medical Advertising News*, November 15, 1983.

Golodner, Linda. "The US Food and Drug Administration Modernization Act of 1997: The Impact on Consumers." *Clinical Therapeutics* 20, 1998, C20–C23.

Gorman, Christine. "A Prescription for Scandal." *Time*, August 28, 1989: consulted online at http://www.time.com/time/magazine/article/0,9171,958423,00.html.

Goyan, Jerry. "FDA Aim: Meeting the 75-Year Challenge." *U.S. Medicine*, January 15, 1981, 63–64.

"It was a very good year." *Drug Topics*, July 2, 1984, 22–23.

Jones, Laurie. "Dr. Young Leaves the FDA." *American Medical News*, November 24, 1989, 3.

"Laetrile Crackdown." *Time* 107, 1976, 84.

"Laetrile Flunks." *Time* 117, May 11, 1981, 63.

Lapham, Lewis. "Tentacles of Rage." *Harper's*, November 2004, 32–41.

Lawler, Andrew and Richard Stone. "FDA: Congress Mixes Harsh Medicine." *Science* 269, August 25, 1995, 1038–1041.

Loewenberg, Samuel. "Sidney Wolfe." *Lancet* 373, 2009, 537.

Magnuson, Ed. "Three Steps Forward, Two Back." *Time* 122, August 29, 1983, 16.

Moertel, C.G. "A Trial of Laetrile Now." *New England Journal of Medicine* 298, January 26, 1978, 218–219.

Morris, Charles. "Interview with Arthur Hayes." *Food Engineering*, October 1983, 14–19.

Mundy, Alice. "Risk Management: The FDA's Deference to Drug Companies is Bad for America's Health." *Harper's*, September 2004, 83–84.

Pike, Jesse M. "Letter to President-elect Reagan." *NARD Journal*, January 1981, 21.

"PMA rift healing, exec says." *Advertising Age*, November 12, 1984.

"PPI Users Know Less Than Nonusers, APhA Says." *Drug Topics*, June 15, 1979.

"Products in Development: Progress Continues in Search of New AIDS-related Drugs." *AIDS Patient Care*, August 1988, 28–33.

Relman, A. "Closing the Books on Laetrile." *New England Journal of Medicine* 306, 1982, 236.

Rhein, Reginald. "Industry Laments a Weak FDA." *Chemical Week*, June 12, 1985, 10–12.

———. "Why Reagan's FDA is All Stuffed Up." *Business Week*, June 17, 1985, 112.

Rheinstein, Peter H. "Overview of the US Food and Drug Administration's Reform Legislation." *Clinical Therapeutics* 20, 1998, C6–C7.

Robinson, Bill. "Frank Young takes over 'new challenges' at FDA helm." *Drug Topics* September 3, 1984, 24–26.

———. "Get on the Bus FDA chief tells health professions." *Drug Topics*, October 15, 1984.

Scherer, Michael. "The Side Effects of Truth." *Mother Jones*, June 2005, 71.

Scheibla, Shirley Hobbs. "Drug on the Market: Examining What's Wrong with the FDA." *Barron's National Business and Financial Weekly*, April 16, 1984, 22.

Scheibla, Shirley Hobbs. "Young Ideas: Meet the New Head of the FDA." *Barron's National Business and Financial Weekly*, June 4, 1984, 13.

Stacks, John. "It's Rightward On." *Time*, June 1, 1981, 12–13.

"Search for Hayes' successor will be tough one." *Drug Topics*, September 5, 1983, 10.

Stetler, C. Joseph "It's Your Business." RADIO TV REPORTS, INC., June 3, 1984: FDA Daily Clipping Service, FDA Biomedical Sciences Library.

———. "What Happened to FDA Regulatory Reform?" *Pharmacy Times*, July 1984, 6.

Stone, Richard. "Kessler's Legacy: Unfinished Reform." *Science* 274 December 6, 1996, 1603–1604.

Sun, Marjorie. "Laetrile Brush Fire Is Out, Scientists Hope." *Science* 212, May 15, 1981: 758–759.

"Testing Medicines to Death." *Economist*, January 30, 1988, 52.

Thompson, Dick, "What's the Cure for Burnout? Budget Cuts Leave FDA Sickly and Corporations Concerned." *Time* 134, December 25, 1989, 68.

"The FDA Hits a Snag over Issuing Drug Data." *Business Week*, December 3, 1979, 48.

Walsh, John. "Laetrile Tops FDA's Most Unwanted List," *Science* 199, 1978, 158–159.

Wiener, Janet Ochs. "FDA Scandal: White Hats, Black Hats, Gray Areas." *Medicine & Health*, December 11, 1989, 12–13.

Wolgemuth, Richard. "Realizing the Promise of the US Food and Drug Administration Modernization Act." *Clinical Therapeutics* 20, 1998, C29–30.

FDA Today:

"Action Plan II Is Here Now." *FDA Today*, August/September 1987, 1.

"AIDS Activists Stage Day-Long Demonstration at FDA." *FDA Today*, November 1988, 1.

"FDA Rates in Top Three Among Federal Agencies." *FDA Today*, February/March 1987, 1.

"Former FDA Commissioner to Chair 'Blue-Ribbon' Panel." *FDA Today*, April 1990, 1.

"Hayes Departs for Academia." *FDA Today* 10 (2) September 1983, 1.

"New Division to Review Drugs for AIDS and other Viruses." *FDA Today*, April 1988, 1.

"New Regs Proposed, Ex-FDAers Sentenced." *FDA Today*, November 1989, 1.

"President Asks for More Funds, Added Staff in 1988." *FDA Today*, March 1987, 1.

"President Reagan's Budget Request." *FDA Today*, March 1988, 1.

"Studies Give Nod to Review Process." *FDA Today*, July 1982: 3

"Vox Populi." *FDA Today*, January 1982, 4.

"Vox Populi." *FDA Today*, July 1982: 2.

FDA Consumer

Cooper, Richard M. "Regulation: Looking to the Future." *FDA Consumer* 14 (5) 1981: 52–53.

"Fast-tracking the First AIDS Drug." *FDA Consumer* 21 (8) October 1987: 14–15.

"FDA Crackdown on Illegal Products." *FDA Consumer* 38 (2) 2004: 36–37.

FDA Consumer 21 (8) October 1987: 1–19. Special issue.

Gilston, Samuel M. "Drug Regulation Today: How Much is Appropriate?" *FDA Consumer* 14 (5) 1981: 46–50.

"New Commissioner Finds No Lack of Challenges—Or Satisfaction." *FDA Consumer* 15 (9) 1981: 17–19.

Segal, Marian. "A Progress Report on AIDS Research." *FDA Consumer* 21 (8) October 1987: 11.

"Talking With Industry About Drug Lag, Generics, and Breakthrough." *FDA Consumer* 14 (1) 1981: 26–28.

"What the Experts Know About AIDS." *FDA Consumer* 17 (7) September 1983: 16–18.

SECONDARY SOURCES

Journal Articles

Arno, Peter S., Karen Bonuck, and Michael Davis, "Rare Diseases, Drug Development, and AIDS: The Impact of the Orphan Drug Act." *The Milbank Quarterly* 73 (1995): 231–252.

Abraham, John. "Distributing the Benefit of the Doubt: Science, Regulators, and Drug Safety." *Science, Technology & Human Values* 19 (4) Autumn 1994: 493–522.

Akard, Patrick J. "Corporate Mobilization and Political Power: The Transformation of U.S. Economic Policy in the 1970s." *American Sociological Review* 57 (5) October 1992: 597–615.

"A Question of Competence: The Judicial Role in the Regulation of Pharmaceuticals." *Harvard Law Review* 103 (3) 1990: 773–793.

Bandow, Doug. "Demonizing Drugmakers: The Political Assault on the Pharmaceutical Industry." *Policy Analysis* 475 (2003): 1–55.

Barkdoll, Gerald L. "Scoping Versus Coping: Developing a Comprehensive Agency Vision." *Public Administration Review* 52 (4) 1992: 330–338.

Birkhead, Guthrie S., "Reagan's First Term." *Public Administration Review* 45 (6) (1985): 869–875.

Bosch, Jean-Claude and Insup Lee. "Wealth Effects of Food and Drug Administration Decisions." *Managerial and Decision Economics* 15 (6) (1994): 589–599.

Carter, Dan T. "Legacy of Rage: George Wallace and the Transformation of American Politics." *Journal of Southern History* 62 (1) (1996): 3–26.

Drezner, Daniel. "Ideas, Bureaucratic Politics, and the Crafting of Foreign Policy." *American Journal of Political Science* 46 (4) 2000: 733–749.

Eizenstat, Stuart. "Economists and White House Decisions." *The Journal of Economic Perspectives* 6 (3) (1992): 65–71.

Epstein, Steven. "The Construction of Lay Expertise: AIDS Activism and the Forging of Credibility in the Reform of Clinical Trials." *Science, Technology, & Human Values* 20 (4) (1995): 408–437.

Fallows, James. "The Passionless Presidency: The Trouble with Jimmy Carter's Administration." *Atlantic Monthly* 243 (5) (1979): 33–48.

———. "The Passionless Presidency II: More From Inside Jimmy Carter's White House." *Atlantic Monthly* 263 (6) (1979): 75–82.

"FDA Reform and the European Medicines Evaluation Agency." *Harvard Law Review* 108 (8) (1995): 2009–2026.

Fuchs, Edward P. and James E. Anderson, "The Institutionalization of Cost-Benefit Analysis." *Public Productivity Review* 10 (4) (1987): 25–33.

Gieringer, Dale H. "The Safety and Efficacy of New Drug Approval." *Cato Journal* 15 (1) (1985): 177–202 consulted at http://www.cato.org/pubs/journal/cj5n1/cj5n1.html on February 12, 2009

Grabowski, Henry. "An Analysis of US International Competitiveness in Pharmaceuticals." *Managerial and Decision Economics* 10 (1989): 27–33.

Grabowski, Henry and John Vernon. "Longer Patents for Lower Imitation Barriers: The 1984 Drug Act." *American Economic Review* 76 (2) (1986): 195–198.

Grabowski, Henry G., John M. Vernon, and L.G. Thomas. "Estimating the Effects of Regulation on Innovation: An International Comparative Analysis of the Pharmaceutical Industry." *Journal of Law & Economics* 31 (1) (1978): 133–163.

Goyan, Jere. "The Future of the FDA Under a New Administration." *Food Drug Cosmetic Law Journal* 36 (1981): 61–66.

Himmelstein, Jerome L. and James A. McRae Jr. "Social Conservatism, New Republicans, and the 1980 Election." *The Public Opinion Quarterly* 48 (3) (1984): 592–605.

Hoover, Kenneth R. "The Rise of Conservative Capitalism: Ideological Tensions within the Reagan and Thatcher Governments." *Comparative Studies in Society and History* 29 (2) (1987): 245–268.

Horowitz, Robert B. "Understanding Deregulation." *Theory and Society* 15 (1986): 139–174.

Hughes, Sally Smith. "Making Dollars Out of DNA: The First Major Patent in Biotechnology and the Commercialization of Molecular Biology, 1974–1980." *Isis* 92 (3) (2001): 541–575.

Jennings, Kent M., and Ellen Ann Anderson. "Support for Confrontational Tactics among AIDS Activists: A Study of Intra-Movement Divisions." *American Journal of Political Science* 40 (6) (1996): 311–334.

Joskow, Paul. "Inflation and Environmental Concern: Structural Change in the Process of Public Utility Regulation." *Journal of Law and Economics* 17 (2) (1974): 291–327.

Krauss, Michael I. "Loosening the FDA's Drug Certification Monopoly: Implications for Tort Law and Consumer Welfare." *George Mason Law Review* Spring (1996): 1–19, consulted on March 11, 2005 athttp://classweb.gmu.edu/mkrauss/FDAmonopoly.html.

Liebenau, Jonathan. "Review of Peter Temin's Taking Your Medicine: Drug Regulation in the United States." *The Economic History Review* 35 (1) (1982): 161–162.

Light, Paul. "Review: Reagan's Regulatory Reform." *Public Administration Review* 48 (6) (1988): 1012–1013.

Lipset, Seymour Martin and William Schneider. "The Public View of Regulation." *Public Opinion.* January–February (1979): 6–13.

Lowe, Mary Frances. "Pharmaceutical Regulatory Policy: A Departmental and Administrative Perspective." *Food, Drug, Cosmetic Law Journal* (39) 1984: 504–509.

Lourie, Alan D. "Patent Term Restoration: History, Summary, and Appraisal." *Food, Drug, Cosmetic Law Journal* 40 (1985): 351–371.

Miller, Henry I. "Failed FDA Reform." *Regulation* 21 (3) (1998): 24–30.

Miller, Henry I. and David R. Henderson, "The FDA's Risky Risk-Aversion." *Policy Review* 145 (2007): 3–27, consulted at http://www.hoover.org/publications/policyreview/10183506.html.

McCubbins, Matthew. "The Legislative Design of Regulatory Structure." *American Journal of Political Science* 29 (4) (1985): 721–748.

Mitnick, Barry M. "Deregulation as a Process of Organizational Reduction." *Public Administration Review* 38 (4) (1978): 350–357.

———. "Review of The Politics of Regulation." *The Academy of Management Review* 9 (2) (1984): 361–364.

Moe, Terry. "Control and Feedback in Economic Regulation: The Case of the NLRB." *American Journal of Political Science* 79 (4) 1985: 1094–1116.

Morgan, Iwan. "Jimmy Carter, Bill Clinton, and the New Democratic Economics." *The Historical Journal* 47 (4) (2004): 1015–1039.

National Journal Opinion Outlook Briefing Paper. Washington: Government Research Corporation 2 (1982): 3–5.

O'Keefe Jr., Daniel. "Technical Problems With the Drug Regulation Reform Act of 1978." *Food, Drug, and Cosmetic Law Journal* 33 (1978): 674–680.

Olson, Mary K. "Regulatory Agency Discretion Among Competing Industries: Inside the FDA." *Journal of Law, Economics and Organization* 11 (2) (1995): 379–405.

———. "Substitution in Regulatory Agencies: FDA Enforcement Alternatives." *Journal of Law, Economics and Organization* 12 (2) (1996): 376–407.

Pape, Stuart M. "Market Exclusivity Under the Drug Price Competition and Patent Term Restoration Act of 1984—The Five Clauses." *Food, Drug, Cosmetic Law Journal* 30 (1985): 310–316.

Peltzman, Sam, Michael E. Levine and Roger Noll. "The Economic Theory of Regulation After a Decade of Deregulation." *Brookings Papers on Economic Activity, Microeconomics* (1989): 1–59.

Quirk, Paul. "In Defense of the Politics of Ideas." *The Journal of Politics* 50 (1) (1988): 31–41.

Richert, Lucas. "Pills, Policy Making and Perceptions: Inside the FDA During the 'Reagan Revolution.' 1981–1982." *Canadian Review of American Studies* 39 (1) (2009): 41–63.

———. "Reagan, Regulation, and the FDA: The U.S. Food and Drug Administration's Response to HIV/AIDS, 1980–1990." *Canadian Journal of History* 44 (3) (2009): 467–487.

———. "Radical in the White House?" *Ameriquests Journal* 7 (1) 2009: consult at http://ameriquests.org/.

Roberts, Peter W. "Product Innovation, Product-Market Competition and Persistent Profitability in the U.S. Pharmaceutical Industry." *Strategic Management Journal* 20 (1999): 662.

Rothstein, Henry, "Review of Science, Politics and the Pharmaceutical Industry: Controversy and Bias in the Drug Regulation." *Science, Technology & Human Values* 21 (4) (1996): 487–489.

Shapiro, Robert Y. and John M. Gilroy, "The Polls-Regulation I." *Public Opinion Quarterly* 48 (2) (1984): 531–542.

Sherrill, Kenneth, Carolyn M. Somerville, and Robert W. Bailey, "What Political Science is Missing by Not Studying AIDS." *Political Science and Politics* 25 (4) (1992): 688–693.

Shiner, Roger A. "Deregulation and Distributive Justice." *Journal of Business Ethics* 3 (1984): 235–256.

Siegel Joanna E. and Marc J. Roberts, "Reforming FDA Policy Lessons from the AIDS Experience." *Regulation Magazine* 14 (4) (1991): consulted at https://www.cato.org/pubs/regulation/regv14n4/reg14n4-siegel.html.

Siplon, Patricia. "A Brief History of the Political Science of AIDS Activism." *Political Science and Politics* 32 (3) (1999): 578–581.

Smith, R. Jeffrey. "Califano Tells Tales of the Top Post at HEW." *Science* 212 (1981): 142–144.

Stanbury, W.T. "Review: Instead of Regulation: Alternatives to Federal Agencies." *Canadian Journal of Political Science* 15 (3) (1982): 628–629.

Taylor, John B. "Changes in American Economic Policy in the 1980s: Watershed or Pendulum Swing?" *Journal of Economic Literature* 33 (2) June 1995: 777–784.

Tobbell, Dominique. " 'Who's Winning the Human Race?' Cold War as Pharmaceutical Political Strategy." *Journal of the History of Medicine and Allied Sciences* 64 (4) 2009: 429–473.

Tolchin, Susan J. "Presidential Power and the Politics of RARG." *Regulation* 2 (4) 1979: 44–49.

Vodra, William W. "The Drug Regulation Reform Act of 1978: Putting Some Economic Issues into Context." *Managerial and Decision Economics* 1 (4) (1980): 184–196.

Wardell, William. "Rx More Regulation or Better Therapies?" *Regulation* 2 (5) (1979): 25–33.

Wettergreen, John Adams. *The Regulatory Revolution and the New Bureaucratic State II.* The Heritage Foundation Policy Research & Analysis (1989): consulted at http://www.heritage.org/Research/Regulation/HL181.cfm on March 15, 2006.

Weingast, Barry R., and Mark Moran. "Bureaucratic Discretion or Congressional Control? Regulatory Policymaking by the Federal Trade Commission." *The Journal of Political Economy* 91 (5) (1983): 765–800.

Whittington, Dale, and W. Norton Grubb, "Economic Analysis in Regulatory Decisions: The Implications of Executive Order 12291." *Science, Technology and Human Values* 9 (1) (1984): 63–71.

Winston, Clifford, and Robert Crandall. "Explaining Regulatory Policy." *Brookings Papers on Economic Activity, Microeconomics* (1994): 1–49.

Young, Frank, and James Norris, "Leadership Change and Action Planning: A Case Study." *Public Administration Review* 48 (January/February 1988): 564–570.

Young, James Harvey. "Review: Peter Temin's Taking Your Medicine: Drug Regulation in the United States." *The Journal of Economic History* 41 (1981): 246–248.

BOOKS

Abramson, John. *Overdo$ed America: The Broken Promise of American Medicine.* New York: HarperCollins, 2004.

———. *Science, Politics and the Pharmaceutical Industry: Controversy and Bias in Drug Regulation.* New York: St. Martin's Press, 1995.

Agrawal, Madhu. *Global Competitiveness in the Pharmaceutical Industry: The Effect of National Regulatory, Economic, and Market Factors,* New York: Haworth Press, 1999.

Altman, Dennis. *AIDS in the Minds of America: The Social, Political, and Psychological Impact of a New Epidemic.* New York: Doubleday, 1986.

Anderson, Martin. *Revolution.* New York: Harcourt Brace Jovanovich, 1988.

Anderson, Oscar E. Jr. *The Health of a Nation: Harvey W. Wiley and the Fight for Pure Food.* Chicago: University of Chicago Press, 1958.

Angell, Marcia. *The Truth About Drug Companies: How They Deceive Us and What to Do About it.* New York: Random House, 2004.

Arno, Peter and Karyn L. Feiden. *Against the Odds: The Story of AIDS Drug Development, Politics and Profits.* New York: HarperCollins, 1992.

Avorn, Jerry. *Powerful Medicines: The Benefits, Risks, and Costs of Prescription Drugs.* New York: Alfred A. Knopf, 2004.

Bartlett, Bruce. *Imposter: How George W. Bush Bankrupted America and Betrayed the Reagan Legacy.* New York: Doubleday Books, 2006.

Berkowitz, Edward D. *Something Happened: A Political and Cultural Overview of the Seventies.* New York: Columbia University Press, 2006.

Berman, William C. *America's Right Turn: From Nixon to Clinton,* 2nd edition. Baltimore: John Hopkins University Press, 1998.

Birkland, Thomas. *After Disaster: Agenda Setting, Public Policy, and Focusing Events.* Washington, D.C.: Georgetown University Press, 1997.

———. *Lessons of Disaster: Policy Change After Catastrophic Event.* Washington, D.C.: Georgetown University Press, 2006.

Biven, W. Carl. *Jimmy Carter's Economy: Policy in an Age of Limits.* Chapel Hill, NC: The University of North Carolina Press, 2002.

Black, Earl, and Merle Black. *The Rise of Southern Republicans.* Cambridge: Harvard University Press, 2002.

Bogner, W., and H. Thomas. *Drugs to Market: Creating Value and Advantage in the Pharmaceutical Industry.* London: Permagon, 1996.

Boskin, Michael J. *Reagan and the Economy: The Successes, Failures, and Unfinished Agenda,* San Francisco: Institute for Contemporary Studies, 1987.

Broder, David. *Changing of the Guard,* New York: Simon and Schuster, 1980.

Brownlee, Elliot and Hugh Davis Graham. *The Reagan Presidency: Pragmatic Conservatism and its Legacies.* Lawrence: University of Press of Kansas, 2003.

Burkholz, Herbert. *The FDA Follies.* New York: Basic Books, 1994.

Busch, Andrew E. *Ronald Reagan and the Politics of Freedom.* Lanham, MD: Rowman and Littlefield, 2001.

Cannon, Lou. *President Reagan: The Role of a Lifetime.* New York: Public Affairs, 2000.

———. *Reagan.* New York: G.P. Putnam's Sons, 1982.

Carpenter, Daniel. *Reputation and Power: Organizational Image and Pharmaceutical Regulation at the FDA.* Princeton, NJ: University of Princeton Press, 2010.

Carter, Dan T. *From George Wallace to Newt Gingrich: Race in the Conservative Counterrevolution, 1963–1994.* Baton Rouge: Louisiana State University Press, 1996.

Ceccoli, Stephen J. *Pill Politics: Drugs and the FDA.* New York: Lynne Rienner Publishers, 2004.

Cohen, Jay. *Overdose: What's Wrong with the FDA? And What Can be Done About it?* New York: Tarcher-Putnam, 1999.

Collins, Robert M. *More: The Politics of Economic Growth in Postwar America.* Oxford: Oxford University Press, 2000.

———. *Transforming America: Politics and Culture in the Reagan Years.* New York: Columbia University Press, 2007.

Daemmrich, Arthur. *Pharmacopolitics: Drug Regulation in the United States and Germany.* Chapel Hill: University of North Carolina, 2004.

Dallek, Robert. *Ronald Reagan: The Politics of Symbolism,* 1st ed. Cambridge: Harvard University Press, 1984.

Danzon, P.M. *Pharmaceutical Price Regulation: National Policies Versus Global Interests.* Washington, D.C.: American Enterprise Institute Press, 1997

Dugger, Ronnie. *On Reagan: The Man & His Presidency.* New York: McGraw-Hill Book Company, 1983.

Dunn, Charles W. and David J. Woodard. *The Conservative Tradition in America*, revised edition. Lanham, MD: Rowman and Littlefield, 2003.

Dyck, Erika. *Psychedelic Psychiatry: LSD From Campus to Clinic.* Baltimore: Johns Hopkins University Press, 2008.

Ehrman, John. *The Eighties: American in the Age of Reagan.* New Haven: Yale University Press, 2005.

Eisner, Marc. *Regulatory Politics in Transition.* Baltimore: Johns Hopkins University Press, 2000.

Engerman, Stanley L. and Robert E. Gallman, eds. *The Cambridge Economic History of the United States, vol. 3, The Twentieth Century.* New York: Cambridge University Press, 2000.

Erickson, Paul D. *Reagan Speaks: The Making of an American Myth.* New York: New York University Press, 1985.

Feldstein, Martin, ed. *American Economic Policy in the 1980s.* Chicago: The University of Chicago Press, 1994.

Fink, Gary M. and Hugh Davis Graham, eds. *The Carter Presidency: Policy Choices in the Post- New Deal Era.* Lawrence: University Press of Kansas, 1998.

Friedman, Barry. *Regulation in the Reagan-Bush Era: The Eruption of Presidential Influence.* Pittsburgh: University of Pittsburgh Press, 1995.

Gambardella, Alfonso. *Science and Innovation: The U.S. Pharmaceutical Industry During the 1980s.* New York: Cambridge University Press, 1995.

Gerstle, Gary and Steve Fraser, eds. *The Rise and Fall of the New Order, 1930–1980.* Princeton, NJ: Princeton University Press, 1989.

Gilmore, Grant. *The Ages of American Law.* New Haven, CT: Yale University Press, 1977.

Ginzberg, Eli. *The Medical Triangle: Physicians, Politicians, and the Public.* London: Harvard University Press, 1990.

Goozner, Merrill. *The $800 Million Pill: The Truth Behind New Drug Costs.* Berkeley: University of California Press, 2004.

Green, Mark, ed. *Changing America: Blueprints for the New Administration.* New York: New Market Press, 1992.

Greene, Jeremy A. *Prescribing by Numbers: Drugs and the Definitions of Disease.* Baltimore: Johns Hopkins University Press, 2007.

Haig, Alexander M. Jr. *Caveat: Realism, Reagan, and Foreign Policy.* New York: MacMillan Publishing, 1984.

Halberstam, David. *War in a Time of Peace: Bush, Clinton, and the Generals.* New York: Scribner, 2001.

Hamilton, Nigel. *Bill Clinton: Mastering the Presidency.* New York: Public Affairs, 2007.

Hawthorne, Fran. *Inside the FDA: The Business and Politics Behind the Drugs We Take and Food We Eat.* Hoboken, NJ: John Wiley & Sons Inc., 2005.

Hayward, Steven. *The Age of Reagan: The Fall of the Old Liberal Order, 1964–1980.* Roseville, CA: Prima Publishing, 2001.

Healy, David. *Pharmageddon.* Berkeley: University of California Press, 2012.

Herzberg, David. *Happy Pills in America: From Miltown to Prozac.* Baltimore: Johns Hopkins University Press, 2008.

Himmelstein, Jerome L. *To the Right: The Transformation of American Conservatism.* Berkeley: University of California Press, 1990.

Hilts, Philip J. *Protecting America's Health: The FDA, Business, and One Hundred Years of Regulation.* New York: Alfred A. Knopf, 2003.

Johnson, Haynes. *Sleepwalking Through History: America in the Reagan Years,* Revised edition. New York: W.W. Norton & Company, 2003.

Karaagac, John. *Between Promise and Policy: Ronald Reagan and Conservative Reformism.* New York: Lexington Books, 2000.

Kenney, M. *Bio-Technology: The University-Industrial Complex.* New York: Yale University Press, 1986.

Kessler, David. *A Question of Intent: A Great American Battle with a Deadly Industry.* New York: Public Affairs, 2001.

Kleinknecht, William. *The Man Who Sold the World: Ronald Reagan and the Betrayal of Main Street America*. New York: Nation Books, 2009.

Kolassa, E.M., Greg Perkins, Bruce Siecker, and Mickey C. Smith, eds. *Pharmaceutical Marketing: Principles, Environment and Practice*. New York: Haworth Press, 2002.

Kolko, Gabriel. *Railroads and Regulation, 1877-1916*, Princeton: Princeton University Press, 1965.

———. *The Triumph of Conservatism*. London: The Free Press of Glencoe, 1963.

Kramer, Larry. *Reports from the Holocaust*. New York: St. Martin's Press, 1989.

Kuzmarov, Jeremy. *The Myth of the Addicted Army: Vietnam and the Modern War on Drugs*. Boston: University of Massachusetts Press, 2009.

Kwitny, Jonathan. *Acceptable Risks*. New York: Simon & Schuster, 1992.

Lewis, David E. *The Politics of Presidential Appointments*. Princeton: Princeton University Press, 2008.

Marks, Harry M. *The Progress of Experiment: Science and Therapeutic Reform in the United States, 1900–1990*. Cambridge: Cambridge University Press, 1997.

McCraw, Thomas K. *Prophets of Regulation*. Cambridge: Harvard University Press, 1984.

———, ed. *Regulation in Perspective: Historical Essays*. Cambridge: Harvard University Press, 1981.

McGirr, Lisa. *Suburban Warriors: The Origins of the New American Right*. Cambridge: Harvard University Press, 2001.

Meadows, Donella H., Dennis L. Meadows, Jorgen Randers, and William W. Behrens III. *The Limits to Growth: A Report for the Club of Rome's Project on the Predicament of Mankind*. London: Pan Books, 1974.

Meese III, Edwin. *With Reagan: The Inside Story*. Washington, D.C.: Regnery Gateway, 1992.

Melnick, R. Shep and Morton Keller, eds. *Taking Stock: American Government in the Twentieth Century*. New York: Cambridge University Press, 1999.

Micklethwait, John and Adrian Wooldridge. *The Right Nation: Why America is Different*. London: Penguin Books, 2004.

Morgenthaler, John and Steven William Fowkes, eds. *Stop the FDA: Save Your Health Freedom*, Menlo Park, CA: Health Freedoms Publications, 1992.

Morris, Edmund. *Dutch: A Memoir of Ronald Reagan*. New York: Random House, 1999.

Moss, Ralph W. *The Cancer Industry*. New York: Equinox Press, 1980.

Neustadt, Richard E. *Presidential Power and the Modern Presidents*. New York: Free Press, 1990.

Niskanen, William. *Bureaucracy and Representative Government*. Chicago: Aldine-Atherton, 1971.

Noll, Roger, ed. *Regulatory Policy and the Social Sciences*. Berkeley: University of California Press, 1985.

Noll, Roger G., and Bruce M. Owen. *The Political Economy of Deregulation: Interest Groups in the Regulatory Process*. Washington: American Enterprise Institute for Public Policy Research, 1983.

Noonan, Peggy. *When Character Was King: A Story of Ronald Reagan*, New York: Penguin, 2002.

Patterson, James. *Restless Giant: The United States from Watergate to Bush v. Gore*. Oxford: Oxford University Press, 2006.

Pemberton, William E. *Exit with Honor: The Life and Presidency of Ronald Reagan*. Armonk, NY: M.E. Sharpe, 1998.

Pertschuk, Michael. *Revolt Against Regulation: The Rise and Pause of the Consumer Movement*, Berkeley: University of California Press, 1982.

Pines, Wayne, ed. *FDA: A Century of Consumer Protection*. Washington: Food and Drug Law Institute, 2006.

Quick, Perry. "Businesses, Reagan's Industrial Policy." In *The Reagan Record*. Edited by John L. Palmer and Isabel V. Sawhill. Cambridge: Ballinger, 1984.

Ranney, Austin, ed. *The American Elections of 1980*. Washington, D.C.: American Enterprise Institute, 1981.

Ranney, Austin, ed. *The American Elections of 1984*. United States of America: Duke University Press, 1985.

Reagan, Ronald. *An American Life*. New York: Pocket Books, 1990.

———. *A Life in Letters*. New York: Free Press, 2004.

———. *The Reagan Diaries*. Edited by Douglas Brinkley. New York: HarperCollins, 2007.

Regan, Donald T. *For the Record: From Wall Street to Washington*. New York: Harcourt Brace Jovanovich, 1988.

Reinhard, David W. *The Republican Right Since 1945*. Lexington: University Press of Kentucky, 1983.

Relman, Arnold. *A Second Opinion: Rescuing America's Healthcare*. New York: Public Affairs, 2007.

Rusher, William. *The Rise of the Right*. New York: National Review, 1993.

Schaller, Michael. *Reckoning with Reagan: America and Its President in the 1980s*. New York: Oxford University Press, 1992.

———. *Right Turn: American Life in the Reagan-Bush Era, 1980–1992*. Oxford: Oxford University Press, 2007.

Schaller, Michael and George Rising. *The Republican Ascendancy in American Politics, 1968-2001*. Wheeling, Illinois: Harlan Davidson, 2002.

Schoenwald, Jonathan M. *A Time For Choosing: The Rise of Modern American Conservatism*. New York: Oxford University Press, 2001.

Schneider, Eric. *Smack: Heroin and the American City*. Philadelphia: University of Pennsylvania Press, 2008.

Schumacher, E.F. *Small is Beautiful: A Study of Economics as if People Mattered*. London: Blond and Briggs, 1973.

Schweitzer, S. *Pharmaceutical Economics and Policy*. New York: Oxford University Press, 1998.

Shilts, Randy. *And the Band Played On: Politics, People, and the AIDS Epidemic*. New York: St. Martin's Press, 1987.

Shrum, Bob. *No Excuses: Concessions of a Serial Campaigner*. New York: Simon & Schuster, 2009.

Silverman, M., and Philip R. Lee. *Pills, Profits, and Politics*. Berkeley: University of California Press, 1974.

Sloan, John W. *The Reagan Effect: Economics and Presidential Leadership*. Lawrence: University Press of Kansas, 1999.

Speakes, Larry and Robert Pack. *Speaking Out: The Reagan Presidency from Inside the White House*. New York: Charles Scribner's Sons, 1988.

Stein, Herbert. *Presidential Economics: The Making of Economic Policy From Roosevelt to Clinton*, 3rd. ed. Washington D.C.: The American Enterprise Institute Press, 1994.

Stockman, David. *The Triumph of Politics: Why the Reagan Revolution Failed*. London: Bodley Head, 1986.

Tanner, Michael. *Leviathan on the Right: How Big Government Brought Down the Republican Revolution*. Washington, D.C.: Cato Institute, 2007.

Tobbell, Dominique. *Pills, Power, and Policy: The Struggle for Drug Reform in Cold War America and Its Consequences*. Berkeley: University of California Press, 2012.

Vietor, Richard H.K. *Contrived Competition: Regulation and Deregulation in America*, Cambridge: Harvard University Press, 1994.

Viguerie, Richard A. *The New Right: We're Ready to Lead*. Falls Chuch.: The Viguerie Company, 1981.

Visuci, W. Kip, John M. Vernon and Joseph E. Harrington Jr. *Economics of Regulation and Antitrust 2nd edition*. Cambridge, MA: MIT Press, 1998.

Wallison, Peter J. *Ronald Reagan: The Power of Conviction and the Success of his Presidency*. Boulder, CO: Westview, 2003.

Werth, Barry. *The Billion Dollar Molecule: One Company's Quest for the Perfect Drug*. New York: Touchstone, 1995.

Wilentz, Sean. *The Age of Reagan: A History, 1974–2008*. New York: HarperCollins, 2008.

Wills, Garry. *Reagan's America: Innocents at Home*. London: Heinemann, 1988.

Wilson, James Q., ed. *The Politics of Regulation.* New York: Basic Books, 1980.
Woodward, Bob. *The Choice: How Clinton Won.* New York: Simon & Schuster, 1997.

Index

About the Author

Lucas Richert is a postdoctoral fellow at the University of Saskatchewan. He has written a number of articles in the field of American medical and political history.

Lightning Source UK Ltd.
Milton Keynes UK
UKOW04n1903030215

245606UK00001B/30/P